Books by Elmer Gertz

Charter for a New Age: An Inside View of the Sixth Illinois Constitutional Convention (with Joe Pisciotte)

For the First Hours of Tomorrow: The New Illinois Bill of Rights

Frank Harris: A Study in Black and White (with A. I. Tobin)

A Handful of Clients

Henry Miller: Years of Trial and Triumph, 1962–1964. The Correspondence of Henry Miller and Elmer Gertz (edited by Elmer Gertz and Felice Flanery Lewis)

Moment of Madness: The People vs. Jack Ruby

The Odyssey of a Barbarian: The Biography of George Sylvester Viereck

Quest for a Constitution: A Man Who Wouldn't Quit. A Political Biography of Samuel Witwer of Illinois (with Edward S. Gilbreath)

The Short Stories of Frank Harris: A Selection

To Life: The Story of a Chicago Lawyer

■ *Gertz v. Robert Welch, Inc.*
The Story of a Landmark Libel Case

Elmer Gertz

Southern Illinois University Press
Carbondale and Edwardsville

Copyright © 1992 by the Board of Trustees
   Southern Illinois University
All rights reserved
Printed in the United States of America
Edited by Robert K. Burdette
Design and production by Natalia Nadraga
95 94 93 92   4 3 2 1

Library of Congress Cataloging-in-Publication Data

Gertz, Elmer, 1906–
   Gertz v. Robert Welch, Inc.: the story of a landmark
libel case/Elmer Gertz.
      p.   cm.
   Includes bibliographical references and index.
    1. Gertz, Elmer, 1906–   —Trials, litigation, etc. 2. Robert Welch,
Inc.—Trials, litigation, etc.   3. John Birch Society—Trials, litigation, etc.
4. Trials (Libel)—Illinois—Chicago.   I. Title.
KF228.G47G47   1992
345.73'0256—dc20
[347.305256]   91-39403
ISBN 0-8093-1813-X   CIP

The paper used in this publication meets the minimum requirements
of American National Standard for Information Sciences
—Permanence of Paper for Printed Library Materials,
ANSI Z39.48-1984. ∞

For Wayne B. Giampietro,

with pride in having given him his start in the practice of law;
with joy in his steady and heartening progress in his profession;
with gratitude for what he has accomplished in pursuing my
   landmark case.

Contents

	Acknowledgments	*ix*
	Chronology	*xi*
1.	I Am Defamed by the Birchers	*1*
2.	The Birchers and the Sixties	*7*
3.	It Began with a Murder	*11*
4.	The Nelsons Sue Nuccio and the City	*18*
5.	What to Do?	*25*
6.	I Strike Back	*36*
7.	The Laborious Course of Our Case	*42*
8.	First Trial	*51*
9.	The Unraveling of a Victory	*69*
10.	The Supreme Court	*83*
11.	Slowly, Slowly Creeps the Case	*112*
12.	A New Trial: A Resounding Victory	*127*
13.	An Interminable Case Is Terminated	*196*
14.	The Meaning of a Landmark Decision	*213*
	Bibliography	*251*
	Index	*283*

■ Acknowledgments

This book deals with one case, my libel action, and principally one person, myself. Thus I am peculiarly well suited to write it from my own resources. But as the poet Donne said long ago, "No man is an Island, intire of it selfe," so I gladly acknowledge the assistance of others.

I owe a great debt to many people for their indirect assistance in the writing of this book, indirect because when they tendered their assistance, it was in connection with the trial of my case rather than my writing about it. The one to whom I owe the most is the person to whom this book is dedicated, Wayne B. Giampietro, my law associate and partner, who was involved in every phase of the case, as this book attests. It is an understatement to say that he was invaluable.

Then there are the witnesses who performed so well: four now departed friends—Eli E. Fink, John Ligtenberg, Albert E. ("Bert") Jenner, Jr., and Frank Greenberg—and Carol Bellows, Irv Kupcinet, Professor Jon R. Walz, Ralla Klepak, Julius Lucius Echeles, Michael Kachigian, and Mary Giampietro.

One person's aid was direct and inestimable in value. My wife, Mamie Gertz, attended every session of both trials and constantly counseled with me. When I began to write this book, she typed all drafts of it, work that required the most painstaking care.

This book in its final form owes much to Carol Rausch Gorski. At times, her help amounted to virtual collaboration.

There are numerous quotations in the text from many sources and references to other sources. I must thank each of the authors, even those who have confused rather than helped me.

Because of the nature of the case and of the book, it has been necessary for me to incorporate much more quoted matter than is my wont. I hope that this helps the reader.

My aim has been to give an analytical narrative of an important case in which I was the protagonist. Through it, I hope to make the case and the legal process itself understandable to both lawyers and laypeople. I hope that lawyers will forgive any oversimplification and that laypeople will excuse the necessary dwelling upon the technicalities of the law.

I must also thank those who have permitted me the luxury of talking about this case to their law classes and thus expanding my understanding of it, especially Professors David Gordon, David Protess, Michael Pollelle, Craig Peterson, Arthur Sabin, and George Trubow. There are, I am sure, many others whose names have slipped from my memory. After the Supreme Court handed down its decision in my case in 1974, we discussed the case and its implications each semester in my privacy and civil rights seminars at the John Marshall Law School, and from time to time, students wrote papers on the case. These things too helped to clarify my thinking.

I owe a special debt to Michael Rodak, Jr., the clerk of the Supreme Court of the United States, for his kindness in providing me with a transcript of the oral argument before his Court.

As one reads my exposition, other debts of gratitude will become apparent. I want to thank all, named and unnamed. The case and writing about it have been intellectual and emotional adventures.

■ *Chronology*

Spring 1968.	Peace demonstrations in Chicago, violently resisted by the police. The Sparling Commission is formed by the Roger Baldwin Foundation to study the situation. Elmer Gertz becomes chief counsel for the commission. It issues a report, *Disent and Disorder*.
Summer 1968.	Peace demonstrations in connection with the Democratic Convention in Chicago, violently resisted by the police.
June 4, 1968.	Chicago Police Officer Richard Nuccio kills Ronald Nelson.
July 12, 1968.	The Nelson family, through attorneys Elmer Gertz and Ralla Klepak, files civil-rights suits against Nuccio in federal court and two suits in Cook County Circuit Court.
July 26, 1968.	The inquest into the death of Ronald Nelson returns "open verdict."
July 29, 1968.	Nuccio is indicted for murder.
August 1968.	Nuccio's first bench trial before Judge Richard Fitzgerald.
August 1968.	Judge Fitzgerald convicts Nuccio of murder.
April 1969.	John Birch Society magazine, *American Opinion*, published in March 1969, includes an article, "Framed," that defames Elmer Gertz. Reprint is also published.
June 17, 1969.	Gertz files libel suit in U.S. district court in Chicago against Robert Welch, Inc., the publisher of *American Opinion*. Case is assigned to Judge Bernard Decker.
November 18, 1969.	Judge Decker denies Welch motion to dismiss suit.

November 26, 1969. First conviction of Nuccio for murder is reversed by the Illinois Supreme Court.

September 21, 1970. First trial of Gertz libel suit before Judge Decker begins; jury awards Gertz $50,000.

October 13, 1970. Nuccio's retrial for murder starts before a jury. Nuccio is convicted and appeals.

December 8, 1970. Judge Decker sets aside jury verdict in favor of Gertz in libel case and dismisses suit. Appeal of dismissal to Court of Appeals for Seventh Circuit.

January 22, 1971. Judge Alexander Napoli grants summary judgment in Nelson civil-rights suit on issue of liability.

January 31, 1971. Oral argument before court of appeals in libel suit.

February 26, 1971. Illinois Appellate Court rules in the suit of Ronald Nelson's mother, finding cause of action for mental distress against Nuccio but dismissing suit against the city of Chicago.

August 1, 1972. Court of Appeals for Seventh Circuit affirms dismissal of Gertz libel suit.

October 17, 1972. Gertz files appeal (petition for certiorari) to Supreme Court regarding the dismissal of libel case.

February 20, 1973. Gertz petition for certiorari allowed by U.S. Supreme Court.

March 20, 1973. Illinois Supreme Court affirms murder conviction of Nuccio in second trial.

November 14, 1973. Oral argument in U.S. Supreme Court in libel appeal.

June 25, 1974. U.S. Supreme Court reverses dismissal of libel suit and sends back for retrial. The Court lays down important new constitutional guidelines for libel suits of private persons.

February 15, 1978. Judge Joel Flaum, to whom libel case is assigned for retrial, grants summary judgment for Gertz on the issue of truth, finding Welch statements about him false.

June 12, 1980.	Judge Flaum denies Welch motion for summary judgment.
April 13, 1981.	Retrial of Gertz libel case begins before Judge Flaum, lasts five days, and jury brings in verdict in favor of Gertz: $100,000 compensatory damages, $300,000 punitive.
September 4, 1981.	Welch files appeal in Seventh Circuit Court of Appeals.
February 8, 1982.	Oral argument before Seventh Circuit.
June 16, 1982.	Seventh Circuit Court of Appeals affirms Gertz judgment.
December 14, 1982.	Welch files petition for appeal in U.S. Supreme Court.
February 22, 1983.	U.S. Supreme Court denies Welch appeal petition.
May 17, 1983.	Welch pays judgment in full.

Gertz v. Robert Welch, Inc.

1 ■ I Am Defamed by the Birchers

If I had to pick one sentence out of the defamatory article that obsessed me for so many years, it would be "The file on Elmer Gertz in Chicago Police Intelligence takes a big Irish cop to lift."

This sentence appeared in an article published in the April 1969 issue of the John Birch Society magazine *American Opinion*. It caught my attention at once, and it still intrigues me more than the other defamatory material that prompted my libel litigation. In the midst of my anger at the lies about me in the article, I could not help being amused at the very thought that it would take "a big Irish Cop" to lift the fictitious police file about me. Why not a Jewish cop, a black, a Pole?

As it turned out, the file consisted of a couple of sheets telling of such horrendous crimes as presiding at a dinner in honor of Albert Einstein by a prestigious Jewish lawyers' group and serving as a pallbearer at the funeral of my ill-fated client Jack Ruby, the hapless slayer of the killer of President Kennedy. I had been one of the lawyers responsible for getting the conviction and death sentence of Ruby set aside in the Texas Court of Criminal Appeals.

My long struggle with the Birch Society began in late March 1969. Mary Giampietro, the wife of my young law associate (later partner) Wayne B. Giampietro, telephoned. She had been shopping, and her armload of groceries had not stopped a young lady from trying to hand her some printed material. Despite Mary's evident lack of interest, the woman dropped the pamphlet on top of a grocery bag. Her curiosity piqued, Mary picked up the material and glanced through it. It was headed: "FRAME-UP— Richard Nuccio and the War on Police." She had vague recollections of the Nuccio imbroglio, which had arisen not far from her home. A picture of her husband's employer caught her attention. It bore the caption "Elmer Gertz of Red Guild Harasses Nuccio." Reading here and there, she sensed that serious charges had been made, so she called us. We asked her to come down to the office as soon as possible.

I went through the pamphlet rather hurriedly at first, then carefully, with increasing surprise and anger. Stamped on the paper cover was "Support Your Local Police Committee." The pamphlet was bylined Alan Stang, a name unfamiliar to me. Inside the cover was the pledge that "these reprints will be sent postpaid to any address in the United States." The reader was also informed that "this article first appeared in the April 1969 issue of AMERICAN OPINION, an internationally circulated Conservative journal."

I learned later that the magazine was an organ of the John Birch Society. The article began with a small picture of the author, Alan Stang, and a few biographical words. I learned that Stang was "a former business editor for Prentice-Hall, Inc., and a television writer, producer, and consultant... a frequent contributor to AMERICAN OPINION," and the author of various best-sellers. In addition, I learned that Alan Stang had "just returned from an investigative trip to Chicago, where he conducted extensive research into the Richard Nuccio case."

The article presented the results of this "extensive research." By the time it appeared, Nuccio had been convicted of the murder of a youth, Ronald Nelson, by the Criminal Court of Cook County, Judge Richard Fitzgerald presiding. Nonetheless, Stang set forth the "facts" on the assumption that Nuccio had been "framed." Thus the "facts" were those of the defense witnesses, not the state's. They charged that Nelson was under the influence of drugs, a drunk, and a leader of a gang of toughs who drew obscene pictures on the tables of Benjamin Citron's Franksville restaurant across from the Chicago Cubs ballpark.

On the night of June 4, 1968, Nelson, violating a judge's order, appeared at the restaurant and played with a knife. Citron, frightened, called the police. Officer Nuccio promptly appeared with other officers. Nelson fled, and Nuccio pursued. Warned that Nelson was throwing a knife at him, Nuccio fired and hit Nelson, who died almost immediately at the hospital to which he was taken. According to prosecution witnesses, Nelson was shot in the back from a distance of seventy to ninety feet.

Stang then told of the excitement that followed the death of Nelson. "Revolutionary agitators," he said, "were now hard at work to 'get Richard Nuccio.'" Stang gave examples of the revolutionary tone of the opposition to Nuccio and summed up: "Yes, the comrades now had the lines: Get Richard Nuccio!" He gave further details of the conspiracy and asserted: "In short, the Nelson incident was used by revolutionaries of the Far Left to try to turn the people against the police—and vice versa—at a time when criminals with official sanction are tearing our country apart."

Stang then lost no time in driving home his charges, and I was the target:

> By now you are thinking that there is more to this matter than some teenagers hanging around a hot dog stand. Teenagers at a hot dog stand would not know how to arrange the carefully orchestrated publicity the case soon acquired. And of course you are correct. They wouldn't.
>
> But Elmer Gertz for instance would. On behalf of the Nelson family, attorney Gertz has filed three suits against Officer Nuccio and the City of Chicago, two in state court and one under the Federal Civil Rights Act, asking for a total of almost a million dollars....
>
> The file on Elmer Gertz in Chicago Police Intelligence takes a big, Irish cop to lift. According to the Communist *Worker* of December 8, 1964, he has signed a petition to abolish the House Committee on Un-American Activities. On May 12, 1966, he sponsored another such petition, published by the Illinois division of the American Civil Liberties Union—founded by Harry F. Ward, one of the top Communists in the United States. Gertz also was a pallbearer for Jack Ruby, the "lone fanatic" who killed the "lone fanatic" who killed the President of the United States. He has been an official of the Marxist League for Industrial Democracy, originally known as the Intercollegiate Socialist Society, which has advocated the violent seizure of our government.
>
> On April 27, 1968, the Chicago Peace Council conducted a "peace parade," as part of an operation coordinated around the country by the National Mobilization Committee to End the War in Vietnam, a Communist outfit headed by Communist David Dellinger—which also coordinated the terrorist attack on the police at the Democrat Convention in August. The Chicago Peace Council is also a Communist outfit. It is headed by a Communist named Jack Spiegel. Its headquarters are at 1608 W. Madison in a building owned by Communist John Rossen, an official of the defunct Communist Fair Play for Cuba Committee. Also headquartered in the building is the Communist S.D.S. Indeed, the Chicago Peace Council chose a former National Secretary of S.D.S. named C. Clark Kissinger to organize its Communist parade last April twenty-seventh. Kissinger, too, was later active in the terrorism against the police at the Chicago Convention.
>
> The Communist parade in April included the usual Communist violence. Apparently, the traitors were practicing for what they planned to

do in August. And just as the phony Walker Commission and its *Walker Report* followed the terrorism in August, so a Commission and a report called Dissent and Disorder followed the terrorism in April, financed by the Roger Baldwin Foundation of Communist Harry Ward's A.C.L.U. After an "impartial investigation," the A.C.L.U.'s Commission ridiculed "the inaccurate impression that the April 27 event was a left-wing affair"; exonerated the Communist Chicago Peace Council, which ran it; and naturally blamed the violence the Communists caused on the Chicago police: "On April 27, at the peace parade of the Chicago Peace Council, the police badly mishandled their task. Brutalizing demonstrators without provocation, they failed to live up to that difficult professionalism which we demand."

And the Chief Counsel for the Commission which committed Dissent and Disorder was the same Elmer Gertz who now turns up as lawyer for the Nelsons in the attack on Officer Nuccio.

In fact, the only thing Chicagoans need to know about Gertz is that he is one of the original officers, and has been Vice President, of the Communist National Lawyers Guild—which has been described by the House Committee on Un-American Activities as "one of the foremost legal bulwarks of the Communist Party"—and which probably did more than any other outfit to plan the Communist attack on the Chicago police during the 1968 Democrat Convention.

Yes, Gertz is good at publicizing "police brutality." On July twenty-fourth, two days after the "open hearing" at the Lake View Presbyterian Church, he was active at the inquest, which had the flavor of a trial.

Five days later, Richard Nuccio was indicted for murder.

Stang went on with his version of the facts about the criminal trial arising out of the shooting of Nelson, with a picture of me, not a very good one. Although I was not actually mentioned in the account of the trial, it was clear that Stang wanted his readers to think of me as he recited his version of what happened.

On Thursday, August 29, 1968, Judge Fitzgerald found Police Officer Nuccio guilty of murder—only a few hours after hordes of Communist and young toughs and dupes attacked his fellow officers the evening before, a short walk away at the Conrad Hilton. If, like millions of other Americans, Judge Fitzgerald was watching television on the evening of Wednesday, August Twenty-eighth, he saw not those Communist attacks, but just the Chicago police responding to the attacks, which created the impression of an unprovoked "police riot," as the *Walker Report* put it. He heard such humanitarians as Walter Cronkite express-

Defamed by the Birchers ▪ 5

ing indignation. Like millions of other Americans, he was watching an organized attempt to discredit our local police—organized primarily by the Communist National Lawyers Guild, preeminent in which is the same Elmer Gertz who now appears as the Nelsons' lawyer.

He went on to tell of interviews with various people who had protested Nuccio's killing of Nelson. He characterized them as Communist dupes, among them a well-known Roman Catholic priest, Father Carl Lezak.

"Are you associated with the Chicago Peace Council?" I asked suddenly.
His eyes narrowed warily, which doesn't prove anything, of course. But you see, I already knew that one of the reasons he could be on the subversive list is the fact that he has contributed money to the Chicago Peace Council. The C.P.C. as you will recall, is the Communist outfit headed by a Communist and defended by Leninist Elmer Gertz, who now turns up as lawyer for the Nelsons.
"I think I'm on the mailing list," he said.
Interesting, isn't it? Gives you a tingly feeling all over.

Having completed his account of the various ramifications of the Nuccio case, he wrote:

So you see, what ran over Richard Nuccio is the Communist War on Police. Indeed, Chicago Police Intelligence has already established that what you have read here is just the proverbial scratch on the surface. And the purpose of the Communist War on Police, as always, is to demoralize, discredit, and destroy our independent, local police, so that Communists can impose their totalitarian dictatorship. One major part of the plan is the rioting run by Communists in the streets—which their allies in government forbid the police to suppress—to create the impression that our local police are inadequate in training, manners, and capability. The other major part is the current attempt by conspirators in government to seize our local police—with the usual weapon of federal "aid" coupled with federal "guidelines" (that is, controls) inflicted by the new federal "anti-crime" law—allegedly to satisfy demands for "law and order."

Perhaps fearing that readers might forget his earlier charges and insinuations against me, he now phrased them somewhat differently:

Mayor Richard J. Daley has refused to see Mrs. Nuccio, but he had time the other day to see Hubert Humphrey, who calls himself the "biggest victim" of the Convention. Two Chicago Assistant Corporation Counsels warned Nuccio not to testify at the coroner's inquest, for fear what he said might jeopardize their defense against Communist-fronter Gertz. Nuccio obeyed and was charged with violation of Rule Number Fifty-One: refusing to testify at a coroner's inquest.

He rephrased what he had written earlier when he charged me with fomenting the publicity campaign that sealed Nuccio's fate: "As we have seen, it was publicity and organization that led to Richard Nuccio's conviction. And it is only publicity and organization that can lead to his release."

He ended his article: "One thing already stands out clearly: Richard Nuccio is innocent. *He must be freed.*"

At least one thing was clear to me: I had to take action of some kind to redeem my reputation.

I wrote to *American Opinion* for extra copies of the pamphlet and also obtained copies of the April 1969 issue of the magazine. It supplemented what was said in the reprint.

As will appear presently, I filed suit against Robert Welch, Inc., the parent organization of *American Opinion*, charging that it had defamed me by publishing harmful lies impugning my reputation and patriotism.

2 ■ The Birchers and the Sixties

Some twenty years later, Alan Stang's accusations seem bizarre. Why did he think readers would believe that sinister forces were plotting to discredit the police? Did he really expect readers to accept his assertion that "criminals with official sanction are tearing our country apart"? What sorts of backers provided *American Opinion* magazine with a secure base from which to launch such outrageous attacks?

To understand why my attackers behaved as they did in their libel of me and in the subsequent legal proceedings, one must know something about the Birchers and the sixties.

The John Birch Society was founded in Indianapolis in 1958 by its permanent leader, Robert Welch, a Massachusetts candy manufacturer, and a small group of wealthy businessmen. By the late 1960s, the society had 60,000 to 100,000 members, including about 25,000 active participants and some 250 staff members.

At that time, the Birch Society was "the only national, permanently-organized, grass-roots organization set up to effectively marshall right-wing forces in the United States." But its position was far to the right of any established party's, and today many of its assertions seem fantastic. The Birchers saw a Communist under every bed. Their list of covert Communists or Communist "tools" included Presidents Dwight D. Eisenhower, John F. Kennedy, Richard M. Nixon; Secretary of State John Foster Dulles; Chief Justice Earl Warren; and Martin Luther King, Jr. All of these villains were in one way or another engaged in a plot to enslave the world.

Behind the plot, however, Welch detected its real brains, a group he called the Insiders. He believed the Insider conspiracy to be "a continuous, secret, historical and dedicated procession of diabolical human beings," many of them Jewish. The cabal was "200 years old and... rooted in European secret societies that planned and ignited the French Revolution." This combine was responsible for catastrophes ranging from World War I to the Arab-Israeli conflict and the civil-rights movement. As part of their effort to weaken the U.S. government, the Insiders were plotting to undermine local police departments by promoting charges of police brutality.

The Birchers recruited people to their cause by exploiting fear and igniting a desire to be among the elite who grasped the "real truth." According to Gerald Schomp, a former John Birch organizer:

You're told things a suspicious person can readily agree with. America's going to pot. They're just messing around in Vietnam. The politicians are afraid of the punks rioting in the streets. Unions are getting way out of hand. Too many deadbeats leeching off us hard-working people. Supreme Court is atheistic. Taxes will ruin us. Police being persecuted. Communists in State Department. Crime soaring. Drugs rampant. Too much sex. Corruption. Immorality, Propaganda, Anarchy. Pretty soon it dawns on you: sounds sensible to me. They're absolutely right. By golly, these are my people!

At meetings there were

ministers disgusted with the social gospel, doctors alarmed over Medicare, mothers concerned about schools and safe streets, businessmen worried about taxes and property values and teachers distraught over permissiveness. Yet, the mystery, adventure, and atmosphere of underground secrecy were definitely there. Although these things were more imagined than real, planning to impeach Earl Warren, to get the "U.S. out of the UN," and to expose the civil rights movement as a Communist plot seemed pleasurably naughty—but immeasurably noble.

Why did these people accept such beliefs? No one can know another's motives with certainty, but one can speculate. Surely the political and social climate of the sixties sent some recruits into the arms of the Birchers. During the early sixties, many people went to bed harboring a real fear of nuclear destruction. In 1961, three years after the Birch Society's beginnings, John F. Kennedy and Nikita Khrushchev went nose-to-nose over the removal of Russian missiles from Cuba. Khrushchev blinked first, and the missiles were shipped out, but for many Americans, nuclear holocaust had seemed imminent. At neighborhood barbecues, people discussed backyard bomb shelters.

At the same time, blacks were agitating for their right to vote and otherwise participate in the common life. In 1963, some

200,000 people traveled to Washington, D.C., to hear Martin Luther King, Jr., proclaim "I have a dream." In 1965, about 1,500 black and white marchers converged on Selma, Alabama, to promote voting rights for blacks. The sheriff greeted them with electric cattle prods.

The U.S. military involvement in Vietnam evolved from a police action to a full-fledged war. At home, young people protested the war, grew their hair long, and smoked marijuana at "love-ins." To many Americans, these developments were deeply disturbing, calling into question assumptions on which they had built their lives.

Thus developed the conflicts of the sixties. The issues were "not at all simply about America's involvement in Vietnam. [They were] over how the American political system worked and over how Americans found meaning in their lives. In the adversarial mood that gripped the nation, members of the 'youth culture,' war opponents, and certain civil libertarians were on a collision course with the forces that claimed to represent 'law and order.' The 'greening of America' impinged upon the 'thin blue line'" (Gerald Schomp, *Birchism Was My Business*).

Which brings us to Chicago in 1968. The city was already tense in the wake of the assassinations of Bobby Kennedy and Martin Luther King, Jr.—the latter followed by days of rioting in the black ghettos. Ronald Nelson was shot that summer. Perhaps the general level of tension and the distrust between generations fatally exacerbated the conflict between Nelson and Nuccio.

Then came the violence between police and protesters, first during the spring in the Civic Center, then during the summer outside the Democratic National Convention, which brought Chicago worldwide notoriety. Charges of "police rioting" could only have underlined the Birchers' belief in a conspiracy to discredit the police. Nuccio's conviction one day after the riots must have made it seem to some an integral part of the "plot." And since I served as counsel of a blue-ribbon panel of inquiry into the riots whose conclusions were published as *Dissent and Disorder*, in their eyes I must have been part and parcel of the conspiracy.

In a sense, we could not have expected the Birchers to discuss their fears in a rational manner. That year, few elements of our society could carry on a rational dialogue with one another. Each group could hardly comprehend the others' notions of what our society was about and where it should be headed. Too often, people talked at, not with, one another, and the common rules of discourse were strained past their limit. The Birchers' reckless statements about me exemplified the extremes that could occur when debates were displaced by shouting matches. To them, I was "the enemy." Never mind truth. They thought the truth could be known only by the few who were privileged to comprehend it — themselves.

Slowly the country returned to greater sanity. Paradoxically, the libel suit that the Birchers prompted contributed to the turnaround. The suit resulted in one small but vital step in the restoration of discourse in our land. By delimiting more clearly than ever before the responsibilities of the press, the judicial system established critical guidelines.

These significant results, however, began with the saddest outcome of conflict. They began with a murder.

3 ■ It Began with a Murder

My libel case had its origin in a murder—the senseless killing of a nineteen-year-old youth, Ronald Nelson, by a police officer, Richard Nuccio. This event led to two murder trials for the police officer and appeals by him to the Illinois Supreme Court; three civil lawsuits against him and the city of Chicago in which I was the lead attorney for the plaintiffs (the persons filing the suits); and a claim for libel that I filed in response to the article in the Birch Society magazine.

The libel complaint led to much so-called pretrial discovery, numerous motions and other legal maneuvers, a trial, appeals to the U.S. court of appeals and the Supreme Court, a retrial, another appeal to the U.S. court of appeals, and a second appeal to the U.S. Supreme Court. The libel actions have prompted countless law-review and media articles and many pages in learned treatises and popular books. Many not yet born may be reading about the matter when they are mature and I am gone.

One must begin at the unexpected beginning of *Elmer Gertz v. Robert Welch, Inc.*—the murder of a young man. Some of the facts of that dismal tragedy are in dispute, but as far as the law is concerned, the essential situation is incontrovertibly established: Police Officer Richard Nuccio "shot and killed Ronald Nelson with a gun, knowing that such shot with a gun created a strong probability of death or of great bodily harm to said Ronald Nelson without lawful justification," as charged in the indictment handed down on July 29, 1968, in the Criminal Division of the Cook County Circuit Court.

The dispute over some of the facts was a central issue in all that followed, including my libel action, but not all the facts were disputed. We know that directly across from Wrigley Field, the Cubs baseball park on the North Side of Chicago, there had long been a large parking lot containing a Tastee-Freez stand and the Franksville Restaurant. These spots had been hangouts for the sometimes wild and undisciplined youths of the neighborhood, much to the distress of Ben Citron, who ran Franksville. He had complained to the police that these young men (and sometimes their girlfriends) were boisterous and insolent, dangerous smokers of marijuana and drinkers of hard liquor.

Saul Epton, a judge of the Boys Court, had ordered Ronald Nelson and a friend to stay away from Franksville for six months. They had ignored the judge's order and had returned. Thereupon, Citron had phoned the police that they were creating a disorder. Richard Nuccio and other police officers familiar with the youths had assembled on the scene. When accosted by one of the police officers, Nelson had sprinted away, down one of the adjacent alleys. It was then that Officer Nuccio, in pursuit (why, no one knew), had shot him in the back and killed him. Nuccio claimed that the young man was throwing a knife at him.

Nuccio was twice convicted of the murder of Ronald Nelson. He was defended originally by a competent and intriguing criminal defense lawyer, Julius Lucius Echeles. Echeles's very appearance suggested television drama. His courtroom oratory was mellifluous, his strategy unorthodox, his achievements considerable.

When the case came before Judge Richard Fitzgerald, the chief justice of the Criminal Division of the Circuit Court of Cook County, Echeles decided that he would defend the case to the judge rather than a jury. Judge Fitzgerald is generally regarded as one of the most honorable, fair, learned, and able presiding judges in the history of the court. A jury might be inflamed by the recital of the facts—the slaying of a probably unarmed youth who had committed no felony and possibly no misdemeanor. As it turned out, Judge Fitzgerald was just as disturbed by the situation as a jury might have been. He found Nuccio guilty of murder and sentenced him to fourteen to fifteen years' imprisonment, a rather mild sentence in view of the seriousness of the offense.

In his decision, Judge Fitzgerald gave an exposition of the relevant, rather complicated law. He then applied these principles of law to the facts of the case and found:

> It is the judgment of this court that the evidence reflects the distance between the police officer and the decedent was between 70 and 90 feet. And it would be illogical, therefore, to assume that the deceased could have in any manner caused the officer great bodily harm; and the court therefore must conclude that the defendant acted in an unreasonable manner and that his assumption that the force he used was

necessary to prevent great bodily harm to himself was formed hastily and without due care and his belief was unreasonable.

Judge Fitzgerald added:

> In reaching its decision, the court has considered the great ramifications and implications of this case and is aware of the theory propounded in these days of civil disobedience and unlawful disturbances and the great responsibilities placed upon the police officers in the City of Chicago, and the court is also aware of the theories advocated that deadly force should be given a wider latitude than those specifically set forth in . . . [the statute].
>
> However, the court is of the opinion that the legislators deliberated long and hard before placing restrictions on police officers, such as those imposed in [the statute], and it was the purpose and the intent of the Legislature that deterrence should not be the controlling factor upon which the justified use of deadly force is based.
>
> If deterrence is our main consideration then every crime and every escape from arrest should be punishable by death. Several jurisdictions have abolished the use of the death sentence as an instrument of punishment and deterrence. A conscious decision has thus been reached to restrict the use of deadly force, even where all the safeguards of a judicial proceeding have been exhausted. To allow the use of deadly force in making an arrest or preventing an escape merely as a means of deterring crime appears to be totally illogical. There is something within the human soul which cries out against sacrificing a 19 year old on the altar of deterrence.

The usual motions, some technical, were made by the highly resourceful Echeles, the chief defense counsel (assisted throughout by his associates Jo-Anne F. Wolfson and Michael M. Kachigian), but all such maneuvers were thwarted by the court. Nuccio was left with the necessity of appealing his conviction. Echeles handled the appeal with skill. The Supreme Court of Illinois accepted his contention that the prosecutors' cross-examination of various witnesses had created an impression, not substantiated by any credible evidence, that Nuccio and his colleagues had grossly mistreated Nelson and his friends in the past and had even made death threats against them.

Chief Justice Robert Underwood delivered the opinion of the court (*People v. Nuccio*, 45 Ill. 2d 375, filed November 26, 1969), commenting at the outset: "The testimony is voluminous and

14 ∎ *Gertz v. Robert Welch, Inc.*

conflicting, with few matters undisputed." He then summarized the evidence and concluded: "The defendant's claim that the proof does not establish guilt beyond a reasonable doubt is, therefore, not sustainable, for the testimony of the state's witnesses, if believed by the trier of fact [Judge Fitzgerald], is sufficient to justify the verdict."

Why, then, the reversal of Judge Fitzgerald's judgment against Nuccio and the remand of the case for retrial?

Where, as here, the guilt of the accused is not manifest, but is dependent upon the degree of credibility accorded by the trier of fact to this testimony and that of the witnesses who testify on his behalf, and there appear in the record substantial numbers of unsupported insinuations which, if considered, could have seriously impeached the credibility of the defendant and his witnesses, and there is no indication of the court's awareness of this impropriety even though it is brought to his attention, it is our opinion that justice and fundamental fairness demand that the defendant be afforded a new trial free from such prejudicial misconduct.

So Echeles was given a second chance by the Supreme Court of Illinois. This time, after a six-day trial in Judge Felix M. Buoscio's courtroom, a jury brought in a guilty verdict. Everyone was shocked, particularly Nuccio and Echeles, who expected Nuccio to win and had confidently predicted that result.

Chicago Sun-Times columnist Tom Fitzpatrick, known as "Fitz" in the newspaper world, devoted his December 1, 1970, column to an amazing episode in the Nuccio saga. It bears repetition here in view of subsequent events.

NUCCIO WALKED OUT of the court and into the hall. It was out in the hall that the most unusual thing of the day happened.

A tall, thin woman approached Nuccio.

"Dick Nuccio," she said, "they should have given you 50 years for what you did."

"They should have given it to you because you tried to make a liar out of me, too."

"Get out of here," Nuccio said. "Get away from me." Nuccio headed down the hall and to the elevator.

The woman, Mrs. Margaret Tischner, sat down on a marble bench in the hall.

"I'm afraid to leave the building right now," she said. "All those people here are with Dick Nuccio. They hate me for what I've done, but I hate them too."

MRS. TISCHNER LOOKED AROUND before continuing:

"Dick Nuccio came to me and wanted me to lie that I was an eyewitness to the killing. He told me that kid had a knife and I believed him and so I went to the state's attorney, Matt Walsh, and told him this."

"But later I found out that boy didn't have a knife. So I went back to Matt Walsh and told him how Dick Nuccio and his friends had come to me with maps and graphs all drawn out to show me how to testify."

The story is incredible. If that's true, why didn't she take the stand in this trial and tell the jury what she knew?

"Mister," Mrs. Tischner said, "that Matt Walsh is one smart lawyer. He knew the defense would only point out that I'd lied once and might be lying again."

MRS. TISCHNER LEFT THEN, and I went looking for Matt Walsh.

"There are a lot of strange things in this case," Walsh said, "and Mrs. Tischner is only one of them."

"Her story about coming back to me and telling me how Nuccio had asked her to lie is true. And she's right about why I didn't put her on the stand, too."

Fitz's story about the knife adds an interesting piece to the puzzle of whether such a weapon did exist. Despite the testimony of Nuccio, no knife was received in evidence, and there was no testimony that Nelson's fingerprints or palm prints were found on a knife.

At the second trial, Ben Citron, proprietor of Franksville, said that he had not told the police officers of any knife or mentioned such a weapon when he called to complain of the young people's creating a disturbance. This differed considerably from his prior testimony. At the trials of Nuccio, virtually all the witnesses other than Nuccio and some of his close police associates testified that there was no knife.

In contrast, spread across the entire top of a page in the *American Opinion* article is a photograph of an ominous-looking object, with the caption "Shown here is the knife which hoodlum Ronald Nelson used in attack on Officer Nuccio."

What had caused the jury, despite all expectations, to convict Nuccio? We need not guess, for Ron Weiss, a young advertising man who was the foreman of the jury, told the story in an article that appeared in the once lively but now defunct *Chicago Free Press* (November 9, 1970). He seems to have kept a sort of journal of what occurred, either in his memory or in written form. He commented on the contrast between the soft-spoken, conservatively attired prosecution lawyers Matthew Walsh and Richard Jalovec and the boisterous, informally dressed defense counsel Echeles.

Weiss was much impressed by the testimony of the Cook County pathologist, who declared that his findings were not consistent with the description of the Nelson shooting given by the police. But Echeles was good, if highly dramatic, in his closing argument. One of the jurors remarked later, "I damn near applauded, it was that moving."

Two questions were of continuing concern to the jury. Why had Nelson run away if he hadn't done anything? Why hadn't any of the state's witnesses seen a knife? The foreman had remained undecided through several votes. He began to ask himself why Nuccio had been the only police officer to draw his gun; the others had not. And he remembered that Nuccio had admitted that he had stopped Nelson sixty to a hundred times in the previous eighteen months and had never found any weapons on him. Why would he now suddenly believe that Nelson was armed with a knife? Weiss might also have asked why Nuccio needed to pursue Nelson, since the officer knew where the young man lived.

So Nuccio was convicted by his peers. They had been turned around by the force of the facts as they finally saw them.

The John Birch Society and its local police committees were not alone in the defense of Nuccio. A Cleveland police newspaper, the *Blue Line*, raised $1,300 for his appeal and presented the money to him at a banquet. Nuccio was solemn, stoic, and laconic at the event. "At first, I thought I was pretty much alone in this," he said. But the previous week he had received $4,275 from another group, and more was coming in from strangers. Whether the Birch Society assistance was only verbal I do not know. Later Birch publications dwelt only on the poverty of the "lonely" police officer.

After Nuccio lost the jury trial, he appealed to the Illinois Supreme Court. It sustained the conviction and sentence (*People v. Nuccio*, 54 Ill. 2d, 39, filed March 20, 1973): "This court cannot say that the evidence here is so palpably contrary to the verdict or so deficient as to cause a reasonable doubt of the defendant's guilt."

I never saw Ronald Nelson and had nothing to do with Nuccio's trial. I became associated with the matter when the boy's parents asked me to file some civil suits on their behalf. As the family's attorney, I attended the inquest into Nelson's death. I tried to question Nuccio about the circumstances of the death. Nuccio, availing himself of the constitutional privilege against self-incrimination, would not take the stand. I questioned one or two other witnesses rather briefly.

Why, then, is it necessary to deal with the case at such length? In the defamatory article that gave rise to my suit against Robert Welch, Inc., I was charged with being the architect of a Communist plot against the police and the frame-up of Richard Nuccio for murder. These falsifications, coupled with other untrue statements about me, aroused me to do what others defamed by the Birch Society had not done. I decided to call the defamers to account.

4 ■ The Nelsons Sue Nuccio and the City

Ralla Klepak, the attorney who brought Ronald Nelson's parents to me, was an old friend. Our association began at a garden party and grew through a common interest in the theater. In time, Ralla gained confidence in my ability as a trial lawyer, particularly in the field of civil rights (I was a pioneer litigator in that area). Thus, when Ralla became interested in the complications that arose from the shooting of Ronald Nelson, she introduced me to Ronald's parents and asked me to represent them with her in suits based upon this ultimate deprival of civil rights—the taking of a life. I took the lead and so became the Birch Society's target. When I sued them, Ralla became a witness, a good one.

When Ralla brought Ronald Nelson's parents to my office, I told them about the federal Civil Rights Act, based upon the Fourteenth Amendment to the Constitution. This amendment was enacted in the post–Civil War period so that those deprived of their rights by those acting under color of law might recover money damages.

Since Ronald was dead, there was a question about who might sue for the wrong done to him and the extent of the recovery. The problem was complicated by the fact that Ronald was not really a Nelson, although he was known by the last name of his stepfather, his mother having divorced his father and married Nelson. There was a question too about who could be sued. Obviously Richard Nuccio could be sued, but he probably had no assets from which we could collect a judgment. It would be more practical to sue the city of Chicago if we had the legal right to do so because the city presumably had funds available for such a purpose. The law at that time seemed to preclude a suit against the city for a willful act like Nuccio's, but there might be recovery for negligence.

We decided that we would file the usual civil-rights suit in the federal district court and a suit in the Cook County Circuit Court for the wrongful death of Ronald. There could be only one recovery, but we would pursue both remedies simultaneously. We would make Nuccio and the city parties to at least one of the suits, regardless of an ultimate lack of success against the city. Perhaps we would be paid out of the insurance carried by the city, or the city would voluntarily settle with us. This had been done. We also hit upon a third alternative—a suit by Ronald's mother for the wrongs done to her in addition to those done to her son. I should say at the outset, because of what the Birch Society people contended later, that neither Ralla Klepak nor I were ever paid a penny in connection with these legal proceedings, nor were the Nelsons. There was some hope of a cash recovery but no fulfillment.

Ralla and I filed the civil-rights suit on July 12, 1968, in the U. S. District Court for the Northern District of Illinois, Eastern Division. We named as plaintiff Ronald's stepfather, Douglas Nelson, "as Administrator of the Estate of Ronald Donaldson, also known as Ronald Nelson, deceased." We named Nuccio as defendant.

We said that on or about June 4, 1968, young Nelson was peaceably going about his business in the vicinity of Clark and Addison streets in the city of Chicago. At approximately 10:00 P.M., he began to sprint through the adjacent parking lot and alley, as was his habit since he had been on a high school track squad. Thereupon, Nuccio began to pursue him without any provocation or reason. At no time did Nuccio call out or command Nelson to stop but suddenly and without warning fired his police revolver at the youth, hitting him in the back and injuring him greatly.

Then Nuccio and another police officer dragged Nelson some distance and laid him on the ground. Despite the seriousness of Nelson's injury, neither Nuccio nor the other police officers called an ambulance. The youth was allowed to lie on the ground for approximately twenty minutes before being taken to a hospital in a police vehicle. He was pronounced dead at the hospital that night.

Nuccio never had a warrant authorizing the arrest or apprehension of Nelson. At no time that day or immediately prior had Nelson committed any crime, nor did Nuccio have any reasonable or probable cause to believe that he had done so.

We declared that Nuccio was known to be a person of violent and ungovernable temper, given to threats, profanity, and abuse as a police officer.

We concluded that what Nuccio had done constituted a violation of the Constitution and laws of the United States in that Nelson was thus deprived of his life, liberty, and property without due process of law, all in violation of the Fourteenth Amendment to the Constitution and Title 28, United States Code, Section 1343(3), and Title 42, United States Code, Sections 1983 and 1985.

Nuccio's attorneys admitted the harmless portions of the complaint but denied everything that created liability. They contended that Nuccio fired his police revolver "in self-defense," the same defense that was made unsuccessfully at Nuccio's trials for murder. They contended further that at the time, Nelson was "committing a breach of peace, contrary to the ordinances of the City of Chicago and the laws of the State of Illinois." The ordinances and laws were not specified. Of course, they declared that Nuccio was in no way liable and that the case should be dismissed.

The civil-rights case went on in the federal court while our county court proceedings were also going on, as well as the murder trials and appeals previously narrated and the libel action, the principal subject of this book.

On December 8, 1970, we appeared before Judge Alexander J. Napoli to ask him to enter *summary judgment* on the issue of Nuccio's liability—that is, a judgment without trial, none of the material facts being in genuine dispute. Damages could be left for later determination. It should be noted that Judge Napoli had been an assistant state's attorney of Cook County and had earlier represented the police individually and as an organization. He was a conscientious judge, and we felt sure that he would follow the law and the facts, regardless of where they led.

We advised Judge Napoli that since Nuccio had already been found guilty of murder on the facts involved in our case, we had proved beyond a reasonable doubt (1) that Nuccio had no reasonable or probable cause to take action against Nelson; (2) that the shooting of Nelson by Nuccio was without lawful justification; and (3) that the shooting deprived Nelson of his constitutionally protected rights without due process of law. Therefore, we contended, summary judgment should be entered against Nuccio. The city counsel filed a memorandum in opposition to our motion for summary judgment; we filed one in support of our motion; and ultimately Judge Napoli filed a memorandum in support of his order granting our motion.

During the course of the legal proceedings, Nuccio was represented from time to time by two other attorneys as well as the corporation counsel of the city. The latter wanted to withdraw from the case because if we were right, Nuccio was guilty of willful misconduct, which the city was not required to defend or compensate. Judge Napoli refused to permit the corporation counsel to withdraw but permitted additional private representation on behalf of the police officer.

On January 22, 1971, Judge Napoli granted our motion for summary judgment on the issue of liability and set the case for trial on damages.

How do you determine the dollars-and-cents value of loss caused a family by the slaying of a youth? One is not supposed to speculate or guess in making the valuation. We produced actuarial tables to project Nelson's life expectancy. We offered evidence of the financial help he had given his family. He was about to enter the army when his death intervened. We told of his decision to have his army compensation paid, at least in part, to this family. We displayed to Judge Napoli, after waiving the jury that we had originally requested, letters from responsible persons attesting to the responsible qualities of Ronald.

One counselor had advised the Army Recruiting Service with candor:

> I have found Mr. Nelson to have a good deal of potential vocational aptitudes and energy which need to be channeled into a meaningful field of work. He would have the ability to do well in a career that he deems worthwhile. He responds well to sound and sincere advice in these matters.
>
> In addition, he has certain personal attributes which could be brought out by a regimented routine; while certain faults would be contained by the military regulations.

One worker attached to Youth Action, a cooperative project of services such as the Chicago Boys Club, the Chicago Youth Centers, the Hull House Association, and the YMCA of Metropolitan Chicago, advised the military:

> As a youth worker involved with this individual, Ronald Nelson, and his peers, I have been able to see him in a leadership position in his group. On occasion he has initiated activities for the group and has assisted me in arranging tournaments for his peers. He has been able to work with others, has shown perseverance in tackling tasks given him.

I believe he is mature enough to be accepted into the United States Army and gain and hold a position of importance.

All this hope had been dashed by a bullet in the back. How much was it worth? Judge Napoli fixed the sum at $20,000, by no means an extravagant judgment. No part of this judgment has ever been paid.

Since it was likely that no judgment against Nuccio alone would be collectible, we worked out a legal theory that would lead to a valid judgment against the city of Chicago. We filed a suit by Ronald's mother, Priscilla V. Nelson. We made several of the same allegations that we had made in the civil-rights complaint and then went beyond it.

The heart of our suit was that Nuccio had an active and unrestrained antagonism for Ronald, shown by his threatening on numerous occasions to arrest him for crimes he had not committed and to injure, maim, and kill him. These actions caused great mental anguish, severe emotional disturbance, nervous exhaustion, and suffering to Ronald's mother. On numerous occasions she had informed officials of the Chicago Police Department that Nuccio was harassing and threatening her son, and pleaded that he be restrained and prohibited from such conduct. Mrs. Nelson also requested Nuccio to cease harassing and threatening her son. All these requests failed, and Nuccio did not change his ways. This continuous ill will led ultimately to Nuccio's killing of the young man.

These charges were supplemented in a second count claiming that the city, the police department, Nuccio, and other police officers at the scene of the shooting—intending to cause Mrs. Nelson great mental anguish, or so recklessly indifferent thereto as to amount to intent—willfully failed and refused to inform Mrs. Nelson that her son had been injured.

Somewhat later, Mrs. Nelson was told that her son had been shot and injured. She immediately placed a telephone call to the Nineteenth District "Town Hall" Station of the Department of Police to learn of his condition. She was told that while her son had been shot, his condition was not serious and he could be visited at American Hospital. However, the police knew that Ronald had been killed or at least seriously injured.

Upon being given this misinformation, Mrs. Nelson immediately went to American Hospital where she learned that her son was dead. Upon learning of the death, having been falsely informed that her son was not seriously injured, Mrs. Nelson immediately collapsed. She then suffered great mental anguish, with resulting physical disabilities and injuries, causing her to be placed under the care of a physician and to lose much time from her employment.

The city corporation counsel moved to dismiss our complaint, claiming simply: "Plaintiff has failed to state a cause of action." This bare statement, unsupported by explanation, was enough to cause Judge Albert Hallett to dismiss our complaint for "legal insufficiency." We then appealed to the Appellate Court of Illinois and won half a victory, the wrong half (*Nelson v. Nuccio*, 131 Ill. App. 2d 2611, February 26, 1971). The action against Nuccio was sustained but not the one against the city, so we were partially thwarted in our plans. (The appellate court made some important pronouncements on the concept of mental anguish, useful to others. Long after the suits were completed and too late to do us any good, the U.S. Supreme Court created municipal liability for civil-rights violations by employees.)

Some perspective on this police shooting is provided by a study entitled *Split-Second Decisions: Shootings of and by Chicago Police* issued by the Chicago Law Enforcement Study Group. The report, issued on May 8, 1981, covers a period somewhat later than that of the slaying of Ronald Nelson in 1968. However, its conclusions are as true for that period as for the years studied:

- More than a third of the 523 civilians shot by Chicago police from 1974 through 1978 were not engaged in life-threatening behavior when shot (14% were shot unintentionally).
- Shootings of civilians by police rose by 62% from 1978 to 1980.
- Almost 40% of the 187 police shot in these five years were shot by themselves or fellow officers.
- 80% of the civilians shot by police are of minorities, although it was impossible, based on the available data, to establish definitively or disprove police racism.

The report made several key recommendations. Among them:

- The Chicago Police Department should adopt a "defense-of-life" shooting policy.

- Intensive "officer survival" training should be instituted to teach officers how better to find and use protective cover and to de-escalate potentially violent encounters. Police service revolvers should be modified, as was done by the Los Angeles Department, to preclude the cocking of weapons prior to firing, a practice which has led to numerous accidental shootings of police and civilians.

These measures might have prevented the shooting of Ronald Nelson. That, in turn, would have precluded the murder trials of Richard Nuccio, the filing of the civil-rights suits, the libeling of me, and the filing of my libel suit.

5 ■ What to Do?

When I helped the Nelsons sue Officer Nuccio and the city of Chicago, I unwittingly made myself a target of the Birch Society. Many Birchers fervently believed that the mysterious Insiders were seeking to undermine America by discrediting the police. When police behavior at the Democratic National Convention was criticized, the Birchers assumed that the Insiders had orchestrated the whole affair. And to them it was obvious that Elmer Gertz must be a tool of the Insiders. After all, I had served as counsel of a blue-ribbon commission that had criticized the police role, and I had helped a family sue a police officer that same year. What *American Opinion* said about me may have seemed the plain truth in their eyes. I *must* have been a Marxist, a Communist-fronter, and a conspirator.

I was by no means the first to be smeared by the Birchers, but I was the first to fight back. To sue them for libel risked dragging my name through the mud again and demands on time, emotion, and pocketbook.

If I took on the Birchers, I could expect a struggle. Confronted with the outrageous article in *American Opinion*, I had to decide what to do about it. I had to act in a relatively brief time; there is a short statute of limitations on libel.

I had to ask, first, What is *defamation* and *libel* (written demation)? Then I had to inquire if what *American Opinion* said of me was actionable and not simply insult and name-calling. Could I prove it? Certainly, the article included false and defamatory statements.

I was dealing with a complex area of law, one that was evolving rapidly. Briefly put, the laws of defamation seek to balance two important areas of public interest: (1) the right of an individual to protect his or her reputation from unjust attack; (2) the right of free speech, as protected by the First Amendment to the Constitution.

Traditionally, protection against defamation had largely been defined by common law—guidelines resting on the accumulation of judicial opinion formed in response to the workaday cases in the courts. Common law regarding defamation was created generally in the courts of the states. If the federal government was involved at all, it may have been to prevent or limit prior restraints on speech. (*Prior restraint* means government or private activity to prevent publication of material believed to be dangerous or disagreeable. One can take action only after publication occurs.) There is also a constitutional basis for the general right to speak out in *fair comment*, including a right to comment upon persons, provided one is fair, nonmalicious, and substantially accurate. (Fair comment does not include obscenity, use of "fighting words," or promotion of some substantive evil that presents a "clear and present danger" to society.)

At common law, a person could sue for damages if a statement about him or her (1) was published, (2) was untrue, and (3) impugned an otherwise good reputation. Generally speaking, fault on the part of the publisher did not need to be proved; there was *strict liability* for defamation. It was only later that the law required proof of fault.

However, at this time freedom of the press had become a matter of increasing concern. Some said that easy collection of defamation judgments by plaintiffs had a "chilling effect" on the press. According to this argument, the press was engaging in self-censorship to avoid costly lawsuits. This in turn supposedly stifled the free debate of issues that is necessary for effective self-governance in a democracy.

The press did find protection in several legal doctrines under the old common law. One was the right of fair comment, described above. The press was also immune from attack, or "privileged," if its source of information was an official government document. A third defense, somewhat difficult to establish, concerned the state of mind of the person responsible for the publication of defamatory material. *Conscientious error* was sometimes a defense; *maliciousness* was likely to cost money.

A few years before my case was filed, the law of libel had begun to change. In 1964, a case was appealed to the U.S. Supreme Court, and defamation, long a common-law issue, became a matter of federal constitutional law. This pivotal case, *New York Times v. Sullivan*, 376 U.S. 254, still stands as a major landmark in the law of defamation. In balancing the right to a good reputation and the right to free speech, the Court made distinctions about the kinds of speech to be protected. It concluded that speech regarding *public officials* in their official conduct would not be actionable unless published with *actual malice*—that is, the publisher's knowledge of falsehood or reckless disregard of truth.

The nation, and particularly the South, was in the midst of the civil-rights ferment. "Freedom riders," mostly from the North, were invading the old Confederacy to assert the civil rights of blacks. Northern newspapers and magazines proclaimed the sins of those who would deprive the blacks of their rights. Naturally, southerners did not cherish this, and they sought means to prevent or to punish interferences with their so-called domestic institutions. They called to their assistance the law of libel and the new concepts of legal *jurisdiction*—the "long-arm" statutes that permitted them to obtain court jurisdiction over distant persons and entities.

Some of the statements in the advertisement that was the basis of Sullivan's libel action were not accurate, and the trial judge submitted the case to the jury under an instruction that the statements were "libelous *per se*," and therefore Sullivan must recover, regardless of the defendant's intent, unless the jury was persuaded that the statements were true in all respects.

The U.S. Supreme Court rescued the defendants: "We hold today that the Constitution delimits a state's power to award damages for libel in actions brought by public officials against critics of their official conduct." In this situation, the Court required proof of actual malice. Such proof of actual malice, the Court continued, must be shown with "convincing clarity." *Actual malice* was defined as knowledge of the falsity of what was published or reckless disregard of truth.

The Court conceded that the advertisement was published without checking its accuracy against material in the *Times*'s files. But this was declared insufficient to prove actual malice.

Then, to show that it truly meant to make recovery by public officials difficult it not impossible, the Court in 1968 set forth rigid standards for proving actual malice in *St. Amant v. Thompson*, 390 U.S. 727. Conceding that the law in this area must be developed on a case-by-case basis, the Court nonetheless declared that "reckless conduct is not measured by whether a reasonably prudent man would have published, or would have investigated before publishing." "There must be sufficient evidence to permit the conclusion that the defendant in fact entertained serious doubts as to the truth of his publication." It was just too bad, but required by the First Amendment, that this policy puts a premium on "ignorance, encourages the irresponsible publisher not to inquire, and permits the issue to be determined by the defendant's testimony that he published the statement in good faith and unaware of its probable falsity."

It was immediately apparent that a defamed public official would have an almost impossible burden. The situation was further worsened by a series of cases holding a vast gamut of minor characters to be "public officials." In Illinois, for example, an ordinary police officer was held to be a public official. And in 1967 the *New York Times* rule was extended to "public figures" in the consolidated cases of *Curtis Publishing v. Butts* and *Associated Press v. Walker*, 388 U.S. 130. Almost everyone with a modicum of notoriety was defined as a "public figure." This was a kind of "bootstrap" operation in which it was enough for a newspaper to mention a person to make him or her a "public figure." Otherwise, why would the person be mentioned?

It appeared at this time that it was only logical to extend the rule requiring proof of actual malice to private persons, provided only that they were mentioned in matters of "public interest." Prurience could make the most private person a subject of inquiry. The rulings seemed to mark the end of defamation actions by anyone—public officials, public figures, or private persons—involved in matters of public interest. The burden of proof had simply become too great for the average person, and the media rejoiced. Almost smugly, they seemed to take the judicial rule protecting them as a matter of course.

My involvement in other libel cases and privacy actions influenced my decision. Almost from the beginning of my career as a lawyer in the early 1930s (and continuing to this moment), I had handled one libel case after another. I learned many things from being a libel lawyer, chiefly that one does not grow rich in Illinois, or elsewhere, by representing plaintiffs. The big money is made in the defense of libel representing the newspapers, particularly the *Chicago Tribune*.

The prodigious influence of the *Tribune* and the media generally in Illinois had helped them gain some unusual advantages in legal precedent. One is the state's unique "innocent construction" rule that if words could reasonably be considered innocent, as a matter of law, there would be no cause of action. This ruling rang the death knell for many libel actions in Illinois, and I was the unsuccessful attorney in a case that helped to establish it. My case did not involve the *Tribune* but a local Hearst newspaper.

I represented a scholar and author of considerable distinction, Dr. Maurice Parmelee. He was connected with a federal agency as an economist, which was surprising in view of the nature of much that he wrote. His book on nudism was the subject of a celebrated obscenity suit, and he also wrote about communism and other controversial subjects. This aroused the interest of Westbrook Pegler and other Hearst writers who were prone to see Communists under every bed and in all governmental agencies. Pegler implied that Parmeleee was of this group. It was injurious for Parmelee, a federal employee, to be considered a Communist; therefore, this was libelous per se. Of course, it was also precarious for a government employee to sue a powerful newspaper, but Parmelee was nothing if not courageous.

The case came before Judge Harry M. Fisher, long an advocate of the right of newspapers to be critical of public officials. Even before *New York Times* his opinions had drastically reduced the possibility of recovery in libel cases. He believed strongly in the marketplace of ideas and was very sensitive to any effort to limit the newspapers' right to speak out.

We discussed my complaint in the *Parmelee* case in light of the judge's well-known views. To my surprise, he found the first count of the complaint (which I regarded as rather weak) strong and the other count (which I regarded as strong) so weak that it did not state a cause of action. He denied the motion to dismiss the first count and approved the motion as to the other count.

In the course of discussion, we reached a settlement of the first count. I thought it was a very modest figure, but I was assured by the house counsel of the Hearst newspapers, Kurt J. Salomon, that it was the largest amount the Hearst papers in Chicago had ever paid in settlement of a libel suit. Strangely, they would not settle the other count, and I was compelled to appeal it.

The argument before the appellate court was proof that one can never tell in advance what such a tribunal will think or do. Only in retrospect, after one has seen the written opinion of the court, can one really size up the oral argument and what it portended. Then it is too late, except for future guidance.

In my characteristic manner before a reviewing court, I was discussing what I regarded as the outrageous nature of the abuse of Parmelee by the Hearst newspapers. One of the justices, Kiley or Lewe, remarked at this point, "You are rather hard-hitting yourself, Elmer, in what you write." I smiled, foolishly pleased that the justices had read my articles and reviews. I then went on to explain the differences between what I had written and the defamatory publication against Parmelee. I had no inkling of how the justices would react. Later I knew that consciously or subconsciously they had given me a preview of their thinking.

Justice Kiley, who played a role in the case that is the subject of this book, wrote the opinion of the appellate court sustaining the defendants' motion to dismiss the Parmelee suit (*Parmelee v. Hearst Publishing Co.*, 341 Ill. App. 339, [1950]). It was, as I have said, the origin for the innocent-construction rule of Illinois.

Most Chicago lawyers (and, I suppose, lawyers in other cities) are in mortal fear of opposing newspapers in litigation, especially in libel actions. Through principle or foolhardiness, I have always had little hesitation about suing the press or writing about it. I have not confined my activities to the *Chicago Tribune* and the Hearst press. I have had cases involving the Field newspapers, both the morning *Sun-Times* and the evening *Daily News* (now defunct), despite my being a sometime contributor to both and a friend of the editors and columnists. It does not seem to have harmed my relations with them, a tribute to them.

One would not think the specialty of libel law dangerous. I had reservations on that score when I received a telephone call from a disbarred lawyer informally representing a man reputed to be a leading member of the crime syndicate in Chicago. His client was about to be released from the county jail where he was serving a sentence on a highly technical charge. I did not know if other accusations against him were true, but I was sure that he should not have been convicted on such slender grounds in this instance.

Just before the call, I had read in at least one newspaper that the man had once committed a brutal murder in which he hung his victim on a meat hook after viciously assaulting him. Of course, I did not know if the charge was true, and I was not going to consider anyone guilty without a trial. I was assured by my caller that the charge was completely untrue. "You are the only lawyer in Chicago with guts enough to represent such an unpopular person and to bring suit for him against a newspaper." I cannot say that this compliment filled me with enthusiasm. I was not too communicative; indeed, scarcely audible. My caller went on: "Will you see my man when he gets out of County?" I decided quickly that at the very least I ought to see the man.

A few days later he called upon me. He did not look the monster he was reputed to be. He gave me an account of his health. Apparently he was dying of a multiplicity of causes. He talked of various matters, including the lies and libels of the press and the sins of their allies in the state attorney's office. Then he got to the point. One newspaper in particular had invented an utterly untruthful story that he had murdered someone. He had done no such thing and could easily prove it. He wanted to sue the paper for libel and collect as much as possible. I was the only lawyer who would handle such a case.

What do you say to such an appeal? I explained the law of libel, especially the defenses and stratagems newspapers have in such cases, the practical difficulties. I recalled that Don Reuben, the *Tribune* lawyer, had cross-examined a plaintiff so mercilessly in a pretrial deposition that he was forced to drop his suit. I then explained that injury to a good reputation is the gist of a libel action. When one's reputation is not good, regardless of the truth, one is unlikely to recover. Defense counsel could trample one's life until nothing was left of it. My would-be client saw the point, and that was the end of the matter. I felt relieved.

There was a bloody aftermath. My would-be client was indicted several years later, charged with the murder of an associate a decade earlier. (Murder has no statute of limitations; charges may be brought at any time.) A short time before the trial was to begin, he was "executed" in gangland fashion in the garage adjacent to his home.

During the years I have opposed Don Reuben in several libel cases. The ill-fated case of Dr. Myrtle Farnsworth against the *Chicago Tribune* (43 Ill. 2d 286, 1969) involved a basic constitutional issue—whether a trial court could refuse to instruct a jury in the very words of the freedom-of-speech section of the Bill of Rights of the Illinois Constitution of 1870. I wanted Judge Henry Dieringer to submit the following instruction to the jury: "Truth is a defense in a libel action only when published with good motives and for justifiable ends." The judge refused to follow the Illinois constitutional provision because he was persuaded by Don Reuben that it was federally unconstitutional by reason of *New York Times* and later cases.

The *Tribune* had published a series of articles about medical quacks and had singled out my client, an osteopath, for special, not to say venomous, attention. All sorts of mischievous and defamatory statements about Dr. Farnsworth had in effect hounded her out of her profession.

The trial was stormy. At one point Judge Dieringer threatened to commit me for contempt, my one such experience. I was not conscious of having uttered one disrespectful word. I had simply persisted in maintaining a viewpoint different from Don's.

In my opinion, many errors had been committed at the trial, and I felt, particularly in view of the constitutional provision, that we ought to prevail on appeal. For example, I thought I had clearly proved that the author of the articles had done insufficient research, had deliberately misstated many basic facts, and was determined to harm Farnsworth; in short, she was actually malicious.

However, the Illinois Supreme Court decided the appeal adversely to us, essentially on the federal constitutional issue. The justices urged that health is a matter of the greatest public importance and that newspapers therefore had the right to deal bluntly with medical quackery and would be protected against judgments in libel suits as long as they were not "malicious" in the constitutional sense, even if they were not accurate in what they published. The court ruled that the provision in the Illinois Constitution of 1870 protecting truthful statements only when they were "published with good motives and for justifiable ends" was federally unconstitutional. This was the first case, federal or state, that had gone that far. Constitutional protection for the public discussion of public issues became accepted practice until my case limited such protection, as we shall see.

From another case I take tremendous satisfaction, even though it is not a great one. The man I represented, Seymour Zeinfeld, is a fine but not famous person. The amount involved was not staggering, the issues fairly common. True, the case became important because of the rules laid down by the Illinois Supreme Court with respect to *conditional privilege*, later to be involved in my libel suit and frequently mentioned in the cases and legal treatises (*Zeinfeld v. Hayes Freight Lines*, 41 Ill. 2d 345, [1968]). The suit was filed in 1959. The final order was not entered until May 1972. The thirteen years of litigation had amazing ups and downs in the Circuit Court of Cook County, the Appellate Court of Illinois, the Supreme Court of Illinois, and again in the circuit court. It was deader than Marley in each court on more than one occasion, but I brought it to life again and again.

Another factor important in my decision concerned practical issues, including the time and place of publication. Had the *American Opinion* article been published in 1957 or 1958 when I was in the news because of my efforts to free Nathan F. Leopold, Jr., a perpetrator of "the crime of the century," and had *New York Times* been decided prior to that time, I would clearly have been a "public figure" and would have had to prove "actual malice" in the *New York Times* sense. Or if the defamatory publication been made in July 1969 or later, shortly after the date of the actual publication, I would have been regarded as a "public official" because I was then running for election as a delegate to the Illinois Constitutional Convention (a position that I won). I would then have had the burden of establishing "actual malice." But in March or April 1969 I was a private person and could prevail, I thought.

The loss of the *Farnsworth* case gave me pause. I reasoned, however, that *Farnsworth* had been decided improperly and that even if it was a fair barometer of the law, it could not be said that I fit within its parameters. I was not then a public figure in the constitutional sense, and I was not then personally involved in matters of great public interest. I had not thrust myself into any controversy. I was simply a private attorney in private litigation, handling it in the courts, not in the media. I had not touched the *Nuccio* murder case in any meaningful fashion; indeed, I did not know Nuccio.

In addition to considering the relevant law, I had to consider the forces against which I would contend. One did not lightly tackle the John Birch Society or any of its emanations. Of course, I already knew a good deal about the Birch Society, and what I knew was not reassuring. In time, I learned more about it. I was shocked later when I was told that declining from its auspicious start, the society was in bad shape at the time it published the article about me, and then it took another turn for the better. On some levels, the society is a clandestine organization, concealing its membership from public scrutiny. On other levels, it is highly visible. Certainly it has made no secret of its views and aims.

I found one book especially helpful: *The Radical Right— Report on the John Birch Society and Its Allies* by Benjamin T. Epstein and Arnold Forster, top staff men of the Anti-Defamation League of B'nai B'rith. I learned that the police question was one of the most important campaigns of the society when the article was published. The campaign, conducted under the slogan "Support Your Local Police," was "both a part of the national Birch program and an intensive local activity; it involves infiltration and it makes use of front groups; it is a holding maneuver against the enemy, a Society recruiting device, a propaganda slogan, a hullabaloo of buttons and bumper-stickers."

The campaign had begun in the society's *Bulletin* of July 1963 and was designed to exploit the white backlash and recruit police into the ranks of the society. The all-knowing Robert Welch said that the police were "the best friends everywhere of anti-Communists like ourselves." In the same issue of the *Bulletin* there was much praise for the handling of black demonstrations by the police in Birmingham, including the use of police dogs. Within a year, hundreds of committees to Support Your Local Police were formed. Many of the police were grateful and joined the ranks, mostly covertly, and enlisted others on and off the forces. A huge quantity of John Birch material was distributed.

The Epstein-Forster book told of the total John Birch Society apparatus. In the corporate structure were Robert Welch, Inc., The John Birch Society, Inc., and the Belmont and Western Islands publishing companies. There were several enterprises bearing the name *American Opinion*, chiefly the monthly magazine by that name, which was owned by Robert Welch, Inc. Its shareholders included the society itself and such wealthy right-wingers as N. B. Hunt of Dallas. Robert Welch purported to be the editor, but he entrusted daily management to Scott Stanley, Jr., a young man who had been active in rightist causes before joining the magazine. As I read the roster of shareholders, associate editors, contributing editors, and advisory editors, and learned some odds and ends of information about them, I could see that I was involved in an enterprise pitting me against the sort of people I had always fought.

As the book concluded:

> In the long run, Americans will . . . reject the false counsels of the Birchers and their allies. What is of deep concern, however, in the years ahead, is the damage that the Radical Rightist manifestation can do to the climate and the processes of democracy before the good sense and moderation of the American people render it a mere footnote in the history books of tomorrow.

I considered the costs, the delays, the uncertainties, the complications, and they did not daunt me. I asked myself if I was contradicting my strong belief in First Amendment freedom of expression.

In the end, I decided to sue, whatever the cost. The conscious process of decision making and my instincts compelled me to take action.

6 ■ I Strike Back

Where to sue, whether to file in state or federal court, whether to request a jury trial—all were initial issues in taking action.

Under the old law when travel was difficult, suit was filed at the defendant's place of residence, for reasons of fairness and due process. But as geographical distances became less important and space could be bridged easily, there arose the concept of "long-arm" jurisdiction. Under this doctrine, an aggrieved person can sue wherever the cause of action arises, regardless of the residence of the one who has wronged him. Obviously, we wanted to sue in Chicago rather than in Belmont, Massachusetts, where Robert Welch, Inc., had its principal place of business. It was incorporated and did business under the laws of Massachusetts. Filing in Chicago would give us and our witnesses ready access to the court; the defendant, away from its home base, would not share such convenience.

There were advantages in filing the case in the federal rather than the state court. Such cases normally belong in state tribunals unless there is complete *diversity of citizenship* (the parties are domiciled in different states) and the damages claimed are in excess of $10,000. The substantive law of the state where the cause of action arises governs, but the procedural rules and practices of the federal trial court govern. Of course, Robert Welch, Inc., and we were worlds apart philosophically, but fortunately we also differed in domicile, and clearly I had suffered damages in excess of $10,000.

As it turned out, the defendant did not contest our filing the case in the federal court. It did not seek to transfer it to the state court as it might have done. Perhaps its attorney felt, as we did, that we were likely to get a better judge and a fairer and speedier trial in the U.S. District Court for the Northern District of Illinois, Eastern Division. But if speed was the objective, we all were doomed to disappointment.

On June 17, 1969, Wayne B. Giampietro, as my attorney, filed suit in the federal court and requested a jury trial. (In that period, before the Supreme Court ruled otherwise, a jury, even in a civil case, consisted of twelve persons. By the time the case was tried a second time, only six were required.) The complaint set forth, in two counts, the basis of my cause of action, at greater length than required. We felt that there were strategic and psychological advantages in telling the story in an engaging fashion.

Plaintiff [Gertz] was born in Chicago, Illinois, and has lived his entire life in this city, except for a few years in his youth, in Cleveland and a few months, during his college years, in Brooklyn. He was educated in the public schools of Chicago, except for the few years he spent in Cleveland. He attended the University of Chicago for six years, receiving his bachelor's degree (Ph.B.) in 1928 and his law degree (J.D.) in 1930. He is married and has children and grandchildren who reside in the Chicago area. His family, friends, acquaintances, colleagues and clients live, for the most part, in the Chicago area. He belongs to professional, literary, historical, religious, educational, philanthropic and civic organizations in the Chicago area. He belongs to and has held numerous offices, including that of president, in such organizations. He belongs to the American, Illinois State, Federal, Seventh Circuit and Chicago Bar Associations, Appellate Lawyers Association of Illinois, and the Decalogue Society of Lawyers, and has served on the committees of these groups and has been president of the latter organization. He has received awards and citations for public services from several groups. He has written books, pamphlets, articles and reviews, some of his work appearing in leading newspapers, magazines and encyclopedias. Biographical notices of him appear in several standard reference works, including *Who's Who in America*, *Who's Who in the Midwest*, and *Contemporary Authors*, all of which are readily available to the public as a whole, including defendant.

....

At all times plaintiff has deservedly enjoyed a good reputation as a lawyer and citizen, continuously throughout his career, and has always been thought of and has always been a loyal and respected citizen of the United States, and has never been thought of or accused of being disloyal to the United States or to its system of government.

Sometime prior to March 22, 1969, defendant caused to be written, printed, published and distributed to the public at large, a certain pamphlet containing an article entitled "Frame-Up, Richard Nuccio and The War on Police." [We attached a copy of the pamphlet to the complaint.]

Copies of the said pamphlet have been shipped to various groups, organizations and individuals within the State of Illinois by defendant and, with the knowledge and approval of defendant, have been distributed to the public at large by said groups and individuals within this State, which is the State where plaintiff lives and carries on his profession. The said article is of and concerning a series of events and alleged events that occurred within the City of Chicago, State of Illinois, where the person who wrote said article for defendant came to obtain the statements placed in said article.

Defendant has continued its distribution of this said pamphlet in Illinois up to the present time, the latest said distribution to the public [before the filing of the complaint] being on June 15, 1969, at Oak Brook, Illinois at a gathering of the John Birch Society, at which the principal speaker was Robert Welch.

As we learned later, the distribution of the magazine and reprint actually continued for months after the filing of my suit, about a year.

We then set forth some of the false and defamatory statements concerning me. Since they are already given in full in a preceding chapter, they need not be repeated here. The complaint was required to give the libelous statements in full, together with any necessary innuendo.

The complaint went on:

The said libelous publications are intended by defendant to, and do in fact, depict and represent plaintiff to his clients, his colleagues, the courts and the public in general in Illinois and elsewhere as a believer in, a follower and advocate of Communism and Leninism, a member of or affiliated with the Communist Party and organizations controlled by it, a leader of or a participant in Communist conspiracies, an enemy of the government, a believer in force, a revolutionary and an enemy of law and order, all and each of which statements were and are utterly false and untrue and were known by the defendant to be false and untrue at the time of printing such article. Such false and libelous publications are intended to hurt plaintiff in his professional reputation and practice as a lawyer and as a citizen and to prejudice him in his relations with his clients, colleagues, the courts, and the community and public generally. As a lawyer he is particularly sensitive to such false and defamatory charges.

In particular, plaintiff has never been connected in any way with the Marxist League for Industrial Democracy, the League for Industrial Democracy, or the Intercollegiate Socialist Society. Plaintiff was not one of the original officers of what defendant styles the "Communist National Lawyers Guild" or the National Lawyers Guild. During the period when plaintiff was a member and officer of the National Lawyers Guild, its membership included lawyers of great reputation, and public officials and jurists of the highest rank, including some who became Justices of the Supreme Court of the United States. Its conventions and other meetings were attended and addressed by Presidents of the United States and others of great stature and reputation. Plaintiff has not been connected in any way with said National Lawyers Guild for over fifteen years. Plaintiff has never been connected in any way with the Chicago Peace Council.

The bad faith and malice of defendant is shown by the fact that neither it, nor anyone connected with it, nor the author of the defamatory article, nor anyone in their behalf, made any inquiries whatsoever of plaintiff, his family or associates as to any of the matters and things set forth in the said article. Defendant made no effort to verify any of the false and defamatory allegations contained in said article, but either relied upon the barest and basest hearsay and misrepresentations or completely fabricated such statements.

A principal theme of defendant's said article is that Police Officer Richard Nuccio was "framed" on a charge of murder by several persons, apparently including the Judge, the State's Attorney, various witnesses, and plaintiff. Since Nuccio's appeal from the murder conviction is now pending in the Supreme Court of Illinois and since the suits filed in behalf of the victims of Nuccio's acts are pending in this and other courts, plaintiff expressly excludes at this time, without waiving any rights with respect thereto, the allegations of the said article with respect to Nuccio, confining himself herein without waiving any rights with respect thereto, to the other defamatory statements made by defendant against him, which do not involve the consideration of the Nuccio suits. Of course, plaintiff expressly denies that there was, or is, any conspiracy to frame Nuccio for any crime whatsoever and denies that he was, or is, involved in any way in any such alleged conspiracy.

The conviction of Richard Nuccio for murder is presently pending on appeal before the Supreme Court of the State of Illinois as are three suits growing out of the acts of Richard Nuccio on June 4, 1968, one presently pending before the United States District Court for the Northern District of Illinois, one presently pending before the Circuit Court of Cook County, Illinois. The publication of the said article by defendant at this time while said suits are pending before various courts of law is an attempt on the part of defendant to interfere with this said litigation and to prejudice the parties thereto, including those persons represented by plaintiff and to interfere with the process of these said courts. These acts are a further indication of the malice of defendant against plaintiff.

As a result of the said article, plaintiff has been, and is, or may be, injured in his good name, credit and reputation, both as an individual and as an attorney at law. At the present time plaintiff does not know how much actual damage he has suffered as a result of this said article, and, therefore, seeks only nominal actual damages. However, the actual malice and viciousness of said article, entitles plaintiff to a large amount of punitive damages.

WHEREFORE, plaintiff demands judgment against defendant in the sum of ten thousand and one dollars ($10,001.00) actual damages and five hundred thousand dollars ($500,000) punitive damages and his costs of suit herein and such further or different relief as to this Court appears to be just.

The second count related to the article from which the reprint was made. After repeating some of the allegations of the first count, the complaint alleged:

Sometime prior to March 24, 1969, defendant caused to be written, printed, published and distributed to the public at large a certain magazine entitled "American Opinion," issue of April, 1969, which said magazine contained an article entitled "Frame-Up, Richard Nuccio And the War on Police," a copy of which is attached hereto as Exhibit and incorporated by reference as though fully set forth herein.

This said magazine has been shipped by defendant to various bookstores, newsstands and other distributors of magazines within the State of Illinois and, with the knowledge and approval and with the assistance of defendant, has been distributed to the public at large by said groups and individuals within this State, which is the State where plaintiff lives and carries out his profession, and the said article is of and concerning a series of incidents which occurred within the City of Chicago, State of Illinois, which is where the person who wrote said article for defendant came to obtain the statements which he placed in said article. . . .

In addition to said statements in said article, there appear on the inside front cover of the April, 1969, issue of "American Opinion," the following statements:

". . . But we do know that when *American Opinion's* Alan Stang goes after the facts in a story he gets them—just as he has, again, in the very important article beginning on page one."

"Mr. Stang reports this month on the framing for murder of an outstanding Chicago police officer—a man with no less than twenty-six formal citations for the excellence of his police work. That this is a part of the Communist war on our police is as certain as the innocence of the officer they have chosen as their symbolic target. So important is this one, in fact, that reprints will be made immediately available."

We then asked for the same amount of damages as in Count One.

As time went on, the setting of the case changed considerably. After our suit was filed, the conviction of Nuccio for murder was upheld by the Supreme Court of Illinois, and dispositions were made of the civil cases that Ralla Klepak and I had filed for the Nelsons. It became apparent too that I had suffered actual damages far in excess of the nominal amount I had requested. Accordingly, the complaint was amended to reflect this.

Here, then, is the setting for the case. In the months and years that followed, the court files became crowded with motions, orders, depositions, and a melange of other material.

7 ■ The Laborious Course of Our Case

Even though the courtroom and its conflicts are not faithfully mirrored by television, the movies, or the stage, many legal battles do have an element of drama. The cast of characters includes the protagonists, their attorneys, the judge, the courtroom personnel, the witnesses, the jury, and the spectators, the buffs, often senior citizens, who take a special joy in judging what goes on. With or without the participation of the media, those who take part in legal proceedings are actors, good or bad. Their histrionics no less than their professional and human capacities, influence—even determine—the results of some cases. Juries, it has been said with some truth, may try the lawyer, not the client. They may be more impressed by the performers than the law and the facts.

The other litigant was a corporation, an impersonal entity, nominally without body or soul. But corporations act through their officers, agents, employees, and lawyers, and these are the ones who impress or depress the triers of fact. In the first trial, Robert Welch, Inc., was visible only through Winfield Scott Stanley, Jr., its managing editor, and James A. Boyle, Jr., its attorney. No one else in the corporate family appeared, not even the author of the article.

It is true that I appeared and spoke, but the presence of my young counsel, Wayne B. Giampietro, counted for much. In a real sense, there was a different Wayne Giampietro in the second trial than in the first, just as there was a different jury. The dramas were different.

Then there were the judges—Bernard B. Decker in the first trial, Joel Flaum in the second. It may be rewarding to discuss the whole cast of characters, not at length but enough to give the flavor of the conflicting personalities and how they may have influenced their words and deeds.

In the long years of delay between the two trials, Wayne B. Giampietro matured as a lawyer and as a person. He was in charge of both trials, under my guidance, but there was a world of difference between the two efforts. In the first, he was competent but not inspired. By the time the retrial came around, he had become a self-assured, resourceful, dynamic lawyer on the way to achieving stature in his profession.

Wayne had to work his way through school; he even drove a bus for the Chicago Transit Authority. But he managed to go to Purdue University and then to Northwestern. He had enthusiasm and brains, and he was not afraid of hard work. He was not especially impressive in appearance, but he made up for this in his drive, devotion, and enthusiasm. I found him very useful in the Ruby case and later when I wrote a book about that case at the urging of the publisher Dwight Follett. I continued to employ Wayne when he left law school, and he remained an associate of mine as long as I continued in the active practice of the law. In time he became my partner.

When I learned that the defendant was represented by James A. Boyle, Jr., I was puzzled, perhaps perturbed. I knew Jim Boyle. He and his partner and I had been associated. Our client was a strange character who faced disbarment, and we rescued him from this embarrassment. Somehow I did not think of Boyle as one who would represent the John Birch Society in any of its guises. However, I could not really describe the kind of attorney who would be appropriate in such company.

Jim Boyle turned out to be better than the usual opponent, better certainly than his successors. Years later, I learned more about him and was intrigued by what I learned. He sent me an attractive pamphlet he had written, *Return to Runnymede*, dealing, among other subjects, with judicial encroachments in the legislative process, and he inscribed it, under date of May 16, 1978, "To Elmer Gertz, a most distinguished lawyer, worthy adversary and good friend."

Jim Boyle accomplished far more than his supposedly tougher successors. He kept us from introducing evidence that would have been harmful to his client; he kept the award of damages down; and he prevailed through a posttrial motion that was set aside only when his successors took over. Would he have won in the end? I do not think so, but as I said earlier of Echeles, he merited the opportunity.

I must confess that it is difficult for me to depict Judge Bernard B. Decker, who presided at the first trial, in a wholly sympathetic light. It is not that I think he was prejudiced against me; indeed, I think he respected me, was as friendly as our conflicting positions permitted, and tried to be as fair as possible. The key may be found in one of our very first in-chambers conversations when he told me bluntly that he thought it was a mistake for me to pursue my case. "It can only result in the repetition of the libel," he said, "and can do you no good. Money cannot compensate you for any harm done to your reputation." He seemed to have a genuine distaste for defamation suits and a respect for the concept of freedom of expression. I wondered how he would have felt if he had been the victim of falsehoods. Yet when the defendant's attorney challenged the sufficiency of my Complaint, and on a few other occasions, he ruled in my favor.

My longtime friend the bookish lawyer Alexander J. Isaacs spoke warmly of Judge Decker, whom he referred to as "Bernie." They had gone to Harvard Law School at the same time, and they had both attended the fiftieth reunion of their class at Cambridge. Much later, one of Judge Decker's district-court colleagues, my dear friend Judge George N. Leighton with whom I had gone on a special mission to the Soviet Union just before the start of the second trial, spoke of Decker with much respect. I did not dislike the judge. I simply did not warm up to him as I had to several others who had places on the federal bench in my time. Some of them were reputed to be cold and unsympathetic, but I had found congenial human qualities in them. Somehow Judge Decker did not affect me that way.

In proceedings in open court, I was careful to let Giampietro take over completely. Despite the temptation to speak out, I generally remained silent. But when we were in the judge's chambers, I occasionally yielded to the urge to participate. After all, it was my case, it meant much to me, and I had considerable experience as a trial lawyer, especially in the field of libel. Judge Decker would caution me, rather good-naturedly, "Elmer, you are the client here, not the lawyer. Let Wayne do the talking."

There was one especially illuminating episode. As required by the pretrial order, we had told the judge that we were going to call Julius Lucius Echeles as a character witness and to prove that I had had nothing to do with the prosecution of Richard Nuccio, as charged in the Stang article. In our judgment, he was strategically situated to be of special help to us because of his intimate relationship with the defense of Nuccio. Judge Decker cautioned me not to use him as a witness. He did not spell out his reasons, but they were apparent and possibly persuasive. Echeles had once been convicted of a felony (selling Post Office jobs), gone to prison, and been disbarred. Later he was pardoned and reinstated as a member of the bar. I had recommended his reinstatement, as had a chief justice of the Supreme Court of Illinois. Then, briefly, Echeles had gotten into trouble again, perhaps because of his exigent manner of conducting criminal defenses. I am sure that Judge Decker was trying to be helpful to me, but at the second trial we did use the controversial attorney as a witness, and he was superb. Undoubtedly, his testimony made a great impression upon the jury, even if they heard him only through a deposition transcript.

We were more troubled when Judge Decker made one especially harmful evidentiary ruling. We wanted to demonstrate to the court and jury that Alan Stang, like other Birchers, was much too quick and careless in calling people Communists or dupes of Communists. Of course, I was not the sole victim of this looseness of terminology. General George C. Marshall; Presidents Dwight D. Eisenhower, Richard M. Nixon, John F. Kennedy, and Lyndon B. Johnson; and many others in high places had been labeled in the fashion that had caused me to sue. We wanted to offer evidence to substantiate our point, but Judge Decker entered an order forbidding us to offer such evidence. In the second trial, no such limiting order was entered, and we made the point very tellingly.

Nor would Judge Decker require the defendant to bring in Stang as an adverse witness. This refusal supported the defendant's claim to have no control over him. We had reason to believe this claim false.

When Judge Decker later dismissed my case, notwithstanding the jury verdict in my favor, he gave what he regarded as sufficient reasons for his judgment. We will discuss this episode in due course.

There were other, more immediate problems.

When I began the practice of law more than sixty years ago, Illinois still based its legal practices and procedures on the common law. The pleadings were highly technical and artificial. Sometimes one did not know what the case was really about when one read the pleadings. Trials were duels in the dark. "Discovery" was virtually unknown. Then Illinois adopted "code pleading," in common with many other states and the federal system. This enabled litigants to take oral depositions more readily, use written interrogatories, examine documents and objects, get admissions of fact. With a resourceful attorney and the financial means to stand the cost, one could learn all about the other side's case before the trial took place. This, we believed at first, was calculated to ensure justice by ascertaining the truth. But like other good things, this extensive discovery process began to miscarry. It could be used by the resourceful attorney and affluent client to wear out litigants who could not afford the process. Justice was often thwarted. The monitors of the legal system are now seeking means to contain the discovery process so that it will be a device for justice.

In my case, the opposing attorneys resorted to every kind of device, supposedly to ascertain the truth and arrive at justice. My deposition was taken more than once. The depositions of others were taken, sometimes duplicitously. There were interrogatories galore, requests for documents—everything in the arsenal of discovery.

And there were motions galore. Boyle was resourceful and ingenious, and indeed there were unresolved issues because of *New York Times* and its progeny. (I do not set forth the various motions because their gist is apparent in the judge's rulings.)

On November 18, 1969, Judge Decker denied the defendant's motion to dismiss my complaint. The judge's memorandum opinion (306 F. Supp. 310) remained of importance throughout the proceedings and in effect was not superseded by the opinion of the U.S. Supreme Court or anything that followed, despite repeated efforts by the defendant to wish it away by various motions and strategems. It requires partial transcription here:

> Plaintiff's complaint alleges that he has been injured in his professional reputation and practice by defendant's publications. The alleged defamatory statements include representations that plaintiff has been an "official of the Marxist League for Industrial Democracy, originally known as the Intercollegiate Socialist Society, which has advocated the violent seizure of our government," that he is "preeminent" in the "Communist National Lawyers Guild," and that he is a "Leninist" and a "Communist-fronter."

Prior cases have uniformly held that it is libel per se under Illinois law to falsely label one a Communist. *Dilling v. IIllinois Publishing and Printing Company*, 340 Ill. App. 303 (1st Dist. 1950): cf. *Ogren v. Rockford Star Printing Company* 288 Ill. 405 (1919). Assuming that the resultant narrowing of the libel per se category is now the law of Illinois, plaintiff's complaint nonetheless establishes a per se case of defamation, for it meets the requirement that the challenged statements "prejudic[e] a particular party in his profession or trade." *Whitby v. Associates Discount Corp.*, *supra*, at 340., cast grave doubts upon an individual's qualification to uphold, apply and interpret our system of laws, a system opposed by Communist theory. *Cf. Grant v. Reader's Digest Ass'n.*, 151 F. (2d Cir. 1945). The instant charges "impart to him a want of the requisite qualifications to practice law . . ." and are therefore actionable per se. *Colmar v. Greater Niles Township Publishing Corp.*, 13 Ill. App. 2d 267, 270 (1st Dist. 1967).

Because plaintiff's complaint sufficiently avers a libel per se, actual and punitive damages may be recovered without pleading special damages. Accordingly, defendant's challenge to the jurisdictional amount must fail. See, e.g., *Lorillard v. Field Enterprises*, 65 Ill. App. 2d 65 (1965).

For the reasons heretofore assigned, an order has been entered today denying the motion to dismiss.

The defendant was now required to file an answer to my complaint. Many of the factual allegations of my complaint, but not its conclusions, were admitted. Some were denied in this same general form.

Defendant's attorney, who could be very shrewd, would occasionally insinuate something that was not relevant to what we had alleged. For example, in dealing with one of the autobiographical paragraphs of my complaint, he pleaded: "Defendant makes no answers to [this paragraph], except to admit that plaintiff is a public figure as contended therein." We had made no such contention. With respect to another paragraph of the complaint, Boyle was almost magnanimous: "Defendant has no specific knowledge of the averments . . . but has no reason to doubt the truthfulness thereof." With respect to our extenuating allegations as to my one-time membership in the National Lawyers Guild, Boyle declared: "The defendant makes no response . . . because of the irrelevances of plaintiff's comments in that regard." Defendant admitted "that it did not make . . . inquiries of plaintiff or of his family" as to the charges made in its article. It thought the references to my "associates" "too vague to require a response."

Then the defendant got to the heart of its defense. It claimed that its widely circulated magazine had an editorial policy to promote what it called "political conservatism and constitutional democracy." It implements this policy by exposing to public view the activities and philosophies of all persons and organizations which are either Communist or which tend to achieve the objectives of Communism. It views the Communist movement as a present-day threat to traditional American institutions and as a matter of grave public interest and concern."

It published the article, the defense claimed, because the purpose of the Communist conspiracy was to undermine law enforcement and the police. Moreover, it believed that Nuccio did not receive a fair trial.

It declared that the words used in the article to describe me did not impute any lack of ability or integrity on my part but that because of my association, especially with respect to the Nuccio matter, the cause of communism was advanced. All that, it said, was fair comment, without malice and in good faith.

Moreover, it said, I was a "public figure" and indeed a "public official," and accordingly the article was privileged.

Then, not having succeeded in its motion for summary judgment, the defendant filed an amended answer, somewhat similar to the original. It then recited a series of so-called separate defenses. These turned out to be extremely important and not for the reasons the defendant may have assumed. We regarded them as admissions of important facts, and the court subsequently agreed with us (as will appear later).

In its new answer, the defendant elaborated on its contention that I was a "public figure" and a "public official." It cited my authorship of books, pamphlets, and articles, which, it said, covered a wide area of public interest and were widely published. It cited my many appearances on public issues before live audiences and on radio and television. It contended that I was a public official because I was connected with various public and quasi-public commissions and was an intended candidate for delegate to the Illinois Constitutional Convention. It contended that I actively participated in the Nelson inquest, that as a result Nuccio was bound over to the grand jury and indicted, and that the trial was widely publicized and a public issue. It declared that the article about which I sued was the result of a prolonged Communist conspiracy to undermine the police and public order and that one result of the conspiracy was the indictment and trial of Nuccio.

Having said these things, it shifted ground, noting that until the publication of the article it had no knowledge of me and that it relied upon Stang's article for its charges against me. It never thought that there would be any challenge to the truthfulness of the article.

For all of these reasons it believed the article was privileged under the First and Fourteenth amendments as fair comment made without actual malice. Then, to drive home its defense, it contended:

> The defendant denies that the words used in the said article, as they related to plaintiff, in their natural and ordinary meaning, impute to the plaintiff any want of ability or integrity as a lawyer, but portray him as one who associates with Communists and whose activities in the Nuccio matter furthered the plan of discrediting the police, thus advancing the cause of Communism. Thus, the allegedly defamatory words were true in the confines of the context intended.

We filed a motion to strike (delete) portions of the amended answer, and Judge Decker struck portions of the defense and the paragraph just quoted. Despite the court's ruling as to that paragraph, the defendant clung to this farfetched interpretation of its articles. Perhaps it had no choice, short of admitting liability. Boyle, like his successors, clung to his position, even when the court ruled against him.

We and Boyle continuously sought shortcuts that would terminate the case. We each filed a further motion for summary judgment. On September 16, 1970, Judge Decker disposed of these motions and hastened the case to trial. His memorandum opinion is significant in view of what followed during the trial. It said in part:

> The only evidence submitted relating to the issue of actual malice is the affidavit of Scott Stanley, Jr., managing editor of defendant's magazine. In brief, this affidavit states that the author of the challenged article was a "free-lance" writer, that a number of his works had previously been used by defendant, and that affiant had received no information

during such time which "seriously" challenged the truth of the factual averments in the author's writings. He further stated that he had therefore come to rely on the accuracy of his articles and conducted no investigation into the truth of the allegations in suit.

When there is a factual dispute as to the existence of actual malice, summary judgment is improper. See *Goldwater v. Ginsburg*, 261 F. Supp. 784 (S.D.N.Y. 1966), aff'd. 414 F.2d 324 (2d Cir. 1969), *cert. den.* 396 U.S. 1049 (1970):

> "The issue of actual malice on the part of defendants seems particularly inappropriate for disposition by summary judgment because it concerns 'motive, intent, and subjective feelings and reactions.'" (Citations omitted) (261 F. Supp. at 788)

In the instant case a jury might infer from the evidence that defendant's failure to investigate the truth of the allegations coupled with its receipt of communications challenging the factual accuracy of this author in the past, amounted to actual malice, that is "reckless disregard" of whether the allegations were true or not. *New York Times v. Sullivan, supra,* at 279–280. And whether these challenges to the author's accuracy were "serious" or not is a matter for the jury, rather than defendant, to determine. See *St. Amant v. Thompson*, 390 U.S. 727, 832 (1968); *Curtis Publishing Co. v. Butts, supra,* at 169–170 (Warren, C. J., concurring). This court cannot conclude, as a matter of law, that defendant either is or is not chargeable with actual malice.

In accordance with the foregoing, an order has been entered denying plaintiff's and defendant's motions for summary judgment.

I have not described all the pretrial maneuvering, but I have given the heart of it. The case proceeded to trial on September 21, 1970. I had been a member of the Illinois Constitutional Convention, but fortunately the convention ended some days before the trial date, affording me a little additional time for preparation.

8 ■ First Trial

We called Wayne Giampietro's wife, Mary, as our first witness. Mary told of "a lady there on the sidewalk handing out these pamphlets to people, and she walked up to me and handed me the pamphlet." At first, Mary pushed away the pamphlet. "She handed it to me again, so I took it."

When she glanced at it, she found that it was about the Nuccio case in which her husband and his employer were involved. She noticed the picture of me and other offensive material, called us promptly, and brought the pamphlet to our office.

When the time came to cross-examine Mary, Boyle declared, "I wouldn't dream of cross-examining counsel's wife."

We called Winfield Scott Stanley, Jr., the managing editor of *American Opinion*, as an *adverse witness* for cross-examination. (This meant that we were not bound by what he might say. In most circumstances, for better or worse, counsel must bear the consequences of the testimony of their witnesses, harmful or helpful. The better prepared one is, the less likely trouble is to ensue. We had previously taken Stanley's deposition.)

Giampietro masterfully pinned Stanley down to admit that he relied wholly upon Stang and had no independent knowledge of anything said in Stang's article. This was confirmed, as we have seen, by admissions in the defendant's pleadings.

In light of what Stanley said at the second trial, his admissions in the first trial must be pondered carefully. It was not always easy to show the differentiations because Stanley displayed a certain skill in evading his prior statements. His testimony bore signs of careful guidance.

One can get the flavor of his story by following the give-and-take of cross-examination—the questions propounded by Giampietro, the answers given by Stanley.

Q: Now, as managing editor of *American Opinion* magazine, what specifically were your duties?
A: My duties were to conceive, plan and prepare what would be in

each issue of the magazine. I decide what we are going to have in a magazine, watching carefully what is happening abroad and in the country and decide what, in my judgment, would make a good issue of that magazine. Then I would contact authors and hire them—not hire them, I would ask them to prepare articles. They would look into the matter, come back to me; I would say, "All right, we are going to go ahead with it." The manuscript would come in. I would go over the manuscript, prepare it for typesetting, I would go over galleys, proofreading, I would go over page proofs. I would locate photographs, decide which photographs were going to be in an issue. I would do, in short, everything that is done within an editorial office except type the manuscripts and answer the telephone.

Q: How long before the issue is actually distributed do you commence putting the articles—putting the magazine together?

A: Well, I may be thinking right now about an article that we would be running in six months or so. It depends upon the issue. Some issues are more immediate; you have to deal with them immediately. Some are long-range issues which will more generally affect the nature of political affairs in the country. So I really can't give you a more specific answer than that. I begin to make an outline of an issue about—about three months ahead of publication date....

Q: So your entire information as to what research was conducted by Mr. Stang come from Mr. Stang himself?

A: That is correct.

Q: Did you yourself make any attempts to verify any of the information appearing in this article other than speaking to Mr. Stang?...

A: No, I relied upon Mr. Stang.

Q: Did anyone else from the staff of *American Opinion* magazine do anything to check on any of the facts which appeared in this article?

A: No one else edited the article, I alone saw it and handled it....

Q: Did Mr. Stang come to you with the idea for this article, or did you come to him with the idea for this article?

A: I went to Mr. Stang with the proposal that he investigate the circumstances around the indictment of Officer Nuccio in Chicago....

Q: The idea was generated within the *American Opinion* magazine?

A: It was.

Q: And this was to fit the specific needs of the *American Opinion* magazine?

A: It was.

Q: Now, at the time this article was received by you in its manuscript form, did you know Mr. Elmer Gertz?

A: No.
Q: Had you ever heard of him before?
A: The only time I had heard of Mr. Gertz was in one of my telephone conversations with Alan Stang.
Q: Now, you also say in your caption underneath the picture of Mr. Gertz that he had been harassing Mr. Nuccio. What did you mean by that?
A: I meant to indicate what Stang says in his article.
Q: And Mr. Stang says in his article that Mr. Gertz had filed three lawsuits on behalf of the Nelson family against Mr. Nuccio?
A: That's correct, yes, he does say that.
Q: And when did you receive the manuscript for the article which we have been discussing, "Frame-up"?
A: The eighteenth of February.
Q: And when was that manuscript sent to the printer?
A: On, within twenty-four hours, I imagine.
Q: I think that it is safe to say, then, that . . . this article was in your hands for a considerably shorter period of time than is normal in the conduction [*sic*] of your business?
A: . . . It was only actually in my hands for about four hours. . . .
Q: Is there any connection between *American Opinion* magazine and the American Opinion Bookstores?
A: We are both children of the same corporate father.
Q: I see. So until the spring of 1970 you were still sending out reprints of this article?
A: We were still providing them to—to our bookstores and people who ordered them, yes, we were.

We requested that the defendant be required to produce Alan Stang as an adverse witness. We were certain that we could establish through him the flimsy nature of his alleged research about me. We were morally certain that he was part and parcel of the Birch Society apparatus, subject to its beck and call. But the defendant repeatedly represented to the court that Stang was simply a freelance writer over whom it had no control. Judge Decker refused to require the defendant to produce him and denied our requested jury instruction on the unfavorable inferences to be drawn from the failure to produce him.

Later we learned that the defendant had deliberately misrepresented the situation to the court, that in fact Stang was a contributing editor of *American Opinion*, contributing editor of another Birch Society magazine, and one of the chief participants in its speakers' bureau—in short, an important cog in its machinery. Besides, what he wrote was simply a reflection of what the managing editor of *American Opinion* had required him to write.

Stang did not escape us in the second trial.

The heart of a claim for defamation is *injury to reputation*. If your reputation is hopelessly bad, it is unlikely that you can recover, even if false charges are made against you. If you have a reputation in your community for truthfulness, integrity, good citizenship, loyalty, patriotism, you have the basis for recovery, all other aspects of your case being proved. So we called several witnesses to attest to my reputation. These included Ralla Klepak, who had brought me into the Nelson civil litigation, and Michael M. Kachigian, who with Julius Lucius Echeles had represented Nuccio in the criminal case (we thought it was in the nature of a coup to have the police officer's attorney vouch for me). But I was especially proud to have three outstanding lawyers speak well of me. There was Eli E. Fink, who had known me since we were both in the seventh grade in public school, a highly successful lawyer, the attorney for Paramount, RKO, Balaban and Katz, and other giants of the motion-picture industry. There was John Ligtenberg, a deeply religious man who had been decorated by Queen Wilhelmina of his ancestral Holland, the general counsel for the American Federation of Teachers and the Chicago Teachers Union. Finally, there was Frank Greenberg, president of the Chicago Bar Association and a strong proponent of judicial integrity.

These lawyers testified impressively regarding my qualities. They affirmed in addition that I had never espoused communism in any form and that a lawyer would inevitably suffer professionally and financially if he was charged with being in sympathy with communism. I am sure that they impressed the jury. We would have loved to have them as witnesses in the second trial, but, alas, Fink and Ligtenberg were dead by then, and Greenberg was too ill to appear.

I should add that we were permitted to read to the jury the transcripts of the testimony of Fink and Ligtenberg at the later trial but could not read Greenberg's testimony because the defendant's attorney raised questions we did not think it wise to argue too much. The law is that in certain circumstances, such as death, illness, distance, unavailability, depositions can be received in lieu of live testimony. Fairness is the basis of this rule. Of course, a deposition can seldom be as effective as live testimony, even though a good lawyer will do his best to give the air of realism to the reading of a deposition.

Defense attorney Boyle tried to discredit the testimony regarding my character and reputation. For example, after Wayne's direct examination of John Ligtenberg, Boyle cross-examined:

Q: Did you read the libel, the ostensible libel, in this case before you came here to testify?
A: I never saw the publication; haven't yet.
Q: Did you read libelous matter before you came to testify in this case?
A: I don't think so. I can't remember it.
Q: Elmer—or Mr. Gertz—never did tell you, then, what it was that he had been called by the defendant in this case?
A: Well, he told me that he had been called a Communist, a Leninist, or something of that kind.
Q: Did that change your opinion of Mr. Gertz in the slightest?
A: No.

The robust Ralla Klepak was a good witness on my behalf. Much of her testimony was invaluable.

Q: Have you had occasion to discuss Mr. Gertz with other members of the legal profession?
A: Yes, I have....
Q: As a result of these discussions, are you acquainted with and do you know the general reputation of Mr. Gertz in the community in which he lives at and prior to April 1969 for truth and veracity, honesty and integrity, being a good and loyal citizen of the United States and as an attorney?
A: Yes, I do. [She testified to the high quality of my reputation in these areas.]
....
Q: During the time that you have known Mr. Gertz, have you ever heard him espouse the Communist doctrine?
A: Absolutely not.
Q: And during the time that you have known him, have you ever heard him espouse the Leninist philosophy?
A: No.

It gave us great satisfaction to produce Michael M. Kachigian as a witness on my behalf; he was associated with Julius Lucius Echeles in the defense of Richard Nuccio.

Q: Now during the time that you have known him personally, have you had occasion to discuss Mr. Gertz or heard him discussed with other members of the legal profession?
A: Yes, I have.
Q: As a result of those discussions, are you acquainted with his reputation in the community of Chicago prior and on April 1969, for truth and veracity, honesty and integrity, being a good and loyal citizen for the United States and as an attorney?
A: Yes. [He testified to the excellence of my reputation in each of these areas.]
Q: During the time in which you have known Mr. Gertz, have you ever known him to espouse the violent overthrow of the United States government?
A: No, I have not.
Q: Have you ever known him to have been a member of the Communist party?
A: No, I have not.
Q: Or a member of any Communist organization?
A: None to my knowledge.
Q: Have you ever heard him espouse the Communist doctrine in any way?
A: None; no.
Q: Do you know a man by the name of Richard Nuccio?
A: Yes, I do. . . .
Q: And did you participate in the defense of Mr. Nuccio in that criminal trial?
A: I did, as cocounsel with Mr. Echeles. . . .
Q: Now, in connection with the Nuccio case, did you ever hear of Mr. Gertz being involved in that case in any manner?
A: None to my knowledge.
Q: Mr. Kachigian, did you ever see Mr. Gertz at the trial of Mr. Nuccio, the criminal trial which was held?
A: I don't believe so.
Q: Were you aware of any conspiracy or any plot to harass or to frame Mr. Nuccio?
A: None has ever been called to my attention, no.
Q: Did you ever hear of any Communist conspiracy to harass or to frame Mr. Nuccio for this alleged crime?
A: No, none to my knowledge.

Q: So, as far as you know, Mr. Gertz was never involved in any way in any prosecution or harassment of Mr. Nuccio—is that correct?
A: Not that I know of, no.
Q: Mr. Kachigian, did you ever hear of a man named Alan Stang?
A: I don't believe so.
Q: Did Mr. Stang ever contact you in connection with the Nuccio case?
A: Not to my knowledge.
Q: And you never talked to him, as far as you know?
A: No.
Q: You never gave him any information of any kind?
A: None; absolutely none.

It was clear to us that my testimony ought to conclude the presentation of our case. Wayne nursed me through the various allegations of the complaint, getting me to testify substantially as we had contended. Boyle did not obstruct the flow of my words. He could not easily complain; in his answer, he had conceded much that we had charged.

I described the nature of my practice during the decades that I had been an active member of the bar: "I have a very general practice; it includes everything from criminal cases to cases involving individuals and property, wills, estates, accounting suits, real estate transactions, trusts—every kind of litigation in various courts-and I have had some criminal cases, although most of my practice has been civil." Very quickly we established that no one had consulted me before the publication of the article.

Q: By the way, was that picture for that article obtained from you?
A: No.
Q: Did anyone ever contact you in connection with the writing of that article?
A: No one.
Q: So when you saw this article for the first time when my wife brought it to you, this is the first knowledge that you had whatsoever of this article?
A: That is right.

We covered every charge made against me in the article.

Q: Have you ever been a member of the League for Industrial Democracy?
A: Never.

Q: Have you ever been a member of any organization which advocated the violent seizure or overthrow of our government?
A: Never.
Q: To your knowledge, is there an Intelligence report in the Chicago Police Department concerning you?
A: I know of no such file and I know of no reason for such file....
Q: Were you ever involved in a peace parade in 1968 in the city of Chicago?
A: No, I was not.
Q: Did you ever have any connection of any kind with the report of the Walker Commission which is sometimes known as the Walker Report?
A: No, I did not.
Q: Do you know, or did you know before today, what the Red Guild was?
A: No, I never heard of any such organization and never belonged to it....
Q: Mr. Gertz, have you ever at any time espoused the Communist doctrine?
A: Never.
Q: Have you ever espoused a Leninist doctrine of any kind?
A: Never.
Q: Have you ever been a Leninist?
A: Never.
Q: Have you ever been a Communist?
A: Never.
Q: Did you have any connection [with] a commission which issued a report called *Dissent and Disorder*?
A: Yes; that was the Sparling Commission. I was retained as general counsel for the commission.
Q: And who sponsored the Sparling Commission, so far as you know?
A: It was a citizens' group. Dr. Edward J. Sparling, President emeritus of Roosevelt University, was chairman. It included Monsignor John Egan; it included Rabbi Edgar Ziskin, Dr. Joseph Evans from the University of Chicago Medical School, and a group of other civic leaders who were called in to make an investigation of circumstances surrounding a parade and demonstration that took place on April 27, 1968, on the way to and around the Civic Center of Chicago.

First Trial ■ 59

Q: This was a purely voluntary organization, was it not?
A: That is right.
Q: Was this commission in any way connected with any Communist organization or with the Communist party?
A: Oh, not at all.
Q: Were there any persons who were members of this commission who were Communists or connected with any Communist organizations?
A: None of them. They were men of the highest reputation.
Q: Now, you stated that you ceased being a member of the National Lawyers Guild some fifteen years ago. Would you state your reason for disassociating yourself with that organization.
A: I was about to become the president of the Decalogue Society of Lawyers, and I felt that I belonged to too many groups, and at that time I was less interested in the Lawyers Guild than others, so I ceased being a member.
THE COURT: Were you ever vice president of the National Lawyers Guild?
THE WITNESS: Yes, for a period of time during my membership. Yes.
Q: Mr Gertz, would you state how you came to become connected in any way with the case of Richard Nuccio?
A: I was asked by Ralla Klepak to associate with her in the filing of some civil actions. I had a good deal of litigation in that field, and after discussing it with Miss Klepak, I agreed to file the actions and did.
Q: In what capacity did you act in that case?
A: Simply as a private attorney handling private litigation.
Q: Representing the Nelson family?
A: The family of the deceased boy.
Q: Did you have any connection of any kind with the criminal case against Richard Nuccio?
A: No. The nearest I came to that was that I appeared at the inquest and asked questions of various witnesses.

. . . .

Q: Did you ever attend any of the sessions of the criminal case against Richard Nuccio?
A: Never.
Q: Did you at any time make any public statements regarding either the criminal case against Richard Nuccio or the civil case against Richard Nuccio?
A: No, I did not.

Q: Did you appear on any radio or television shows at any time wherein that case was discussed?
A: Not at all.
Q: Did you make any statements to newspaper reporters regarding either of those two cases?
A: I think I was called, and I referred them to the complaints that were filed by me. I told them all of the essential facts . . . outside of the courtroom.
Q: Did you ever meet Alan Stang?
A: Never.
Q: Did Mr. Stang ever contact you?
A: Never. . . .
Q: Other than the inquest which you testified you appeared before regarding Richard Nuccio, have you ever had any other contact with Richard Nuccio?
A: No. I tried to take his deposition, but the court ordered it delayed until after the criminal trial.
Q: And that deposition to which you refer was in connection with the civil suit on behalf of the Nelson family?
A: In connection with the civil suit, yes.

. . . .

Q: Were you ever involved in any conspiracy or combination of any kind concerning the prosecution of Mr. Nuccio for murder, or for any other crime?
A: Never.
Q: Were you involved in any Communist conspiracy to harass Mr. Nuccio at any time?
A: Never. . . .
Q: Have you ever held, prior to April of 1969, any public office?
A: Never.
Q: At the time that this article was published and when it was called to your attention in March or April of 1969, were you a candidate for any public office?
A: No.
Q: And you did not hold any public office at this time?
A: That is right.
Q: Did you intend at that time to become a candidate for any public office of any kind?
A: No, I did not.

Boyle had taken my deposition more than once, directed written interrogatories to me, done everything he could to get information about what he regarded as the more public aspects of my career. When I testified at the trial, he cross-examined me to develop the theme that I was a public figure and that public issues were involved in the *American Opinion* article. This was a typical exchange:

Q: How many different radio stations have you appeared on in Chicago, sir, during your lifetime?
A: At one time or another, I suppose practically all of them.
Q: And have you appeared on radio and television programs in cities other than Chicago?
A: When I was the attorney in a case in Dallas, Texas, I was interviewed in connection with that case, and in Cleveland, when I was there in a case, I was interviewed with respect to it, and several other cities. Most of my appearances have been in Chicago.
Q: All right. Have you ever appeared on panel shows in Chicago, on television or on radio?
A: Several times, yes.
Q: Within the last few years, have you appeared on panel shows in Chicago?
A: Yes, I remember appearing on panel shows—a panel show with respect to capital punishment.
Q: Were there any others? Just one in the last several years?
A: No, no; there were several others. I have appeared on panel shows with respect to First Amendment rights.
Q: Did you ever appear on the "Kup Show"?
A: Some years ago.
Q: All right. Well, during the time that you appeared on panel shows and made your various radio addresses, what was the scope of the subject matter covered by you, in a general way? Can you tell us that?
A: When I was on "At Random"—that's the CBS show; it is a conversation show; you can never anticipate what the subject matter will be, almost anything under the sun.
Q: Mr. Gertz, what I am trying to get at is that your presentations over the media of radio or television communications has certainly not been confined to purely legal subjects, has it?
A: I would say most of my appearances have been interviews in connection with cases in which I have been the attorney on one side or the other. But, sometimes, other matters.
Q: But you have spoken—have you spoken on political issues, sir?
A: Political, for candidates, no.

Q: Not for candidates, I mean political philosophies, sociophenomena of, say, communism?
A: No. I don't recall ever appearing on a show devoted entirely to that. I have been on shows in which public issues were discussed and the subject of communism would come up and other subjects would come up which were peripheral to it, but these were all informal, unrehearsed shows where you could never tell what would come up.
Q: How many times in all do you estimate that you were interviewed, either on radio or television, during the year 1969?
A: During the year 1969—that was one of the leaner years—not too many times during that year.
Q: Well, by—what do you mean by "not many times"?
A: Relatively few times, up until the tail end of the year, but that was a year in which I did not appear very often on radio or television.
Q: But you did appear?
A: A few times, yes.
Q: Yes, Mr. Gertz, I will change to another subject, and that is would other people—have other people written articles about you in your lifetime that appeared in the Chicago papers?
A: Yes, I was involved in some cases that you might call well known, or even notorious cases, and in connection with them there were, sometimes, newspaper articles.

The defendant offered little in the way of evidence, confining itself largely to documentation and the testimony of Stanley. Its reliance was on the public nature of the case and any weaknesses in our evidence.

The colloquy between counsel and the court concerning proposed instructions to the jury gave hints, none too clearly, of Judge Decker's ultimate thinking in our case. Perhaps wishful thinking kept us from discerning more sharply what he had in mind.

MR. GIAMPIETRO: Your Honor, may I ask one question? There are a couple of things that I am not clear on, at least as to your holding. There were two ways in which this public issue area may come into being. One is under the general old rules of libel that have developed about fair comment on public issues. The second thing is the *New York Times* rule.
THE COURT: Well, it also has something to do with the whole question of malice, doesn't it?

MR. GIAMPIETRO:	As I understand the *New York Times* and the following cases, they deal with public figures; people who are in the public eye. Under those rules—and I think that this is shown by the cases which I cited in my trial memo—in order to come within *New York Times*, you must speak of a person as a public figure and your comments must be directed to him in that capacity, as a public figure, on that, on any particular issue in which he may have injected himself....
THE COURT:	Well, you are arguing now the question as to "public figure."
MR. GIAMPIETRO:	Well, no, I am trying to make a differentiation, Your Honor, as to the kinds of rules of law that are going to be applied to this, because, under the *New York Times*, the definition of *malice* is very very strictly confined. Under the general rules of libel regarding public issues, it is much, much easier to prove malice, and many other things are admissible to show malice on their part, so I am trying to find out—
THE COURT:	Well, you are trying to find out what I am going to rule on the question of "public figure"—and if you are trying to do that, why—
MR. GIAMPIETRO:	Well, yes. Right.
MR. BOYLE:	Yes.
THE COURT:	Well, if you are trying to find that out, why, you want to smoke me out right now.
MR. BOYLE:	I think that the—
THE COURT:	I will hear your argument—do you necessarily want him [the court reporter] to take it down, or do you just want to make it informally?
MR. GIAMPIETRO:	Secondly, there is no showing that any of those articles [offered in evidence by the defendant] dealt with Mr. Gertz, and that goes to the foundation—
THE COURT:	Well, I will sustain the objection to the exhibits. I don't think that under any circumstances in the case do they have any probative value at all....
	Now, you had better go ahead and make your argument to us as to why you think that this evidence shows that he is a public figure.
	You found out—and the record will show this— that at the time of the voir dire examination [of prospective jurors] there was not, as I recall, a single

member of the panel who had ever heard of Elmer Gertz; at least I got no response. . . .

That's number one.

Number two, you have shown that he has been active in legal circles. You have shown that he has done some writing. You have shown that he has appeared on some television stations, and so has one of his witnesses, Frank Greenberg, who testified here.

Now, is it your contention that when a lawyer becomes prominent and gets into—and becomes engaged in some type of other activities as well as his law practice, his law business, that he becomes a public figure to the point where he can be used in a situation like this and find himself helpless to defend himself against libelous material on the basis that he is privileged? I mean under the First Amendment?

MR. BOYLE: It is my contention, Your Honor, that the philosophy behind extending the language of the ruling of the *Sullivan v. Times* case to a public figure was basically the access of the public figure to the mass media in order that he might respond to any kind of remarks.

THE COURT: Do you think that Mr. Gertz should have taken the podium and said, "I am not a Communist"?

MR. BOYLE: I think that Mr. Gertz certainly would have had, and continue to have, the public eye for that purpose and that his comments as a public person have, in the past, covered a great range of subjects and I think that he would have at his disposal a continuing availability, an ear to the public to give the public his own views on any subject, including the most vituperative argument against the John Birch Society or anything else, because he has had this access, and, with that philosophy, I would say that if—if a lawyer had achieved notoriety by being a great golfer and that's all, then I would say, now, there is a real question. But when this kind of a lawyer, whose great prominence arose dually, both through his notoriety that was achieved by his handling of prominent cases and by his altogether different role as an author, as a newspaper writer, his—he really has an identity that makes him, I think, officer of the court and as a public figure by virtue of his totally disassociated activities of author, etc.

	Now, in addition to that, when one looks at the evidence, the evidence simply shows that the reputation of Mr. Stang was such that an editor relied upon him.
	The record further shows that there was no knowledge of Mr. Gertz—
THE COURT:	Well, I understand that.
MR. BOYLE:	All right. So that I say that if Mr. Gertz is held to be either a public official or a public figure, and if Mr. Gertz is held to have been associated with those two issues, then Mr. Gertz is bound by the rule of the *Times* case, and he must prove actual malice.
	My contention is that there was not publication with knowledge of the probable falsity of the promulgated matter with the strong degree of knowledge required to overcome this privilege, and I don't think that there is an issue that is submittable to the jury on any one of those points.
THE COURT:	All right. I have no problem. If he is considered to be a public figure, there is a directed verdict. There is no question about that. I mean, there is no issue left. I mean, if he is a "public figure." I mean, and that there has been no malice shown.
MR. GERTZ:	With the distribution of the article for a year afterward—
MR. GIAMPIETRO:	Plus the fact that they didn't even talk to Nuccio's attorney. I think that's enough.
THE COURT:	I can say now, without any question, and it will appear of record in the case, that on the basis of the evidence that I have heard, that if I—if I should hold, or some other court should hold, that he is a public figure, that so far as the rest of the evidence is concerned, I would direct a verdict on the question of malice on the evidence that I have heard. I wouldn't even submit it to the jury.
MR. GIAMPIETRO:	First of all, it has been specifically held that an attorney is not, in and of himself, a "public official."
THE COURT:	I understand that.
MR. GIAMPIETRO:	First of all, in response to Mr. Boyle's statement, there was no trial involved in which Mr. Gertz participated.
THE COURT:	I know that.
MR. GIAMPIETRO:	So he can't say that there was a public issue on a trial because Mr. Gertz wasn't involved in that at all. He didn't speak out in any way on the matter. He did not

thrust himself into this issue. He made no public statements. Not of any kind. He wasn't available—did not open himself up to return comment. . . .

As to any notoriety or knowledge as to articles and books which he may have written, this article here about which we are suing does not refer to him in that capacity, and of course the best evidence of that is the fact that these guys at *American Opinion* never heard of him. They couldn't have been talking about him as a public official because they didn't know who he was.

I think that those cases specifically hold he must have spoken out in his public, official capacity.

THE COURT: I am not going to direct a verdict. I am going to submit the case to the jury on the basis . . . that this is a simple libel action in which a lawyer is involved, and the question will be to give them proper instructions under that theory of the case. If I am wrong, it can be taken care of, either by myself or by some other court at a later time.

So the judge arrived at the instructions he was going to give to the jury after the closing arguments. Of course, he gave the jury the usual guidance regarding its role as the trier of the facts—instructions given in virtually every case at the time—honored touchstones for arriving at the essential truth. Then the court went into the heart of the case, giving the following instructions (although not necessarily in this order; I have reorganized them for clarity):

The plaintiff's claim has two essential elements, as follows:
First, that the defendant published the magazine article and reprint pamphlet complained of herein.
Second, that the said libels were read by persons other than the plaintiff, namely, members of the general public.
The plaintiff has the burden of establishing the essential elements of his case by a preponderance of the evidence. If you find that he has done so, you will find for the plaintiff. If you find that plaintiff has not so established either of these elements, then you must find for the defendant.
In reading defendant's articles, the articles must be read as a whole and the words given their natural and obvious meaning. The headlines,

subheadlines, pictures, and captions in the articles must be construed in the context of the articles when read as a whole.

The article and reprint pamphlet involved herein, insofar as it relates to plaintiff, is libelous per se, because in calling plaintiff a Leninist and Communist-fronter, it imputes to him a want of the requisite qualifications to practice law, in that a belief in communism is inconsistent with his oath to support the Constitution and laws of the United States government, and casts grave doubts upon his qualifications to uphold apply, and interpret our system of laws, which is opposed to Communist theory.

Since this article and reprint pamphlet are libelous per se, plaintiff need not show that he has suffered any actual damage as a result of this article in order to entitle him to a verdict in this matter.

The fact that false statements are obtained from another source does not provide a defense to a libel suit. Put simply, a defamatory statement can be repeated, and repetition or republication does not render the statement true or correct nor excuse the defendant from liability therefor. The defendant may not rely upon the author to justify its actions.

Where the publication complained of is libelous per se and the defendant has not proved the truth, the plaintiff is entitled to recover compensatory damages such as will fairly compensate him for the injury he has sustained, if any. Mental suffering and injury to reputation as the result of a libelous publication need not be proved, but may be inferred from the nature of the injury.

In assessing damages, you may also award plaintiff such amount as will punish defendant for publishing the untrue defamatory statements concerning plaintiff.

If you decide for the plaintiff on the question of liability, you must then fix the amount of money which will reasonably and fairly compensate him for any damages he has suffered that were directly and proximately caused by the articles complained of. When I use the expression "proximate cause," I mean that cause which, in natural or probable sequence, produced the injury complained of. In fixing the amount of damages, you are to take into account the following elements:

1. his prominence in the community where he lives
2. his professional standing
3. his character
4. his good name
5. his reputation
6. the mental suffering and anguish occasioned by the publication
7. the extent of the circulation and republication of the libels

Gertz v. Robert Welch, Inc.

In general, we could not complain of the instructions as given. Our difficulty was in coping with restrictions imposed on our evidence. We were prevented from demonstrating the defendant's propensity for calling people Communists. We found it particularly trying to be thwarted in our plan to call Alan Stang as an adverse witness.

Boyle's closing argument was surprisingly restrained. We were especially pleased with his fairness as he concluded his talk to those who were to decide the fate of his client, at least for the moment:

> *As I stand here today, I can speak on behalf of my client and say that we don't think Elmer Gertz is a Communist.* We do think that we are a counterforce. My client is against not just against witches but something that is real, something that is out there now, and our editor spoke, or this magazine spoke, with a lot of hair on its chest, and we are content to let the kind of government that we are trying to save be perpetuated by giving you the control over that voice by your verdict. [Emphasis added.]

Wayne, who had been the first to argue the case, now closed it with his final arguments, the practice in trials as in debates. Then the instructions were given, and the jury retired for its deliberations.

The jury brought in a general verdict for me in the sum of $50,000.

The defendant was given time to file its posttrial motion, and in due time Boyle filed it. Frankly, we did not take it seriously. We thought it would be denied as a matter of course; that is usually what happens to such motions. But we were in for a devastating surprise.

9 ■ The Unraveling of a Victory

The defendant filed a motion for a *judgment notwithstanding the verdict* (despite the jury's decision) or a new trial. We thought it simply reargued what had already been determined by Judge Decker. But in view of what subsequently happened, we should review this motion in detail. It began with the old contention that I was a public figure

by virtue of being the author of books, newspaper columns, pamphlets, all of which covered wide areas of public interest and which were published all over the United States, and by virtue of having lectured in public and private forums, appeared in the State of Illinois and nationally on radio and television, many times as a panelist or guest speaker.

It then declared that its contention was supported by my Complaint, efforts to limit the scope of the deposition of me taken by the defendant, testimony during the trial, and the copies of newspaper articles that had been offered in evidence by the defendant.

It also declared that I had thrust myself into matters of great public interest:

The undisputed evidence in this case reveals that the plaintiff injected himself into a controversy of great public interest, involving a charge of murder against a Chicago policeman, Officer Richard Nuccio; and, in connection therewith, the plaintiff appeared at the Coroner's inquest upon the body of Ronald Nelson, whom Officer Nuccio was charged with murdering; and, during the course of such inquest, the plaintiff actually interrogated witnesses, and participated in the proceeding, in a capacity as legal representative of the family of the decedent. By reasons of such activity, participating in a statutory hearing, the plaintiff became a de facto public official.

By reason of the status of plaintiff as a "public figure" and a "de facto public official," he was precluded from recovering from defendant damages for alleged libel, without proof that such libel was published by the defendant, with actual malice; and there is no evidence in the record of this cause establishing such actual malice.

Defendant then outlined its contentions why a new trial should be granted if its primary motion for judgment was not allowed. It listed all the rulings of Judge Decker against it that it regarded as erroneous. One such alleged error was especially interesting:

> The Court erred in giving to the jury, over the objection of defendant, instructions which were contrary to the Constitution of the United States, and the law of Illinois, particularly instructions which charged the jury that the statements of defendant concerning plaintiff were libelous per se, and instructing the jury as to awarding damages to plaintiff in such amount as "will punish defendant for publishing the *untrue defamatory statements* concerning plaintiff."

Another of the stated grounds for a new trial was interesting in view of what happened at the *retrial* of the case: "The court erred in refusing defendant's tendered instructions concerning 'fair comment on a public issue,' and presenting the case to the jury in such manner as to deprive the defendant of its defense of fair comment upon a matter of public importance."

Judge Decker was taking an inordinately long time to dispose of the defendant's motion. I was beginning to worry; I had no clear sense that he was in our corner. Indeed I detected a kind of hostility to our cause not necessarily involving a personal dislike of me. I had a feeling that the courts were increasingly distrustful of libel cases that had any public aspects. *New York Times* seemed to have set in motion an inexorable process. Finally we were summoned to hear our fate. Judge Decker came to the point quickly:

> I am ready to give to you gentlemen this morning a memorandum opinion disposing of the motion for judgment notwithstanding the verdict, or, in the alternative, for a new trial, and that will explain the reasons for doing what I am about to do. It will explain the reasons for the judgment that I have reached that I have no alternative under the law, as the law now exists, except to grant this motion for judgment notwithstanding the verdict and, in effect, vacate the verdict of the jury awarding the plaintiff damages in the amount of $50,000.
> You gentlemen, I think, already know that I have spent some considerable time on this case already. I wrote two opinions.
> I permitted the case to go to the jury and I got, at least, for the benefit of the plaintiff, the jury's judgment about the—the jury's judgment

as to what the damages in this case reasonably should be, based on what the jury heard and based on the instructions that I gave the jury.

But subsequent to the trial of the case, I made a more thorough investigation into the law, and I am convinced in my own mind that the law as it now exists, and until the Supreme Court does something to change it, has extended the *Times* rule to not only public officials, public figures, but also to matters of public interest, and all this is outlined in the opinion.

Not only is that true insofar as the courts of appeal, a number of court of appeal decisions, but, as Mr. Gertz well knows, it has also been true in Illinois. The Supreme Court of Illinois, in *Farnsworth v. The Tribune* [one of my cases], certainly did the same thing, and, by analogy to all of these cases, I don't think that I have any alternative here except to follow the law as I think that the law has been set forth in these cases.

I will make this one personal observation, and then that will finish any statement that I may want to make. A trial judge's views as to what the law should be—I think you will agree with me—can't be substituted for what—and in this case where a member of the legal profession was involved I think that I had some difficulty in being objective, and particularly where there was a lawyer involved who was on the face of it at least maligned by what proved to be a baseless charge, and while I strongly favor a free press, I also favor a press that is responsible. And I think that a responsible press should be subject to the same requirements for meeting ordinary standards of decent behavior as other citizens. And I would hope that the Supreme Court—which I understand in considering this very subject now—would arrive at that same conclusion. But with the law, as I think that it has clearly been stated in these opinions, I don't think that this verdict can stand.

Judge Decker handed down his bombshell of an opinion on December 8, 1970. He summed up the factual situation with some restraint before arriving at his devastating conclusion.

At trial, Gertz testified as to his stature and reputation in the community. He is a prominent attorney in Chicago, having represented clients who sometimes command a wide following in the press and media. He has written books, articles and reviews which have enjoyed wide circulation. He has appeared frequently on radio and television, and has delivered numerous speeches. And he has long been involved in civic affairs.

Despite the above, the court held, in effect, that Gertz was not a public figure. In instructing the jury, the court determined that the publication in question was libelous *per se*. All issues were withdrawn from the jury except the proper measure of damages.

A closer examination of the article shows that its theme was more general and far reaching than just the trial of one Chicago policeman for murder. Instead, it painted the picture of a conspiratorial war being waged by the Communists against the police in general. Caught up in the web of the alleged conspiracy, aside from Gertz, was such a disparate cast of characters as the Lake View Citizens Council, the Walker Report, a Roman Catholic priest, and the Chicago *Seed* (an underground newspaper). In fact, although Gertz's picture was displayed in the body of the article he did not play a very prominent role in the article expose of the purported war on police.

This, it seemed to us, was a distortion of the whole case. If I "did not play a very prominent role in the article's expose of the purported war on police," how could I be regarded as an integral part of a matter of great public concern?

Judge Decker summed up the testimony of the managing editor of *American Opinion*: "While it may be that the failure to check the accuracy of the article was negligent, Stanley clearly did not act with actual malice or with reckless disregard for the truth. See *New York Times Co. v. Sullivan*, 376 U.S. at 287–288." He posed the issue confronting him:

> Plaintiff having failed to establish actual malice on the part of defendant, the issue presented in this motion is whether the court properly concluded that Gertz was not a public figure. If the conclusion was proper, then the award of $50,000 by the jury was not constitutionally impermissible. However, if the court erred in holding that Gertz was not a public figure then under the rule in *N.Y. Times v. Sullivan, supra* at 279–280 and *Curtis Publishing Co. v. Butts, supra* at 155, the article would be privileged under the First and Fourteenth Amendments, and the award of damages therefor would have been improper.

It did not seem to occur to the judge that I had not been given the opportunity to prove malice. If I failed to do so (and this we disputed), it was because he had decided that it was not necessary. I did not see why I should bear the consequences of any assumed error of judgment on his part. At that point in Judge Decker's opinion I had the right to assume that he would grant a new trial rather than dismiss the suit.

Unraveling of a Victory ■ 73

He resumed:

The issue is not as simple, of course, as the question of whether Gertz is a public figure. The penumbra of material protected by the guarantee of freedom of speech has been extended to include matters of public interest, whether or not public officials or public figures are involved.

The rationale for affording First Amendment protection to matters of public interest, as implied by *Hill, supra,* is that our system of government places great value on society's open discussion of not only public officials (*Sullivan*) and public figures (*Butts*), but also matters of public interest (*Hill*). A person allegedly defamed by matter pertaining to the public interest must satisfy a heavy burden, i.e., a showing of actual malice, in order to recover therefor. The rationale of *N.Y. Times v. Hill* [*sic*] has been applied to several decisions of the Courts of Appeal recently, all of which extend the guarantee of free speech to matters of public interest.

By analogy to the above cases, and to those cited in *Bon Air Hotel, Inc. v. Time, Inc., supra* at 861, n. 4, I think that the subject matter of "Frame-Up" was clearly one of public interest protected by the First and Fourteenth Amendments. A Chicago policeman's killing of a criminal suspect, and the policeman's subsequent indictment for murder at a time when the police generally were the subject of attacks within the community, commanded wide public attention and interest. By representing the victim's family in litigation brought against the policeman, Gertz thrust himself into the vortex of this important public controversy. *Curtis Publishing Co. v. Butts, supra* at 155. In affording First Amendment protection to defendant's publication, I reiterate that Gertz played a small part in the vast sweep of the whole article. What this court concerns itself with primarily is the public's right to become informed on a matter of public interest, rather than with any right to know about persons who have injected themselves into the limelight on that matter. See *United Medical Laboratories v. Columbia Broadcasting System, supra* at 712. The penumbra of First Amendment protection falls equally on references to Gertz, the Lake View Citizens Council, the policeman charged with murder, and the Chicago *Seed*.

Accordingly, the verdict for plaintiff is set aside and defendant's motion for judgment notwithstanding the verdict is granted. F. R. Civ. P. 50(b).

Embedded in the judge's opinion was an issue that gave the case its greatest significance. The judge said, in effect, that any person, public or private, involved in a *controversy of public interest* thereby lost ordinary protection against defamation. He said that "a person allegedly defamed by matter pertaining to the public interest must satisfy a heavy burden, i.e., a showing of actual malice, in order to recover therefor." In other words, according to Judge Decker's reading of the law, private persons have no more protection from defamation than public figures. Whether the *subject* in question was public or private was the criterion that determined a person's degree of protection from defamation. In a private controversy, a defamed person need demonstrate only a defamatory publication to collect damages. But a person unfortunate enough to be swept into a public controversy must show actual malice to recover.

To me, this accommodation between freedom of speech and protection of reputation seemed to lack balance. People who deliberately become public movers and shakers must accept a certain amount of "flak." But for private persons in public controversies, I believed a different balance should be struck.

Even accepting Judge Decker's questionable premise, however, I simply failed to grasp his logic. If I "played a small part in the vast sweep of the article," then surely I was not an integral part of any matter of public interest. I was disappointed in the judge and chagrined that we could not dissuade him. More than that, I was hurt, angered. I would not let the matter rest where the judge had left it. We gave formal notice that we were appealing to the U.S. court of appeals from the order that set aside the jury verdict and entered judgment for the defendant.

The defendant thereupon cross-appealed from that portion of Judge Decker's order that conditionally denied defendant's motion for a new trial. This was a technical requirement, to preserve the defendant's rights if it did not wholly prevail on our appeal. In the end, as we shall see, we did prevail in the Supreme Court but not in the court of appeals, and we had to retry the case almost seven years later.

We filed our appellant's brief in the U.S. Court of Appeals for the Seventh Circuit in my name (*pro se*) and in the name of Wayne B. Giampietro. The court did not take exception to this (as was later the case in the U.S. Supreme Court).

Our brief was lengthy. Of course, we thought it persuasive, but as it turned out, it did not persuade the panel of judges, who took an inordinately long time deciding the case, as if they were in

Unraveling of a Victory   ■   75

doubt or awaiting enlightenment from the highest court. Our brief made the following arguments:

1. In a magazine article and reprints of it, plaintiff falsely called me a Communist, Communist-fronter, Leninist, and Marxist. In addition, the article falsely alleged that I was a part of a Communist conspiracy to discredit and harass the police, in particular one Richard Nuccio, a police officer of the city of Chicago. Nuccio had been found guilty of murdering a nineteen-year-old boy. I had no connection with the criminal proceedings in the case but had represented the boy's family in a civil claim for damages against Nuccio. I had not made any public statement regarding this case, nor had I in any other way thrust myself into the vortex of public controversy.

2. At the time, I was clearly a private figure. The article referred to me as a private attorney, and no witness testified that I was a public figure. My various activities as a lawyer, community leader, and author did not make me a public figure within the meaning of *Curtis Publishing Co. v. Butts* or *New York Times v. Sullivan*.

3. Even though I was a private figure and did not need to prove actual malice, defendant's actions toward me constituted actual malice. Plaintiff had commissioned the author to write the article and had a preconceived notion of its contents. Neither the author nor the defendant made any effort to verify its seriously damaging allegations against me, even though the publication was a monthly and there was little deadline pressure. Nevertheless, defendant's managing editor elsewhere in the publication strongly vouched for the statements in the article. He also said the author was not connected with the magazine when in fact he was a contributing editor. Reprints of the article were forced upon residents of my neighborhood; distribution continued even after I filed a Complaint.

At the trial, not only did the defendant make no effort to prove the truth of its statements, but defendant's counsel admitted to the jury that I was not a Communist. All these factors together strongly demonstrated that the defendant indeed acted with actual malice. However, I had no opportunity to prove this because of inconsistent rulings of the trial court. Both prior to and during the trial, it ruled that I was neither a public official nor a public figure so need not demonstrate actual malice. However, after I received a jury verdict of $50,000, the court granted judgment notwithstanding the verdict, holding that I had failed to prove actual malice. Thus, at the very least, I should be granted a new trial at which to introduce evidence proving actual malice, and the author of the article should be required to appear for cross-examination at this trial.

Although no order was entered then or later with respect to the appearance of Alan Stang at the trial, we did take his deposition in due course. At the second trial, he finally appeared as a defense witness, and we had full opportunity to expose him to cross-examination. At that time, we understood why the defendant had not previously called him as a witness or permitted us to do so. Stang's allegations collapsed when he was subjected to an in-depth interrogation about them.

It will be remembered that the victorious defendant, not content with having prevailed on its motion, had filed a cross-appeal. Boyle was joined by Clyde J. Watts, of Oklahoma City. General Watts had been the attorney for General Edwin Walker in the latter's famous unsuccessful libel suit. Walker had been in charge of maintaining order when a southern university was desegregated. His was one of two cases in which the Supreme Court ruled that a "public figure," like a "public official," is subject to the *New York Times* rule requiring proof of "malice."

The defendant's cross-appeal brief declared that the trial court committed error

1. when it overruled the defendant's motion for a continuance when the defendant's then counsel was prohibited from completing necessary discovery;
2. when it struck certain allegations from defendant's answer to the complaint;
3. when it excluded certain evidence, which impaired the defense;
4. when it gave certain instructions to the jury;
5. when it directed the jury that defendant's article referring to me as a Leninist or a Communist-fronter was libelous per se;
6. when it instructed the jury that I need not show that I had suffered any actual damage to entitle me to a verdict; and
7. when it refused the defendant's requested instruction concerning fair comment.

Common sense teaches that one ought not to raise too many points in any argument lest what is really substantial lose its effectiveness. Defendant may not have suffered from such excessiveness since we lost this proceeding. But we and they were to learn that an interim victory or loss fades away.

In our response to the defendant's cross-appeal, we argued that the defendant was not prohibited from completing any necessary discovery, that it was not deprived of any defenses to which it was entitled, that it was not precluded from introducing any relevant evidence, and that the jury was properly instructed.

I have excluded all references to the defendant's answer to our original brief (or our reply to it) because we ultimately had to raise all the necessary arguments in the highest court of the land. For the sake of the narrative, I remain silent on these points; however, we fumed with frustration at the time.

Jim Boyle and General Watts appeared together for the oral argument before the court of appeals on January 31, 1971, Wayne Giampietro for me. The panel consisted of Senior Judge Win Knoch and Judges Roger Kiley and John Paul Stevens, jurists of competence, integrity, and experience. It was not the best panel from our viewpoint, nor was it by any means the worst. The judges knew me and respected me. One could be sure that they would not be influenced by personal considerations.

Wayne, as the appealing counsel, opened and closed the argument. He performed more than adequately in summarizing our case and answering the questions of the panel. One could not be sure how they reacted to him. The long interval between the oral presentation and the ultimate decision, handed down seventeen months later on August 1, 1972, indicated the care with which they considered the case (and, perhaps, their perplexity).

Ostensibly, General Watts, lanky and military in bearing, had the lead role for the defendant. He did well enough in presenting the basic points of the defense; the trial court's ruling in favor of the defendant lent him assurance. But whenever any of the judges asked a question, he turned to Boyle for the answer. Clearly, he was not sufficiently familiar with the record. As a matter of fact, he never became familiar with it, even for the argument in the Supreme Court. After a time, Boyle tired of the charade; when questions were asked, he answered them directly.

Unfortunately, no transcript of the oral argument before the court of appeals is now available, since the clerk of the court destroys such transcripts after six months. In a landmark case, this is unfortunate, but who could predict that this was to become such important litigation?

Judge John Paul Stevens (soon to be elevated to the Supreme Court) wrote the opinion of the court of appeals. The court disposed of the cross-appeal of the defendant in a short footnote: "Our disposition of plaintiff's appeal... makes it unnecessary to consider or decide any of the issues raised in the cross-appeal."

Judge Stevens pointed out that my appeal presented two issues: (1) whether the *New York Times* rule applied to plaintiff's false and scurrilous statements about me; (2) if the privilege did apply, whether the jury had heard evidence insufficient to permit it to find that these statements had been made with actual malice. He assumed, without deciding, that the article was libelous per se under Illinois law and that defendant had been either deliberately or recklessly mendacious. His concern centered on the tension between the publisher's responsibility and its First Amendment freedoms. Stevens then summarized the evidence. His summary was notable, I thought, for a couple of statements:

Stanley made no effort to verify the accuracy of anything said in Stang's article. Based on statements in the text, Stanley drafted an introductory comment and captions for illustrations. Before the article was conceived, Stanley, whose office is in Boston, had never heard of the plaintiff.

Plaintiff is mentioned because he was retained by the Nelson family to assert a civil claim for damages against Nuccio. In that capacity, he attended the coroner's inquest into Nelson's death. Notwithstanding his limited, professional interest in the matter, the article implied that plaintiff was the architect of a gross miscarriage of justice. A purported relationship to a nationwide conspiracy was suggested, in part, by frequent references to the National Lawyers Guild, of which plaintiff had been a member and which Stang repeatedly described as a Communist front.

The judge pointed out that "no proof of actual damages was offered" because the trial judge instructed the jury that injury was presumed as a matter of law.

In another important finding, the court concluded that even if I was not a public figure, the subject matter was of *significant public interest*. Furthermore, although the defendant had been negligent, actual malice had not been proved. My principal contention, said Stevens, was that I was not a public figure and that the subject matter *as it pertained to me* was not of significant public interest. My claim to be a private figure was arguable, but the court accepted it.

The question then turned upon whether the *subject matter* was of significant public interest. Both the specific focus of the article (the trial of a police officer for murder) and its broader theme (the possibility of a nationwide Communist conspiracy to discredit local police officers) did have significant public interest, Stevens concluded. The lower court had been correct in so ruling. Furthermore, discussion and debate about such public matters deserved the protection of the *New York Times* rule.

Stevens assumed the charges of a nationwide conspiracy to be false.

Nevertheless, under the reasoning of *New York Times Co. v. Sullivan*, even a false statement of fact made in support of a false thesis is protected unless made with knowledge of its falsity or with reckless disregard of its truth or falsity. It would undermine the rule of that case to permit the actual falsity of a statement to determine whether or not its publisher is entitled to the benefit of the rule.

If, therefore, we put to one side the false character of the article and treat it as though its contents were entirely true, it cannot be denied that the comments about plaintiff were integral to its central thesis. They must be tested under the *New York Times* standard.

Judge Stevens refined the issue further: "There is no evidence that Stanley actually knew that Stang's article was false; defendant did not 'deliberately publish falsehoods.' The question is whether the publication was made recklessly." He disposed of the issue of recklessness almost curtly: Failing to verify possible defamatory statements did not constitute recklessness. "On several occasions the Court has expressly stated that the record must reveal a 'high degree of awareness of . . . probable falsity' before a publisher may be found to have acted recklessly. In this case there is no evidence that Stanley knew anything at all about plaintiff except what was contained in Stang's article."

In addition, Stevens went on, "the Court has plainly stated that the evidence establishing reckless disregard for the truth must be clear and convincing," but "to assume that Stanley must have known... that the comments about plaintiff were false, would itself be reckless." Thus, actual malice had not been demonstrated with convincing clarity. Stevens also took into account the opinion of the trial judge, who heard the testimony and did not find undoubted recklessness. "[I]f, therefore, we put to one side the false character of the article and treat it as though its contents were entirely true, it cannot be denied that the comments about plaintiff were integral to its central thesis. They must be tested under the *New York Times* standard."

He concluded with the kind of elevation that often distinguishes defenses of freedom of the press:

> We cannot, however, apply a fundamental protection in one fashion to the New York Times and Time Magazine and in another way to the John Birch Society. Whether we are moved to applaud or to despise what is said, our duty to defend the right to speak remains the same.

The conclusion was eloquent, but it did me no good.

Judge Kiley, who it may be remembered had written the opinion years previously in my *Parmelee* case in which the Illinois innocent-construction rule was established, wrote an intriguing concurring opinion:

> I concur. Judge Stevens has written a persuasive opinion. It is with considerable reluctance, however, that I concur. The reluctance is due to my fear that we may have in this opinion pushed through what I consider the outer limits of the First Amendment Protection against liability for libelous statements and have further eroded the interest of non-"public figures" in their personal privacy.
>
> Gertz, a reputable attorney, is virtually called a Communist in an article written by Stang and adopted by Stanley without the latter making any inquiry on his own as to whether there was a reasonable basis for calling Gertz a Communist.
>
> This is not the *Rosenbloom* case, 403 U.S. 29 (1971). Rosenbloom was the publisher of "nudist magazines," and the news broadcast by defendant implicitly referred to Rosenbloom as a "smut distributor" and a "girly peddler." The involvement of the non-"public figure" with an issue of public interest is a consideration which moved the Supreme Court to apply the *New York Times* rule in *Rosenbloom*. I cannot find that Gertz was closely involved with the asserted national Communist conspiracy, as Rosenbloom was with the "smut literature racket."

Yet Judge Stevens shows that the trend of the Supreme Court decisions requires "in this close case" the conclusion that the district court did not err in entering the judgment for defendant, notwithstanding the verdict for Gertz.

Here again the pivotal issue is highlighted: Should ordinary protections against defamation be stripped from a private person who becomes embroiled in a public controversy, thereby rendering one a public person? Relying on the trend of Supreme Court decisions at that time, Judge Kiley ruled that it did.

Kiley did acknowledge the nature of my involvement and the injury to me, and in other circumstances, I might have derived pleasure from his words. I confess that I was angered. I felt that I had to take the case to the highest court when the court of appeals denied my motion that it exercise its discretion to eliminate or cut the court costs assessed against me. After all, they had conceived the case as "close," and I had been defamed. There was no principle involved in penalizing me. I recalled how the harsh English law of libel had pauperized Harold Laski years earlier.

Abigail Spreyer wrote analyses of both the Seventh Circuit and the later Supreme Court decisions in my case for the *Chicago-Kent Law Review* (1974, vol. 51, no. 2). It was a part of the annual Seventh Circuit review, although it culminated with the aftermath in the highest court. Spreyer's analysis of the Seventh Circuit opinion was, in my judgment, strikingly bright and fresh. She thought the Seventh Circuit could have found an opposite conclusion "equally tenable." The court could have reversed the district court and ordered the case remanded for a new trial. It could have decided that while the general subject of the *American Opinion* article may have been of public interest, my involvement may not have been sufficient to sustain the district-court ruling.

The question should have been "Did Gertz, by filing civil suits on behalf of the Nelsons, or by representing the Nelsons at the coroner's inquest, or by acting as counsel for the Sparling Commission, or by maintaining membership in the National Lawyers Guild prior to 1955, become sufficiently involved in an event of general or public concern to require that he prove the defamatory falsehoods were published with knowledge or with reckless disregard of whether they were false or not?" The case could have been sent back for determination of that issue.

Or the court could have decided "that the district court erred by not permitting the jury to decide whether the managing editor's circulation of inherently improbable charges not attributed to any source, coupled with his statements vouching for their accuracy without having verified them, constituted reckless conduct." This "might have precluded the Supreme Court decision and the resultant wholesale revamping of the law of defamation."

Or, as I felt, Judge Decker should have granted a new trial so that I would have the opportunity to prove malice. I was not given that opportunity at the first trial. As we shall see, I was compelled to prove malice at the second trial.

Spreyer had less to say of the Supreme Court decision, but I am grateful for her prescient consideration of the Seventh Circuit opinion. She was one of the few writers who made an inquiry in depth about the actual evidence rather than a court's findings with respect to it.

10 ■ The Supreme Court

We filed our appeal in the 1972 October Term. The Supreme Court has only one regular term, which begins on the first Monday in October and ends occasionally in late May, more often in late June, sometimes July. The Court does not immediately decide which appeals it will accept. Such a determination is generally made early in the term so that the briefs may be filed and oral argument heard, if so ordered, within the term of filing. The aim is to dispose of all petitions during the term, although a case may continue to the following term or later, as with the first historic desegregation cases. Sometimes the Court will dispose of a case summarily; that is, without requiring briefs or oral argument. An appeal, when granted, may be general or may be confined to specific issues.

We had filed our petition *pro se*—that is, in my name as my own attorney—and in the name of Wayne B. Giampietro. But I was instructed by the Court to remove either my name or Wayne's, and I chose to remove mine, so Wayne was the sole attorney of record. This did not prevent me from counseling with him.

(In the Supreme Court, the party filing the petition to appeal is described in the title of the case as the *petitioner*, and its name appears first, whether it was plaintiff or defendant in the lower courts. The other side is named as *respondent*, whether it was plaintiff or defendant below. In this case, it made no difference. Robert Welch, Inc., the respondent before the Supreme Court, was the original defendant. Sometimes this nomenclature is confusing, but it is somewhat eased by the description of the parties within the body of the petition as they were designated in the trial court. The respondent has the right to answer the petition but often does not do so, on the practical ground that to file a response may dignify the petition. After all, virtually all petitions are denied summarily by the Court. It allows no more than 100 or 150 out of the thousands filed.)

We felt greatly heartened when the Court, through its clerk, notified Robert Welch, Inc., that it should respond. It did so through General C. J. Watts, of Oklahoma City, who had been its cocounsel with Boyle in the successful response before the Court of Appeals for the Seventh Circuit. This time, Boyle's name was omitted. He was out of the case for good. Nor was Watts's tenure permanent. Whether as a result of success or failure, the defendant repeatedly changed its counsel. It did not seem to recognize that settling out of court might be cheaper and more practical.

The usual way of taking one's case from a lower court to the Supreme Court of the United States is by a *petition for a writ of certiorari* to that lower court. It is not enough to declare that the lower court decided your case wrongly. You must show federal constitutional errors to get relief in the Supreme Court. The highest tribunal has virtually arbitrary discretion in determining whether to take a case. Certain rules are supposed to be considered by the justices, but they are confronted with the limits of their crowded calendar and the large number of cases called to their attention. If the Court takes too many cases, it will not be able to give adequate attention to any of them.

Generally speaking, the cases that are accepted involve the most important and timely constitutional considerations. How does one persuade the Court that one's case is of that rare and irresistible nature? First, it must have inherent and apparent importance. Then the matter must be presented so clearly and persuasively that the requisite minimum of four justices will mark it for consideration. Every word must count. There must be no padding or spinning of wheels.

Every petition must incorporate the opinions below, from the first to the last. The basis of the jurisdiction of the Supreme Court must be given. The questions presented must be enumerated succinctly. Then there must be a "statement," a sort of summary of the case and the reasons for granting the writ with supporting authorities of law.

We phrased the questions presented as fairly and persuasively as we could:

1. Whether plaintiff, who was referred to and treated in an admittedly defamatory article as a private attorney, was a public figure within the requirements of the First Amendment?

2. Whether an article alleging a Communist conspiracy to harass the police, with no evidentiary support therefor, is a matter of such

public interest and importance as to require anyone mentioned therein, however peripherally or slightly (as was plaintiff), to prove actual malice in order to recover for libel?

3. Whether plaintiff was denied due process of law as a result of being precluded by the court from introducing evidence of actual malice?

4. Where the court states that in this case, the law limiting recovery in libel has been narrowed, for the first time, to the greatest permissible extent, is it a violation of due process to tax thousands of dollars in costs against an admittedly defamed attorney, in light of the discretion of the court in assessing costs?

In the statement of the case, we summed up the evidence that we had offered at the trial, including everything that we thought would convince the Court that we had been wronged in a constitutional sense. One cannot help but speculate which arguments persuaded the Court to grant a review. Upon reflection, I think that our initial point, that I was not really spoken of in a public capacity, was driven home toward the end of that section of the petition when we wrote:

The gist of defendant's article was that the police in this country are being subjected to an attempt to discredit them by Communists, and that the criminal indictment and conviction of Nuccio was the result of such conspiracy. However, plaintiff had absolutely nothing to do with the criminal proceedings, as attested to by Nuccio's own attorney and even by defendant itself. Gertz represented private clients in a circumspect and inconspicuous manner. The attacks upon plaintiff were no legitimate part of the article or its subject matter.

When does a matter become a public issue of such nature as to bar a defamed plaintiff from recovery short of actual malice or gross recklessness? Is it when any extremist of the right or left or a mere zealot or crackpot declares it to be such, whether or not he is fair or reasonable? And how deeply must a plaintiff be involved in the matter in order to prevent recovery on his part, assuming absence of actual malice or gross recklessness? If defendant's theory is adopted, all of us, including the most reputable lawyers, are at the mercy of those who lightly and without cause defame us.

Is every attorney, representing a client, to be exposed to the most scurrilous attacks, with absolutely no recourse? May a defamer concoct wholly fictitious stories about such an attorney which have no legitimate connection with the matter at hand? Are the members of the legal profession such public figures that they imperil their very livelihood to all unfounded attacks with absolutely no recourse? These issues must be considered very carefully and fully, not in an offhand manner.

It is submitted that these matters were not given the consideration which they require by the Court of Appeals. To say that the actual falsity of a statement does not deprive it of First Amendment protection adds little, if anything, to the policy decision which must be made. If the statements were true, there would be no issue, for this would be defense in itself. The question to be determined is not whether the statements are true or false, but whether the false statements are legitimately entitled to protection despite their falsity.

Our second basic point was that I was denied a fair trial and due process. We stressed that the trial court had declared by its various rulings and opinions that I was not a public figure and that the subject of the article did not concern a matter of public interest and importance. The court had declared that it was unnecessary to offer evidence of malice, since the defamatory falsehoods were libelous per se. Nonetheless, we had introduced evidence that might fairly be found proof of malice. We summarized this evidence. Had we been compelled to offer additional evidence to that effect, we could have done so. After a jury verdict in our favor, the trial judge had then changed his mind and found that public issues were involved. And since in his judgment we had failed to prove malice, judgment in favor of the defendant was entered and the case dismissed, despite the jury verdict to the contrary. This was grossly wrong, we said, denial of a fair trial and due process, because at the very least we should have been given the opportunity through a new trial to establish malice in the constitutional sense. I thought that we were most persuasive when we said:

As was proved by plaintiff at trial, without any attempted contradiction by defendant, defendant's article did not contain simple exaggerations, discrepancies, or slight errors, but monumental misstatements, monstrous lies made out of whole cloth. There was not even the slightest basis for calling plaintiff a Communist, Communist-fronter, Leninist, Marxist, Red, or anything of that nature. These statements were not mere hyperbole or coloration, but completely false fabrication of the most damaging kind to an attorney dealing with private clients. Even if public issues were involved, defendant had no right to drag in an innocent bystander, representing purely private interests. The conclusions reached by this Court regarding the plaintiff in *Curtis Publishing Co. v. Butts*, 388 U.S. 130, 86 S. Ct. 1975 (1967), are clearly applicable to this case. Each of the following elements found in that case are present here: the story was in no sense "hot news"; elementary precautions were ignored; there was no support, independent or otherwise, for the statements made in the article; the author's notes were not viewed by any of defendant's personnel, but were published without substantial independent support; no attempt was made to check with any of the others involved in this situation as to the accuracy of the statements made. As was stated in *Butts*, "the evidence is ample to support a finding of highly unreasonable conduct constituting an extreme departure from the standards of investigation and reporting ordinarily adhered to by responsible publishers."

As a third reason for action by the Court, we declared that the taxation of court costs against me deprived me of due process: "The decision of the Court of Appeals was a close one, as indicated in the opinions filed by the Judges of that court. It extended the previously existing law, as recognized by all parties concerned. Plaintiff had obtained a verdict from a jury, under the instructions given by the District Court, which then radically changed its view of the applicable law."

I am still proud of the conclusion in the final section of the petition:

> This case presents issues of the utmost public importance. A victory for plaintiff would shore up our defenses against extremists of the right and of the left who would destroy the American democratic values and citizen participation in public affairs by misreading and misusing the freedom of expression guaranteed by the First Amendment. This does not constitute a quest for censorship or prior restraint of any kind, but only a plea that those who set out intentionally to defame a private person with no basis whatsoever will be called to a court of law to account for their actions. This is further a plea that a private person, who has no other recourse but the courts, be allowed an opportunity to clear his name and reputation.
>
> Wide leeway has been given to publishers and others to speak to the public where public officials, public figures and public issues are actually involved; provided the defamatory publication really treats the complaining person in his public capacity and the publisher is free from actual malice or such gross recklessness as is tantamount to malice. There can be no license to drag the name of innocent bystanders in the mud by making utterly false and highly damaging charges against them in the most irresponsible manner where the truth is readily available and could easily have been ascertained.

Defendant here made absolutely no attempt to prove the truth of the statements made concerning plaintiff, either at the time of publication or at the trial.

No lawyer's reputation will be safe if the mere fact of his being a lawyer is used to undermine his reputation and standing with clients, the courts and the public. Our system of justice will suffer if a lawyer must hesitate to represent private litigants because extremists may lie about him with impunity. The quality of justice in this country will thus be lowered if an attorney must, before concluding to represent a client, consider whether he is exposing himself to public attacks without an adequate opportunity on his part to vindicate himself. Public policy should favor a strong lawyer-client relationship, rather than weakening it while giving extremists carte blanche.

"Wherefore," we prayed that the Court issue its writ of certiorari (granting appeal) and that the judgment below be reversed.

Watts filed a short, almost curt brief in opposition to our petition. It was almost as if he did not take seriously our petition or the Court's direction to him to respond. Typical of the entire brief, and the essence of its argument, was this passage:

> Certainly, the alleged murder of an individual citizen by a policeman, a public servant, is of general public interest. The act of the policeman is the act of society and all law abiding citizens should be concerned. The Petitioner, while representing the Nelson Family privately, attended the coroner's inquest, which was a public hearing to determine whether or not a public statute had been violated and questioned Officer Nuccio as to his participation in the alleged murderous act. The Trial court stated (Petitioner's Appendix B, page 19a):
>
> "... By representing the victim's family in litigation brought against the policeman, Gertz thrust himself into the vortex of this important public controversy...."
>
> Although Gertz was not the central character of the alleged libelous article, he was alleged to have been involved in the conspiracy to frame Chicago policemen.
>
> Thus the article published by the Respondent was of "public or general interest" and entitled to the shield of the First Amendment.

Watts's lack of care was evidenced by his statement that I had questioned Nuccio at the inquest. In fact, Nuccio had refused to take the stand. His brief could not have impressed the Court. It granted my petition. Thus, we and the defendant would have a further opportunity to brief the case.

While our brief for the original petition was necessarily circumscribed, we had more scope to argue our contentions in the additional brief filed subsequent to the grant of the writ. In federal court briefs, one is required to summarize one's argument in such a way that the judges will readily grasp the essence, which is then supplemented and substantiated by what one says more fully in the body of the brief.

Here is the gist of our initial argument: The Court has reached substantial agreement regarding rules to be applied in libel cases involving public officials but not for private persons involved in issues of public interest and importance. This case is of that genre; it represents "a direct confrontation between the constitutional rights of freedom of speech and privacy."

We proceeded to suggest one way the Court might balance these rights. A person involved in a matter of public interest is judged by actual conduct. It would therefore be just to judge the publisher of false and scurrilous information or conduct similarly—not by a subjective state of mind (as in proving actual malice). Thus, to make out a prima facie case, the libeled person should have to prove falsity. Then, to balance the burdens, the respondent should have to prove probable cause—that there was good reason to believe that what was published was true. "This standard," we argued, "would afford both parties the freedom and protection mandated by the Constitution."

A note of urgency was added by my role as a lawyer. Since an attorney acts for others, an attack on an attorney's reputation also injures the client's.

Even though proof of actual malice should not be required when a private person is involved in public controversy, we could prove it. However, we pointed out, the inconsistent rulings of the trial court had deprived petitioner of a fair trial. Throughout the pretrial proceedings and the trial, we had been told that we need not present evidence to prove actual malice. However, after the jury had found in my favor, the court changed course and said we should have introduced such evidence. "The failure to grant petitioner a new trial in order to give him an opportunity to do so is clearly a deprivation of due process." It was also a violation of due process, we continued, to assess thousands of dollars in court costs against an admittedly defamed attorney.

We analyzed *New York Times* and its progeny, demonstrating that all of the justices—except the "absolutionists," Justices Black, Douglas, and possibly Goldberg—recognized that there are still areas where reputations should be protected.

We asked a question that went to the heart of the case: "But what of the non-public figure who is not involved in a report of official action?" In response, we recapped all the arguments that demonstrated my status as a private person. The editor of defendant's magazine had never heard of me, nor had anyone on the jury. I had not thrust myself into public controversy or done anything else to call attention to myself or my client in the civil case. Nor did the article allege that I had; it referred to my activity strictly as it related to my practice of law in the civil case against Nuccio: "The rest of the statements concerning him were in reference to alleged former activities and his membership in various organizations which were falsely characterized as being Communistic or Communist-dominated." We epitomized the situation as we saw it:

> That the public is entitled to a vigorous, free, and untrammeled press cannot be disputed. That along with freedom must go responsibility is a necessary corollary. There must be some limitation upon freedom, as upon power. Absolute freedom, like absolute power, results in anarchy and corruption. The right of the individual must be protected if we are not to regress to the level of savages.

However, individual rights would indeed be trammeled if the rules were not changed. If a court relied only on the word of the publisher of false information, that publisher could always claim that "it merely took the story as it was given to it and published it verbatim. Such a holding destroys any ability of a private individual to obtain even the slightest recompense for his damage." He could not then prove actual malice. Neither could he easily persuade the media to publicize his rebuttal (as a public figure could).

We phrased the conflict in terms that could be approved by judges who truly believed in dispensing justice:

> We deal here with a collision of great ideals. The worth of the individual, no matter how small or obscure, is the pervasive ideal of our

system. Every individual must be afforded at least an opportunity to seek redress for his injuries. An attitude which postulates that the "public good" is more important than the worth of such an individual will surely lead to a repressive society. Here, the repression is not at the hands of the government, but at the hands of those wealthy and fortunate enough to gain access to the channels of communication of this country. Our anti-trust laws seek to inhibit economic repression. Personal repression must not be countenanced in the guise of freedom of the public to be erroneously informed. No segment of society is entitled to a special right. Yet, all would agree that the press must be allowed to flourish. A balance must be struck which is evenhanded and fair to both interests which are of the utmost importance to the continuation of our society.

We concluded in terms from the Constitution itself:

When a person has not engaged in activity which would call the public attention to him, he is entitled to maintain that anonymity which has been destroyed by the purposeful action of the defendant. It is perfectly justifiable to call upon defendant to show that he had probable cause to make the false statements about plaintiff and bring him unbidden to the public eye.

The temptation is great to quote more of our pearls, but what we said is important only insofar as the Court accepted our views.

The Welch brief in response to ours was much better than its cursory response to our petition had been. We still felt that it was woefully inadequate (not that we mourned its deficiencies). In the very first paragraph of our reply, we minced no words: "Respondent's Brief in Opposition to Petitioner's Petition for Certiorari is tantamount to no opposition at all: as Respondent has sent forth no sufficient reasons why this Court should not grant the Writ. Were it not for the fact that Respondent has made certain material misstatements, Petitioner would rely solely upon his Petition." Perhaps in our enthusiastic belief in our case we were overstating, but we tried to be as free of bias as possible, knowing that the justices would resent any overreaching.

We felt that it was important to stress certain arguments:

This court has not defined extensively what kind of evidence is sufficient to present a *prima facie* case of actual malice. This case presents an admirable vehicle for a clarification of the law. Public policy requires that this Court delve into the special areas presented by this case.

May an extremist publication make it a practice to make irresponsible statements and then avoid consideration of those statements in a determination of actual malice? Should not a publisher be required to vouch for and justify its outlandish and continually distorted attacks? Should not such a tendency be considered by a jury in determining whether such publisher is acting in bad faith and with actual malice?

It remained only to await oral argument before the Court. Before that moment arrived, the Court notified the parties that arguments would take place in tandem with the arguments in another defamation case involving excesses in a labor dispute (*Old Dominion Branch No. 496 v. Austin*). As it turned out, neither case had an appreciable effect on the other.

I decided that Wayne alone would argue before the Supreme Court, that I would not even hear the argument. Instead, I went to Southern Illinois University at Carbondale to address the faculty and students on censorship. I gave scarcely a moment's thought to what was happening in the case that meant so much to me. I felt that I had to contain my curiosity.

Wayne had traveled to Washington with his eldest son and his wife, Mary. From various persons, I learned how well Wayne had acquitted himself. He felt at the time that the most telling inquiry was made when the chief justice stressed the defendant's charge that I had committed crimes of various kinds.

To a lawyer with any sense of professional pride, there is no loftier experience than presenting a matter in the inspiring presence of the nine august justices of the Supreme Court of the United States. One must be thoroughly prepared; every pore of one's being must ooze with knowledge and insight. One must be prepared to answer the most unexpected, difficult, tantalizing, unfair questions, propounded by the least or most knowledgeable justice. One must be able to stand up sturdily if interrupted in the flow of one's argument. If a Justice Felix Frankfurter is the interrogator, one is lucky if one escapes with undiminished self-respect.

But one never really knows how meaningful oral argument is in the Court. One assumes that each justice has read all of the briefs.

One hopes that he or she has gone through the appendix and the whole record. One prays for understanding, tolerance, fairness, and the right decision. However long the time assigned for oral argument, it goes by much too rapidly, except for those moments when a question has been propounded to you and you are struggling for the answer, straining not to destroy the case by misspeaking.

Most lawyers never argue a case before the Supreme Court. Even those who appear several times find each case a unique experience. The greatness of our system is that one feels awe in the presence of the chief justice and the eight associate justices. You count on them to treat you and your cause justly, feeling that they are not swayed by passion or bias, that they are intent upon deciding each case properly.

Wayne freely confesses that at times he was petrified in his first appearance before the Supreme Court. But he was so familiar with the facts and the law of the case that by instinct he handled himself exceedingly well. I learned from friends that Wayne was very impressive; General Watts, for the respondent, less so. Indeed, the general seemed to have the same difficulty recalling the record that he had had in the argument before the court of appeals. This time, Jim Boyle was not there to back him up.

All the justices except Douglas participated in the vigorous questioning of counsel. The chief justice led by observing that I seemed to have been charged with a criminal offense in the publication. Wayne was quick to agree, although frankly he had been less impressed with that argument than the chief justice. Thereafter, we stressed the charge of criminality as much as that of communism; it was indeed defamatory to be charged with obstructing justice and framing an innocent man for murder. Wayne could see that the justices were not in agreement, although they all seemed to take the case seriously. It was disconcerting to observe two of them talking with each other while he was concerned with developing our case.

Wayne became convinced that the Court had not accepted one of his best-thought-out and most original arguments, based upon the Fourth Amendment requirement of probable cause applied to defamatory material. He was relieved that other arguments seemed to be carrying more weight, although he could not tell how the Court was thinking. Probably at this point the justices themselves did not know, except for the First Amendment absolutist Justice Douglas. At any rate, Wayne emerged from his ordeal by fire unscathed. Not least, he had given his wife and eldest son a performance they would never forget.

Reading the transcript of the oral argument years later, one is intrigued by the teasing quality of the interrogation by the justices other than Douglas. The argument came before a full court at 10:48 A.M. on November 14, 1973, and ended at 11:47 A.M., one minute less than an hour later. One cannot always tell which justice is interrogating counsel because it is the practice to omit the names of the justices from the transcript. Generally, the identification here is by implication and may occasionally be in error.

As the attorney for the petitioner, Wayne proceeded first. He had hardly commenced his argument when he was interrupted by the first of many questions, this one from the chief justice: "Under Illinois law, would the acts charged, . . . this conspiracy to frame, be in itself criminal?" Wayne was taken somewhat by surprise, but he replied readily that it would be obstruction of justice and a criminal conspiracy under Illinois law. He was then permitted to expound on this aspect of the defamatory article at some length. He was off to a good start.

Justice Rehnquist wanted to know whether under Illinois law to state that someone is a member of the American Civil Liberties Union is defamatory. No, Wayne said, it is not defamatory in any way. The defamation consisted in the charge that membership in the ACLU made one a Communist. The justice's ensuing question indicated that Wayne's argument was grasped and possibly approved by at least one justice.

Wayne went on to argue at some length that I was not a public official or a public figure and that I had not made any public statements about the Nuccio murder case. I had appeared at the Nelson inquest along with other attorneys to ask questions that might be pertinent to the civil suits in behalf of the Nelson family. He argued that the inquest had no direct bearing upon the trial and conviction of the police officer because the inquest ended in an "open verdict." Therefore, I could not have been part of a conspiracy to frame Nuccio.

A justice inquired whether there had been any argument about this innuendo in the lower courts. Wayne assured him that there was no question that the article had portrayed me as part of a criminal conspiracy to frame Nuccio.

A justice asked if I had been retained by Nelson's parents to initiate civil suits against the police officer, and Wayne assured him that this was the case. In answer to further inquiry, Wayne pointed out that the civil suits had been filed before the publication of the offending article. The justice inquired about the result of the civil action:

Q: I suppose that trial and judgment occurred after the publication?
A: It occurred long after the publication.

Since at least one justice was interested, Wayne went further into the details, then argued that I had a privacy right in the circumstances of being let alone. Wayne was asked by Justice Rehnquist, still pursuing each aspect of the case with great interest, "You don't have to rest your case on that ground, I suppose?" Wayne agreed, pointing out the Illinois constitutional provision that for every wrong there must be a remedy. (He did not mention that I was the chairman of the committee at the Constitutional Convention that had fashioned that right in its present form.)

He continued with a discussion of the conflict between rights of the press and the reputation and privacy rights of private individuals. Justice Powell, who ultimately wrote the opinion of the Court, now joined in: "May I ask this question? You made a statement that there was no public or general interest in the representation in the civil suit by Mr. Gertz. Who determines whether or not there is a public or general interest in a libelous statement?"

Wayne responded that the ultimate arbiter "must be the courts and certainly, ultimately, this Court." Guidelines must be established. In this case, we have a "linking of the plaintiff with something that he had absolutely nothing to do with."

Inquiry was made whether the press in Chicago had referred to my being employed in the private litigation. Wayne said that there had been one or two stories "on one day, and one day only." Now Wayne was asked whether front-page stories about the situation would have made it a matter of public interest. Wayne was sensible enough to concede that this would be a strong factor to be considered, to which Justice Powell responded, "Well, doesn't this enable the press to decide, in almost every case, what you said might be a constitutional question, that is, whether or not a particular story is or is not a matter of general or public interest?" Wayne conceded that this might be the case and that it was something to be guarded against by the Supreme Court.

Justice Stewart suggested to Wayne that this was about what had happened in the *Rosenbloom* case, as far as the lead opinion went, then prodded him further: "Your only answer is, well, that wasn't an opinion of the Court?" Wayne agreed and said that the opinion ought to be reexamined by the Court and that of course they had reexamined the *Metromedia* opinion. Justice Stewart urged that in the Brennan plurality opinion in *Metromedia*, Justice Brennan had pointed out that Rosenbloom "had made himself the central actor and figure." It was not really the press that had done so.

Justice Stewart continued in his analysis of *Metromedia* in a manner that could only encourage Wayne and then went on to examine what had happened in my case. Judge Decker, using a two-step approach, had said, "First, that the killing of a criminal suspect and the policeman's subsequent indictment at a time when the police, generally, were the subjects of attack within the community, commanded wide public attention and interest. Therefore, it was a subject of general public concern." Then, Justice Stewart went on, Judge Decker had said that this was not the only thing that had to be established. It had to be shown that I had thrust myself into the vortex of that controversy, and Judge Decker had concluded, rightly or wrongly, that I had done so by representing the Nelson family in the civil suit.

Wayne agreed. Justice Brennan now asserted that Wayne was arguing that the killing was not a subject of general interest and that in any event I had not thrust myself into the vortex of the controversy. Wayne asserted that it was not necessary to argue whether the killing was a matter of public interest since I was not involved in the situation. The justice then differentiated between the killing and the civil suit, "arguably quite a different matter."

Wayne now argued that I had been deprived of due process. When the trial judge changed his mind about the stance of the case and said that I had to prove malice to recover, he should have granted a new trial so that I would have the opportunity to prove malice. A justice seemed to agree with Wayne. Wayne argued too that we had actually proved malice, although Judge Decker had not recognized this. His interest aroused, the justice wanted to know if we had filed the complete trial record, and Wayne assured him that we had.

Wayne cited a libel defendant's protections under Illinois law: First, he need prove only the general truth or thrust of the offending article, not each detail of it; second, the innocent-construction rule applied. Wayne reminded the Court that publication of the article had continued long after my suit had been brought. Finally, he argued that taxing substantial costs against me where the court was extending for the first time the constitutional limits of libel was grossly unfair.

Reading the transcript now, one can say that Wayne had done very well in his maiden argument before the highest court of the land. He had not shown excessiveness or unfairness; he was informed, balanced, and persuasive. The justices must have been impressed that so young a man could do so well.

It was now the turn of Clyde J. Watts, an army general and counsel for the defense. He was older than Wayne and more experienced. He had been before the Court previously, had had a long and distinguished career, and he was supported by the assurance of rulings in his client's favor in the lower courts. He expressed great sympathy for my position; he had been on both sides of similar issues (no doubt including the case involving General Edwin Walker in which the Court had ruled against him). He dwelt upon the vast literature on freedom of speech.

He referred to the reluctant review of the case by Judge Decker. The chief justice interrupted: "The reluctance didn't show up very much when there was this extraordinary assessment of costs." Clearly, Wayne had struck home with his final comment. Watts, surprisingly, conceded that the chief justice might be right in his remark on the costs.

Watts was asked, "It was a great change of heart, wasn't it, from the beginning of this case to the end?" Watts remarked that he was at a disadvantage; he had not participated in the trial of the case, so he could not answer the chief justice's question accurately. He said that the trial court had considered the implications of *New York Times* and reached the proper conclusion—that there had to be proof of malice. The reviewing court, he added, carefully and exhaustively considered what Judge Decker had decided and agreed in a very penetrating decision. He read from Judge Stevens's opinion in the court of appeals (at least one justice carefully monitored his quotation; sometimes the Court is misled by unfair or inaccurate quotation).

He dwelt, with not much clarity, on the John Birch Society's views of General Eisenhower to which we had referred in our brief and opined that it was perhaps difficult to muster sympathy for the society but that it was entitled to the same degree of constitutional consideration as the *New York Times* or *Time* magazine. He told of the strategy by Communists to undermine the police by making false charges against them. He was questioned closely whether this was the impact of the article, and he said it was. He added, "The reference to Mr. Gertz is very, very incidental to this article."

At this point, an embarrassing question was put to him: "I understand counsel for the petitioner to say that it had been conceded at the trial that the article was libelous. Do you deny that?"

Somewhat lamely, Watts responded: "Well, sir, I was—as I say, I was not at the trial."

"What does the record show?"

Watts fumbled and then admitted: "It was conceded that some of the remarks in the article were false."

Justice White cited the language of the article: "'The file on Elmer Gertz in Chicago Police Intelligence takes a big Irish cop to lift.' Now, as a lawyer, "I assume you would concede that that is libelous, per se."

MR. WATTS: I doubt it, sir.
Q. You doubt it?
MR. WATTS: Mr. Justice, I doubt that, in fact, the police investigations could have a file on a lawyer without anything criminal appearing in the file.

He then meandered in explanation, stating once again that he had not participated in the trial. Stripped of its verbiage, his argument was that my appearance at the inquest may have had an impact on the charge against Nuccio.

Justice Rehnquist interrupted to inform Watts that the Court was not as interested in Illinois law as in the *New York Times* issues. Watts responded again that *American Opinion* was entitled to the same protection as the *New York Times*, *Time*, or *Life*. A justice punctured his argument: "On relevance, Mr. Watts, you know, there is question of whether *New York Times* applies at all." Watts, puzzled, asked for more enlightenment on the point, and the justice responded: "Well, isn't there an issue in the case as to whether or not the knowing or reckless falsehood rule of *New York Times* applies at all in this case?"

Watts tried to defend his position but was again interrupted: "That isn't my question. My question is whether that rule applies at all or not." Watts tried to make his point and was once more interrupted: "I know, but under the *New York Times*, the *New York Times* talked about a public official." Watts tried desperately to respond but was thwarted at every turn. The justice finally made his viewpoint unmistakably clear: "The issue is whether it was of any necessity at all to prove malice." This observation proved prophetic indeed.

When he could proceed, Watts said of me, "I think very definitely he is a public figure." He was reminded by Justice Brennan that the trial court had said that I was not a public figure, that the case involved an *issue* of public interest into which I had injected myself. Brennan continued: "What are you going to say—what would you say if we disagreed with you that this lawyer was either a public figure or a public official? Let's assume we disagreed with you on that. Are we to conclude . . . that the *New York Times* would therefore not apply?"

Watts now insisted that I was involved in a matter of vital public interest. At the same time, he said that my involvement was indirect and in a minor capacity. The justice reminded him that the language used was whether I had "thrust" myself "into the vortex of public controversy."

Suddenly a justice interrupted Watts to ask rather brusquely, "Why didn't you just say yes to Mr. Justice Brennan's question?" Watts insisted, "Well, I'd say no, sir." The justice, somewhat startled, repeated: "You'd say no?" Watts tried to defend his position, and the justice asked: "Suppose, instead of bringing a civil suit against the police officers for the death, that Mr. Gertz had been retained by the family to collect on an accident insurance policy where there was some debate? Would you say that he had thrust himself into the vortex of the controversy?" At last Watts admitted, "I should doubt it."

The questioning then turned to my participation in the inquest. A justice suggested, "His part was not as a public official?" Watts argued that I became a de facto public official by participating. A justice suggested that I had a right and duty to participate: "And you said that the whole purpose of the article was to show how he influenced the coroner's inquest. The answer is that the coroner's inquest left it open. It didn't decide anything.... Is that right?"

Watts persisted in quibbling, persisted in reminding the Court that he had not participated in the trial. The justice also persisted: "Well, the record. Is it in the record?" Watts finally admitted that the coroner's inquest left the matter open, and the justice remarked bitingly, "Well, I don't consider that [a] great influence on the result." Watts agreed, and the justice went on in the same vein: "And you keep talking about the persecution of the police officer. Is this the same police officer . . . that was found guilty?"

"Yes."

"And you call that persecution?"

"No, sir, I do not call that persecution."

Watts continued to argue that the case was governed by *New York Times* and freedom of speech. Justice White said that under Watts's interpretation, they would have to apply *New York Times* to almost anything. Watts opined that such would be the case, and the justice went on (was there a hint of irony?): "Or, even insubstantial to the public interest?"

Justice White tried to illustrate the parameters of the *New York Times* rule by an example in the area of health. Watts attempted to cover the situation, but it seemed clear that he was not persuasive as far as Justice White was concerned. The justice questioned him about other aspects of the case, especially my representation of the parents of young Nelson in civil litigation. Watts persisted in seeing something constitutionally special about my participation in the inquest, something that made me subject to the *New York Times* rule. Justice White wanted to know whether any lawyer would lose his rights under *New York Times* if he participated in a coroner's inquest on behalf of a civil client. Watts thought the lawyer would lose his right to say "You have spoken falsely of me."

Justice White played with Watts a bit more, then concluded: "Then, I take it from your response to the questions that you have subjected yourself to being called a John Bircher by appearing in this case?" Justice White suggested: "By your test, everything but the funnies would be privileged, wouldn't it?" Watts responded, "I think so, and I believe even the funnies would be, under certain circumstances . . . if he presented me as a screwball, a crackpot, if he was in reasonably good faith about it."

The chief justice told Wayne that he had only about two minutes for his reply. Wayne corrected his earlier overstatement of the costs taxed against me (the amount was still large and oppressive), then devoted the balance of his time to the demonstration that I had indeed been falsely designated a Communist and that the result could be that all attorneys might be harmed if they got involved in litigation. This, we later learned, affected the chief justice deeply.

After the Court has heard the week's calendar of oral arguments, the Court holds a highly private and significant conference confined to the justices. At this conference, presided over by the chief justice, each justice will have his unfettered say on the cases, and there will be discussion back and forth. Then there will be a vote on the Court's holding on each case and a determination of who will write the majority opinion. If the chief justice is in the majority, he will decide who will write the first draft of the Court's opinion. If he is not in the majority, the senior judge in the majority will make the determination. The other justices may choose to write opinions or join in collective opinions of dissent or concurrence. The opinions will be printed privately, then distributed to all of the justices, and they have the right to suggest changes in the language and the stated reasons. Sometimes this leads to a reversal of the original decision or considerable revision. In the end, the opinions are fixed, then announced at an ensuing public session of the Court. Copies are distributed to interested parties, and ultimately each decision appears in the official reports of the Court.

When the private conference began in my case, the Court had to consider what it had previously decided in *New York Times* and *Rosenbloom* as the necessary background for what it would decide in my case. Although private in nature, what is said ultimately becomes known. Regarding my case, the learned and astute professor Bernard Schwartz has revealed what was said and decided in his authoritative book *The Ascent of Pragmatism—The Burger Court in Action*.

Justice Brennan spoke strongly in favor of following the reasoning of the plurality opinion in *Rosenbloom*. His argument lost its force because Justice Black, who had gone along with Brennan, had been replaced by Powell, who opposed Brennan's views and was joined by another new justice, Rehnquist, in opposition. Chief Justice Burger, who had concurred in *Rosenbloom*, was now ready to reverse his earlier position.

The chief justice began the *Gertz* conference by noting that the basic question was "whether *Times* applies." Burger thought it did not apply: "I reject the idea a lawyer becomes a public figure because his client is. And he seems to be just another lawyer. That's different from *Rosenbloom*, who was a target among the lawbreakers."

As seemed to be indicated by the earlier questioning of counsel in the hearing in open court, Justices Powell, Stewart, Marshall, and Rehnquist agreed that *Rosenbloom* did not apply. Powell, who was selected to write the Court's opinion, said, "I can't accept the 'public interest' standard, because it leaves the power to the press to determine what is 'public interest.'" Stewart added: "Gertz for me is not a public figure in the *Times* sense merely because he's a prominent and well-known lawyer. So I would leave him . . . a state remedy."

Blackmun, who had been part of the *Rosenbloom* plurality, seemed to be ambiguous at the conference, as Professor Schwartz noted. He voted to reverse.

After Powell had drafted the opinion, White wrote to him: "[Y]ou still require fault beyond the damaging circulation of falsehoods. This pretty well forces the States to revise their libel laws substantially. Likewise, requiring that the private plaintiff prove actual injury to reputation imposes a substantial federal limitation on state libel laws, and pretty well scuttles the ingrained idea that there are certain statements that are per se libelous." In yet another letter to Powell, White wrote that there was no "satisfactory evidence or basis for further restricting state court power to protect private persons against reputation-damaging falsehoods published by the press or others."

In short, the brethren recognized that they were faced with new problems in the *New York Times* rule. What they wrote in their opinions reflected this and marked a new departure for the Court in constitutional guidelines regarding defamation.

On June 25, 1974, more than seven months after the oral argument on November 14, 1973, I learned that the Court had decided the case in my favor, at least on the law. It reversed the Seventh Circuit Court of Appeals, and consequently the district court, and remanded the case for further proceedings. I read the first paragraph of the Court's opinion, in which Justice Powell said:

This court has struggled for nearly a decade to define the proper accommodation between the law of defamation and the freedom of speech and press protected by the First Amendment. With this decision we return to that effort. We granted certiorari to reconsider the extent of a publisher's constitutional privilege against liability for defamation of a private citizen. 410 U.S. 95 (1973).

It was now clear that the Court was handing down an important, possibly a landmark, decision. It was significant that the opinion was written by Justice Powell, an appointee of President Nixon, who could well be described as a gentleman scholar, a conservative of principle. His great success in private practice and experiences as president of the American Bar Association gave him a practical and an academic interest in the problems of the law. He was joined in this opinion by another Nixon appointee, Justice Rehnquist, regarded as the most conservative member of the Court; a swing man, Justice Stewart, an Eisenhower appointee; the highly liberal Justice Marshall, the first and only black on the Court, a Johnson appointee; and, in a special concurrence, Justice Blackmun, another Nixon appointee. There were four dissents, two actually in my favor: Chief Justice Burger, named to the Court by President Nixon, and Justice White, a Kennedy appointee like Justice Stewart, a swing man on the Court. The two genuine dissents were by Justice Douglas, the man longest on the Court, a liberal appointed by President Roosevelt, and Justice Brennan, another liberal, appointed by President Eisenhower. Here, certainly, was a varied group. What was said by each demonstrated on the one hand a union of all judicial forces; on the other, the diversity of viewpoints characteristic of the Court.

I thought that Justice Powell summed up the facts admirably, except for one minor error: In Illinois, there were at that time no "degrees" of murder, so that calling Nuccio's conviction a second-degree murder was inaccurate. One is tempted to set forth fully Justice Powell's recitation of the facts. I content myself with his conclusions about the *American Opinion* article:

> These statements contained serious inaccuracies. The implication that petitioner had a criminal record was false. Petitioner had been a member and officer of the National Lawyers Guild some 15 years earlier, but there was no evidence that he or that organization had taken

any part in planning the 1968 demonstrations in Chicago. There was also no basis for the charge that petitioner was a "Leninist" or a "Communist-fronter." And he had never been a member of the "Marxist League for Industrial Democracy" or the "Intercollegiate Socialist Society."

The managing editor of *American Opinion* made no effort to verify or substantiate the charges against petitioner. Instead, he appended an editorial introduction stating that the author had "conducted extensive research into the Richard Nuccio Case." And he included in the article a photograph of petitioner and wrote the caption that appeared under it: "Elmer Gertz of Red Guild harasses Nuccio." Respondent placed the issue of *American Opinion* containing the article on sale at newsstands throughout the country and distributed reprints of the article on the streets of Chicago.

With characteristic clarity, Justice Powell set forth the essence of the case:

The principal issue in this case is whether a newspaper or broadcaster that published defamatory falsehoods about an individual who is neither a public official nor a public figure may claim a constitutional privilege against liability for the injury inflicted by those statements. The Court considered this question on the rather different set of facts presented in *Rosenbloom v. Metromedia, Inc.*, 403 U.S. 29, 91 S. Ct. 1811, 29 L. Ed. 2d 296 (1971).

This Court affirmed the decision below, but no majority could agree on a controlling rationale. The eight Justices who participated in *Rosenbloom* announced their views in five separate opinions, none of which commanded more than three votes. The several statements not only reveal disagreement about the appropriate result in that case; they also reflect divergent traditions of thought about the general problem of reconciling the law of defamation with the First Amendment. One approach has been to extend the *New York Times* test to an expanding variety of situations. Another has been to vary the level of constitutional privilege for defamatory falsehood with the status of the person defamed. And a third view would grant to the press and broadcast media absolute immunity from liability for defamation. To place our holding in the proper context, we preface our discussion of this case with a review of the several *Rosenbloom* opinions and their antecedents.

Justice Powell took the next step in his analysis of the tormenting problem facing the Court:

We begin with the common ground. Under the First Amendment there is no such thing as a false idea. However pernicious an opinion may seem, we depend for its correction not on the conscience of judges and juries but on the competition of other ideas. But there is no constitutional value in false statements of fact. Neither the intentional lie nor the careless error materially advances society's interest in "uninhibited, robust, and wide-open" debate on public issues. *New York Times Co. v. Sullivan*, 376 U.S. at 270, 84 S. Ct. at 721. They belong to that category of utterances which "are no essential part of any exposition of ideas, and are of such slight social value as a step to truth that any benefit that may be derived from them is clearly outweighed by the social interest in order and morality." *Chaplinsky v. New Hampshire*, 315 U.S. 568, 572, 62 S. Ct. 766, 769, 86 L. Ed. 1031 (1942).

Although the erroneous statement of fact is not worthy of constitutional protection, it is nevertheless inevitable in free debate.

Time and again, Powell and the other justices returned to the special situation involving the press: "The need to avoid self-censorship by the news media is, however, not the only societal value at issue. If it were, this Court would have embraced long ago the view that publishers and broadcasters enjoy an unconditional and indefeasible immunity from liability for defamation."

Again and again, he (and the other justices) also returned to the interests of the individual: "The legitimate state interest underlying the law of libel is the compensation of individuals for the harm inflicted on them by defamatory falsehoods. We would not lightly require the State to abandon this purpose."

How, then, could one resolve the problem? "Some tension necessarily exists between the need for a vigorous and uninhibited press and the legitimate interest in redressing wrongful injury."

Justice Powell set forth a step-by-step analysis of the several-tiered situation. His first point was that a public person's protection against libel is defined by the *New York Times* rule. Public figures and holders of governmental office may recover

only on clear and convincing proof that the defamatory falsehood was made with knowledge of its falsity or with reckless disregard for the truth. This standard administers an extremely powerful antidote to the inducement to media self-censorship of the common law rule of strict liability for libel and slander and it exacts a correspondingly high price from the victims of defamatory falsehood. Plainly many deserving plaintiffs, including some intentionally subjected to injury, will be unable to surmount the barrier of the *New York Times* test.

For private persons, though, a different balance should be struck because private individuals have less opportunity to counteract false statements than public figures; therefore, they are "more vulnerable to injury, and the state interest in protecting them is correspondingly greater."

Public figures also deserve less protection, he continued, because by seeking public position, they have knowingly exposed themselves to the risk of public scrutiny, inviting attention and comment. Furthermore, while the media can assume that public figures have voluntarily exposed themselves to increased risk of injury from defamatory falsehoods, they cannot so assume with respect to private parties, who are thus not only more vulnerable to injury but also more deserving of recovery.

We hold that, so long as they do not impose liability without fault, the States may define for themselves the appropriate standard of liability for a publisher or broadcaster of defamatory falsehood injurious to a private individual. This approach provides a more equitable boundary between the competing concerns involved here. It recognizes the strength of the legitimate state interest in compensating private individuals for wrongful injury to reputation, yet shields the press and broadcast media from the rigors of strict liability for defamation. At least this conclusion obtains where, as here, the substance of the defamatory statement "makes substantial danger to reputation apparent."

But this countervailing state interest extends no further than compensation for actual injury. For the reasons stated below, we hold that the States may not permit recovery of presumed or punitive damages, at least when liability is not based on a showing of knowledge of falsity or reckless disregard for the truth.

What should be the extent of recovery? Assuming no malice, only "actual injury" should be compensated:

We would not, of course, invalidate state law simply because we doubt its wisdom, but here we are attempting to reconcile state law with a competing interest grounded in the constitutional command of the First Amendment. It is therefore appropriate to require that state remedies for defamatory falsehood reach no farther than is necessary to protect the legitimate interest involved. It is necessary to restrict defamation plaintiffs who do not prove knowledge of falsity or reckless disregard for the truth to compensation for actual injury.

Powell did not find it necessary to define "actual injury," with which trial courts have had wide experience: "Suffice it to say that actual injury is not limited by out-of-pocket loss. Indeed, the more customary types of actual harm inflicted by defamatory falsehood include impairment of reputation and standing in the community, personal humiliation, and mental anguish and suffering." It was apparent that "actual injury," as defined by the Court, encompassed a wide territory. Without proving special damages, loss of clientele, or the like, it would be possible for an aggrieved private person to recover large sums, as we learned at the retrial of my case.

Thus far, Justice Powell's opinion had dealt with general constitutional principles relating to defamation. Theoretically, a court, including the highest court, is supposed to stick to the facts of the case and what is required by the specific situation. Anything else is called *dictum* and is supposedly not binding in other cases. (This is purely fictional regarding Supreme Court opinions; they are actually used at times as treatises and guidelines on the law.)

At the very end of his opinion, Justice Powell recalled that he was dealing with a specific case, *Elmer Gertz v. Robert Welch, Inc.* Even here, he permitted himself some generalizations on the subject of what constitutes a private person as distinguished from a public figure: "Respondent's characterization of petitioner as a public figure," he observed, "raised a different question." Although I was well known in some circles, I had not achieved general fame or notoriety in the community. In such cases, he continued, "it is preferable to reduce the public figure question to a more meaningful context by looking to the nature and extent of an individual's participation in the particular controversy giving rise to the defamation." And "in this context it is plain that petitioner was not a public figure." I had not been involved in criminal proceedings against Nuccio and had not thrust myself into the vortex of this public issue. Therefore, the Court concluded that the "*New York Times* standard is inapplicable to this case and that the trial court erred in entering judgment for respondent. Because the jury was allowed to impose liability without fault and was permitted to presume damages without proof of injury, a new trial is necessary. We reverse and remand for further proceedings in accord with this opinion."

Justice Blackmun concurred in the majority opinion, but for an apparently unique reason. He had been part of the plurality, with Justice Brennan, in *Rosenbloom*. He then thought it was only logical and inevitable in view of *New York Times*, *Curtis*, and *Butts* to extend the *New York Times* doctrine to events of public or general interest involving private persons. He took a second look at the situation when the majority of the Court refused to go that far, and however illogical it might seem, he agreed with the position now taken by the Court. He did so, he said, for two reasons: (1) The decision would have little if any practical effect on the functioning of practical journalism. (2) The Court needed a definitive ruling in the defamation area, and his vote was needed to create a majority. One might ask (if one were not the beneficiary of his changed position) whether Justice Blackmun had asserted a posture of expediency rather than principle. What he did is really not unusual in the history of the Court. More than one justice has made a principle of judicial harmony. It sometimes seems wise to go along with one's brethren to create a consensus.

Chief Justice Burger dissented, but not in the manner of the dissents of Justices Douglas and Brennan. He thought that the Court should have reversed the Seventh Circuit and the district court and reinstated the jury verdict and judgment in my favor. He said that I "was performing a professional representative role as an advocate in the highest tradition of the law, and under that tradition the advocate is not to be invidiously identified with his client." He went on:

> The important public policy which underlies this tradition—the right to counsel—would be gravely jeopardized if every lawyer who takes an "unpopular" case, civil or criminal, would automatically become fair game of irresponsible reporters and editors who might, for example, describe the lawyer as a "mob mouthpiece" for representing a client with a serious prior criminal record, or as an "ambulance chaser" for representing a claimant in a personal injury action.

Justice Douglas expressed himself briefly but eloquently in support of his well-known thesis that the First and Fourteenth amendments prohibit the imposition of liability for discussions of public affairs, no matter how offensive. His rationale was well expressed:

> The standard announced today leaves the States free to "define for themselves the appropriate standard of liability for a publisher or broadcaster" in the circumstances of this case. This of course leaves the simple negligence standard as an option, with the jury free to impose damages upon a finding that the publisher failed to act as "a reasonable man." With such continued erosion of First Amendment protection, I fear that it may well be the reasonable man who refrains from speaking.

Justice Brennan, allied increasingly with Justice Douglas in his defense of an almost untrammeled right of free expression, agreed with the Court that I was neither a "public official" nor a "public figure." He said that I was involved in an event of public or general interest and that I should therefore be subject to the *New York Times* rule, required to prove "malice with convincing clarity." Inspired perhaps by Justice White's long exposition of the law of defamation, he went into considerable depth in an analysis of the law and why it necessitated a constitutional principle such as that advocated in the plurality opinion in *Rosenbloom*. He thought that only the *New York Times* rule could accommodate the need to protect private reputations without imposing self-censorship upon the press.

The most impressive opinion, in several respects, was that of Justice White. This vigorous jurist, an All-American football player, was sometimes deprecated as less scholarly than his Phi Beta Kappa key would indicate. His dissent showed that he was highly capable of profound inquiry into a subject ancient in origin and consequential in effect. Justice White, like the chief justice, would have reversed the judgment of the court of appeals and reinstated the jury verdict. Thus, it is wrong to think of the ruling as 5–4 in my favor. It was actually 7–2, since only Justices Douglas and Brennan favored the affirmance of the court of appeals and district court rulings against me.

Justice White's dissent began with admirable clarity and forthrightness:

> For some 200 years—from the very founding of the Nation—the law of defamation and right of the ordinary citizen to recover for false pub-

lication injurious to his reputation have been almost exclusively the business of state courts and legislatures. Under typical state defamation law, the defamed private citizen had to prove only a false publication that would subject him to hatred, contempt or ridicule. Given such publication, general damages to reputation were presumed, while punitive damages required proof of additional facts. The law governing the defamation of private citizens remained untouched by the First Amendment because until relatively recently, the consistent view of the Court was that libelous words constitute a class of speech wholly unprotected by the First Amendment, subject only to limited exceptions carved out since 1964.

But now, using that amendment as the chosen instrument, the Court, in a few printed pages, has federalized major aspects of libel law by declaring unconstitutional in important respects the prevailing defamation law in all or most of the 50 States. That result is accomplished by requiring the plaintiff in each and every defamation action to prove not only the defendant's culpability beyond his act of publishing defamatory material but also actual damage to reputation resulting from the publication. Moreover, punitive damages may not be recovered by showing malice in the traditional sense of ill will; knowing falsehood or reckless disregard of the truth will now be required.

He then gave a long and learned history of the law of defamation and cast a critical eye upon what the majority had done in this case. In White's view, the criterion "liability without fault" is virtually meaningless. Certain libels and slanders are inherently damaging. If a publisher, knowing this, publishes anyway, he must *intend* to inflict injury. Even if he is privileged to do so by interpretations of the First Amendment, is he nevertheless "faultless"? White wondered. In these circumstances, when the defamed party is a private citizen, the law had put the risk on the publisher. "The Court would now shift this risk to the victim, even though he has done nothing to invite the calumny, is wholly innocent of fault, and is helpless to avoid his injury."

It is not necessary to revolutionize the law of libel, he continued, to protect the press, which today is vigorous and robust:

> It is difficult for me to understand why the ordinary citizen should himself carry the risk of damage and suffer the injury in order to vindicate First Amendment values by protecting the press and others from liability for circulating false information. This is particularly true because such statements serve no purpose whatsoever in furthering the

public interest or the search for truth but, on the contrary, may frustrate that search and at the same time inflict great injury on the defenseless individual. The owners of the press and the stockholders of the communications enterprises can much better bear the burden. And if they cannot, the public at large should somehow pay for what is essentially a public benefit derived at private expense.

In the same vein, Justice White declared that no case had been made for "razing State libel laws." There must be room, he said, for allowing the fifty states to take diverse approaches to defamation. "Freedom and human dignity and decency are not antithetical." Freedom of the press should not be protected by the Court at the expense of the rights of private persons.

What, then, can be distilled as *Gertz*'s central contribution to jurisprudence?

1. Reaffirming the holding of *New York Times v. Sullivan*, public figures and public officials must prove actual malice to recover for injury to reputation.
2. The states are responsible for determining standards of liability when a publisher or broadcaster injures the reputation of a private person.
3. In setting such standards, the states may not impose liability without fault.
4. Furthermore, if a state chooses a standard less demanding than the *New York Times* rule, it may not assess punitive damages for such injury. Only damages for actual injury may be awarded.
5. *Actual injury* was defined.
6. The expression of mere opinion is not actionable.

11 ■ Slowly, Slowly Creeps the Case

The Supreme Court had reversed the lower courts, sending the case back for retrial. We filed an amended complaint, correcting and supplementing our original complaint. We had discovered the anomalous fact that the reprint had been distributed before the magazine itself and pointed that out. Perhaps most important, we pointed out facts that showed the defendant was in reckless disregard of the truth or falsity of statements concerning me when it published the article. We no longer needed to be circumspect because of pending criminal trial or appeal concerning Nuccio since his conviction had been affirmed by the Illinois Supreme Court.

We said that the defendant had been grossly negligent, having violated its duty to verify the published facts; publication had taken place with reckless disregard for truth or falsity. Furthermore, the publisher was guilty of actual malice. It had made no effort to verify any of the statements prior to publication. Moreover, the publisher knew I was a lawyer and must also have known that calling a lawyer a Communist would seriously jeopardize his professional and community reputation. Thus it should have been on notice to check its facts carefully. Since *American Opinion* was a monthly publication, it did not have to contend with extreme deadline pressure and had ample time to check its facts. It was in an excessive hurry to publish and distribute the article and reprint. To add to the offense, defendant's managing editor vouched for the accuracy of the article, although he had no basis for doing so, and he wrote captions that defamed me. Because the defendant misrepresented the status of Alan Stang, the author of the article, Stang was wrongly excused from cross-examination as an adverse witness. Reprints of the article were literally forced upon people in my home neighborhood, and defendant continued to distribute the article and reprints for months after it had notice of their falsity. All these facts demonstrated that defendant acted with actual malice.

We also made the following points: A principal theme of the article was that Officer Nuccio had been "framed" on a charge of murder. Subsequent conviction of Nuccio, affirmed by the Illinois Supreme Court, demonstrated the falsity of that contention. Moreover, defendant made that charge while the trial was going on—an attempt to interfere with the litigation and prejudice the parties thereto, a further indication of actual malice.

As a result of defendant's malicious activities, I had been injured in my "good name, credit and reputation, and standing in the community, both as an individual and as an attorney at law." In addition, I had suffered mental anguish, humiliation, and public ridicule.

Through these pleadings, I was able to greatly enlarge my claim for actual damages on each count, to $200,000 instead of the nominal sum named in the original complaint, and to ask for $500,000 in punitive damages.

We also sought to file a third count to the complaint. Robert Welch had personally repeated the defamatory statements following the Supreme Court decision, and we believed this action constituted a new claim, grounded in malice. For reasons I found hard to grasp, Judge Decker refused to permit the additional count.

However, he did not remain much longer as the trial judge. He was succeeded by Judge Joel Flaum, and all of us took a new look at the litigation. At the second trial, we were permitted to offer testimony about the additional defamatory statement made by Robert Welch, and we were able to cross-examine Alan Stang, the author of the article. The atmosphere was wholly different.

The defendant's answer to our amended complaint was simple enough. In this, his first pleading, Gerard C. Heldrich, Jr., the defendant's new attorney, was not as prolix and involuted as he later became. The answer consisted for the most part of admissions and denials, and occasionally a statement that the defendant was insufficiently informed to answer.

The name Gerard C. Heldrich, Jr., had a ring of distinction. It was ideal for a profession in which imagery counts for much, but it was totally unfamiliar to me. I could not recall ever having had any contacts with him. I was shocked to learn years after the case was over that Heldrich claimed he had consulted with me in connection with a libel case because "everyone seems to know about

Elmer Gertz as a libel specialist." He had expected much of my office but instead found that it looked like "an old 1939 movie set." In an almost surrealistic manner, Heldrich recalled that virtually every inch of space in my reception room was covered by "frames and frames of photographs of Elmer Gertz with someone—Pope John XXIII, David Ben Gurion, everyone except God." Since I had never been photographed with either the Pope or the Israeli prime minister and knew neither, I was puzzled by Heldrich's recollections and his statement that my tongue had been practically hanging out, presumably at the prospect of getting a big new libel case. This was especially surprising to me, since not even my most notorious cases such as those involving Leopold and Ruby had made me drool.

I was also troubled by Heldrich's statement that General Watts told him when he was hired to represent Robert Welch, Inc., that the prior attorney, James Boyle, was "fired" because he "did not adequately represent" it. Since Boyle had won the first case on motion, had kept Stang, the author of the article, from being forced to testify as an adverse witness, and had kept the damages down to $50,000 before the case was dismissed, I could not understand why Boyle was "fired," especially in view of what followed when Heldrich was the attorney.

Heldrich said later that after reading the article "Frame-Up," which was the basis of my suit, he began to lose heart, but Stang's research cheered him up—Stang might have accurately characterized me "by association." As I learned later, Heldrich reasoned:

> Here was a man, Elmer Gertz, so the record had revealed, who had since the late Thirties, aligned himself with reputed Communist-Front organizations for at least twenty years, only to surface in the great political crusade against the war in Viet Nam.
> Could it have been the last hurrah for an aging social warrior?
> I didn't believe that Stang was right in calling Gertz a Communist-Fronter, a Marxist, or a Leninist. Proving Stang right wasn't my job. All that I had to feel, was that Stang had a right, based upon what he had learned, to accurately express his conclusions in a journal of political opinion.

Long after it could do us any good at the trial, I learned more of Heldrich's reasoning. Stang had given him a box of material about me, principally a large number of newspaper clippings dating back to the 1940s. That was when I had written a pamphlet attacking the then archreactionary *Chicago Tribune* and its imperious publisher, Colonel McCormick. According to Heldrich, Colonel McCormick had written an interoffice memo that called me a "young Red." Apparently Heldrich did not know that the Colonel regarded almost everyone who did not share his extreme views as crimson in coloration.

He noticed my defense of Judge Leighton, who had been criticized for an unpopular decision acquitting three defendants because of "unprofessional police behavior." He noticed other articles about my connection with the Jack Ruby case and my defense of the *Chicago Seed*, which he mistakenly styled "an underground paper." He found articles about my connection with the Sparling Commission report and a number of book reviews I had written. He was especially interested in reviews of a book about the Rosenbergs and one about Alger Hiss and Whitaker Chambers.

He learned more of my personal history. He said that the majority of my friends were writers and journalists, "almost universally Jewish and Black," but that I lived "in a decidedly white neighborhood," which he mistakenly described as Albany Park. Heldrich thought much about the Jews and was given to generalizations about them. He opined, "Jews were just not assimilated into American life at that time in Chicago." He recalled that many early Bolsheviks were Jews. He did not seem to understand that they were few in number and were not practicing Jews or that like Karl Marx, the father of so-called scientific socialism, they were self-hating and anti-Semitic. He felt that in the early twenties, "Soviet political ascendancy [was] deeply admired by the young American Jew."

Heldrich observed: "Gertz was a member of the close-knit Chicago Jewish community. American Jews have reacted strongly whenever one of their own was attacked, as if they were on the endangered species list. Most often, I observed, that when one Jew was in trouble, the others rallied to his cause, regardless of whether the individual was right or wrong." I would have understood Heldrich better had I known these things about him at the time of the trial rather than later when it could do me no good.

Heldrich, like Boyle, took my deposition. His impressions, which came out years later, were intriguing: "I peered across the table at the little grandfatherly-looking man with a beaming round face. He wore a small gray mustache and thick, round rimless glasses. He was only slightly overweight. His hands appeared to be almost feminine. There was no mistaking that he had never performed manual labor. On his rather ordinary head was thin, gray, wispy hair." Obviously enjoying his denigration of me, he went on: "Almost from the beginning I sensed that Mr. Gertz would try to reveal as little as possible. The wily old fox was making his opponent dig out information the hard way."

As I found later, Heldrich's recollections of the details of the case and me were not always accurate. As he purported to tell of my life or what the testimony unfolded, he often misstated the facts or what was said, even when he quoted material. Some inaccuracies were relatively unimportant, but I could not understand how he, an attorney in the case, could state that we had made Alan Stang, the author of the offending article, a defendant.

The case had been transferred to a different judge, as is usual in a retrial. We were exceedingly fortunate that the judge was Joel M. Flaum, who had been appointed to the federal bench in 1974 when he was only thirty-nine. The appointment, by President Gerald Ford, had been widely heralded as brilliant and almost nonpolitical in nature. Flaum's subsequent career made the choice appear increasingly superlative, so it was no surprise when he was suggested as a judge of the U.S. Court of Appeals for the Seventh Circuit and then as a judge of the District of Columbia Court of Appeals while the posttrial motions in my case were still under consideration.

Judge Flaum had early distinguished himself on the *Northwestern Law Review* and then had spent only a year in private practice. He served for four years in the Appellate and Criminal-trial divisions of the Cook County state attorney's office. In 1969, he became an assistant Illinois attorney general under William Scott. He rose rapidly to deputy chief, then chief of the Criminal Justice Division and first assistant attorney general in 1970. From there, he had followed big and promising James R. Thompson to the U.S. Attorney's office, then proceeded to the federal bench.

When the Chicago Council of Lawyers undertook a survey of the federal trial judges in our district in 1978, Judge Flaum ranked third, only slightly behind Judges John Powers Crowley and Prentice H. Marshall. He was called a good judge overall by a remarkable 94.1 percent of those polled. He fared even better, second to Judge Marshall, among those asked which district-court judges would make good court-of-appeals judges. Overwhelmingly, he was regarded as uninfluenced by the identities of the parties in litigation, with no predisposition in criminal rulings (despite his previous tenure as a prosecutor in county, state, and federal prosecutors' offices), no predisposition in civil rulings. He was considered courteous yet firm to lawyers and litigants, refraining from prejudging outcomes, understanding issues in complex and ordinary cases, expressing himself clearly in oral and written rulings. He was familiar with rulings and current legal developments, ruling with decisiveness during trials, adequately researching and preparing, expeditiously handling emergencies. His excellence in other areas also won overwhelming tribute. Only a certain slowness in ruling on pretrial motions and deciding cases was noted, but even here 75 percent expressed approval.

My approval of Judge Flaum was based upon his human qualities. He was likable, without pretense or pomposity, with an unruffled temperament both on and off the bench. He inspired good conduct in all who came before him. You knew that he wanted to be fair to you and your opponent. Sitting in his court during sentencing proceedings, I was amazed at the compassion of this former prosecutor.

I had heard that he welcomed the assignment of my case to him. It would be a test of his knowledge and other judicial qualities. I too found the case fascinating, and not only because I was personally involved. It concerned one of my favorite fields of the law, one in which I had considerable proficiency. I wanted to thwart an attorney who wanted to entangle me in a legal mess, and I was as determined as ever to teach the Birch people that they could not defame me with impunity.

The maneuvering led again to cross-motions for summary judgment. With admirable clarity, the judge set forth what was before him:

> This diversity libel action is before the court on the parties' cross motions for summary judgment. The plaintiff, an attorney, represented in some civil litigation the family of a youth who was killed by a Chicago policeman. The police officer was later convicted of murder for the youth's death. In March of 1969, the defendant published an article

which stated that the policeman had been a victim of a communist conspiracy to frame him for the murder. The article claimed that a participant in this conspiracy was the plaintiff. Following a trial in the Northern District of Illinois and review to the Supreme Court, the case was remanded to this court for a new trial.

The parties in their motions raised four issues: (1) Whether the plaintiff is a public figure; (2) whether the facts of the article are a true statement of Gertz's political leanings and his participation in the alleged plot; (3) whether, pursuant to Illinois law, the defendant was negligent in its publication of the article; and (4) whether the defendant acted with actual knowledge of falsehood or with reckless disregard of the truth, thereby justifying punitive damages under Illinois law.

Flaum denied the cross-motions except for the public-figure issue; on this he entered summary judgment for me. Defendant, he said, was foreclosed from raising the issue because the Supreme Court had already settled it. (On a remand from the Supreme Court, a lower court cannot reconsider a matter on which the Court has ruled.)

What, then, about the other issues of the case? The law-of-the-case doctrine, he said, extends only to matters expressly covered by the appellate court. It is well settled that when a case has been reversed and remanded for further proceedings, all other issues are to be decided as if the former trial had not taken place. Therefore, the court was not foreclosed from considering the issue of liability on the negligence and malice counts. On the merits of the libel claim, the substantive law of Illinois must be applied. He declared, of course, that in Illinois the *Troman* case set forth the standard by which the defendant was to be judged—ordinary negligence.

Next Flaum considered the appropriateness of summary judgment in this case. In a negligence action, he continued, summary judgment is rarely appropriate: "Even when the facts underlying the issue of negligence are undisputed, the issue must still be submitted to the jury if reasonable men could reach different conclusions and inferences from those facts. *Croly v. Matson Nav. Co.*, 434 F.2d 73, 75 (5th Cir. 1970)."

If we could show that there was no genuine issue of material fact, we would be entitled to summary judgment. However, he found that there was indeed "a genuine issue of material fact as to whether the defendant had reasonable grounds to believe that these statements were true." Stang "substantially relied on hearsay statements from news clippings, individuals connected with the policeman's case, as well as on governmental publications." The managing editor stated that Stang had done "extensive research," including a review of the transcript of Nuccio's first trial and consultation with at least nine people who had had some connection with the case.

On the other hand, Stang had failed to contact me, and he admitted he did not know whether I had had any involvement in the criminal case against Nuccio:

In concluding that the plaintiff was involved in communist "front" organizations, Stang relied on a House of Representatives committee report which identified certain organizations of which Gertz had been a member as "subversive." Whether such reliance provided the defendant reasonable grounds to believe that the facts as published were not true is a question which must be decided by the trier of fact.

The second issue was whether the allegations were false:

Gertz testified at the first trial of this case that he never espoused any communist doctrines and that he has never belonged to a communist organization. The defendant seeks to contradict this by arguing that Gertz's alleged association with alleged communist organizations demonstrate that he was in fact a communist. An issue of fact is therefore raised by the parties.

These two considerations, Flaum continued, were relevant to the issue of malice. In Illinois, punitive damages may be recovered if actual malice is shown. He concluded: "Since the court finds that a genuine issue of material facts exists as to whether the defendant might have acted with reckless disregard for the truth or actually knew of the falsity of its statements, the motions for summary judgment on the malice issue are also denied."

Accordingly, Flaum denied both parties' motions for summary judgment regarding the issues of truth, negligence, and malice, but he granted our motion for summary judgment on the public-figure issue. I was not a public figure.

In some respects, we were quite pleased with the court's memorandum; however, we believed that Judge Flaum had not decided the issue of truth properly. We moved that the court reconsider our motion for summary judgment on that issue, pointing out that in the defendant's pleadings and in closing argument before the jury in the first trial, the defendant had admitted that its charges against me were untrue. We said that the defendant had had every opportunity to establish the truth of what it had published but had failed to do so. Most tellingly, we quoted from the majority opinion of the Supreme Court:

> The statements contained serious inaccuracies. The implication that petitioner [plaintiff] had a criminal record was false. Petitioner had been a member and officer of the National Lawyers Guild some 15 years earlier, but there was no evidence that he or that organization had taken any part in planning the 1968 demonstrations in Chicago. There was also no basis for the charge that petitioner was a "Leninist" or a "Communist-fronter." And he had never been a member of the "Marxist League for Industrial Democracy" or the "Intercollegiate Socialist Society."

Judge Flaum, showing a willingness to confess error, sustained our motion for reconsideration and on February 15, 1978, granted summary judgment for us on the issue of truth: "In its earlier pleadings and closing argument in the first trial, defendant conceded that the plaintiff was not in fact a communist and not involved in a conspiracy to frame Officer Nuccio. Such judicial admissions are binding on the defendant on retrial." He emphasized that such admissions have been held to be conclusive. And these findings led him to conclude:

> Accordingly, since defendant admitted in [its] earlier pleadings and closing argument that published statements concerning the plaintiff were in fact false, [it] cannot now raise the issue of truth. Therefore, when this cause comes before the court on retrial, the evidence concerning liability will be limited to the issues of negligence and the existence of malice.

Defendant's counsel had the sometimes admirable trait of refusing to give up. Judge Flaum, on April 6, 1978, denied the motion to reconsider his ruling on the issue of truth and the renewed motion to dismiss the complaint. As will be seen, defendant's counsel persisted in these and similar motions to the end of the case and beyond. Meanwhile, precious time went by. I had the almost forlorn hope that the judge would finally impose sanctions of some sort on the defendant, such as striking its answer and entering a judgment of liability, leaving us to prove damages. A court has the right to do this but seldom does. Judge Flaum, infinitely patient it seemed, did not.

On one point, which turned out to be of no moment, he sustained defendant's argument: Since it was a negligence case, I, as plaintiff, had to plead and prove my lack of contributory negligence. Accordingly, we filed an amendment to the complaint, making the proper allegation.

The court, too hopeful, asked for submission of final pretrial memorandums by May 17, 1978. Instead, the case dragged on for three more years. I reminded Wayne that if I did not survive, the case would not survive either because libel is a "personal" action that ends with the life of the plaintiff unless there has been a judgment. Though vigorous, I was in my seventies. Twice I had surgery, which I used as a warning lesson to Wayne. He promised to do his utmost to bring matters to a head. In three more years, he succeeded.

The defendant's attorney filed another motion for summary judgment, rehashing old material. Months went by without a decision. At last, on June 12, 1980, Judge Flaum brusquely turned down Heldrich's maneuver, denying the motion for summary judgment because it was basically a motion for reconsideration of his court's memorandum opinion of June 7, 1977, and Judge Decker's memorandum opinion of November 18, 1969.

If I presented even the gist of the countless interrogatories filed by the defendant and our answers, summarized the depositions taken, digested the efforts to narrow issues or to get into evidence all sorts of irrelevant documentation, I would consume pages of this book without adding anything to the reader's understanding. For the most part, the maneuvers were transparent and easily overcome, but resisting them took time and ingenuity.

While my case was grinding its way to the long-delayed second trial, I was aided by another libel case. Carol Burnett, one of several Hollywood celebrities who claimed to have been defamed by the *National Enquirer*, won a huge judgment after a protracted trial: $300,000 in general or compensatory damages and $1.3 million in punitive damages. The trial court ultimately cut the award in half to the still substantial sum of $800,000. The publisher declared that it would appeal even this lesser amount. Burnett expressed great satisfaction at her vindication.

I took the verdict as a good omen for the forthcoming trial. After all, the false charges made against me were far more serious than those made against Burnett. The *Enquirer* had published a retraction, but *American Opinion* repeated the libel with no apology. I thought that a reasonable jury would be impressed.

I also thought that the ruling boded well for the health of the publishing industry. Irresponsible publishers like the *Enquirer* were provoking lawsuits that resulted in large punitive-damage settlements. These set a precedent that threatened the publishing industry as a whole in a way that compensatory damages could never do. Many in the media feared that they could be bankrupted or greatly inhibited by the possibility of such large punitive judgments. Some of them organized in self-defense.

The worst offenders, in contrast, apparently believed they could brazen through most situations. The *National Enquirer*, for example, apparently believed that aggrieved parties generally would not sue and thus expose themselves to embarrassment and expense. Even if they did, skillful and sometimes cynical counsel could employ various devices to delay or thwart a day of reckoning.

I felt that the Birch people were guilty of the same tactics, at least in my case. And they were zealots, not likely to act reasonably. Perhaps they counted my not surviving the almost endless delay.

One of the students in my law-school privacy seminars, Ron Chizever, went to the trouble of preparing a scrapbook on the Carol Burnett case and presented it to me. I went through it with mounting interest as my trial approached. From time to time during the pendency of the case, other students had done research on it and written case notes, often of interest and value. I talked to various classes at the John Marshall Law School and elsewhere about the case. The students in Professor David Gordon's class at Northwestern's Medill School of Journalism, and after him, Professor David Protess's class, were especially interested, and I talked with them each semester during the years.

It must not be supposed that the retrial of my case was simply a repeat of the first trial. While there were points of similarity—after all, the case concerned the same article—there were many differences, not merely refinements. The case had been remanded by the Supreme Court for a new trial with instructions that we establish fault (determined by the Illinois Supreme Court in *Troman* to be simple negligence) and prove actual injuries. After the trial got under way, we were confronted by Judge Flaum with the necessity to prove malice in the constitutional sense, not merely negligence, because of the plea of fair comment that he had allowed the defendant to file just before the case came to trial.

The defendant had a new attorney, much less flexible and more cocky than his predecessor, and a house counsel of the Birch Society sat with him at the defense table. Wayne had come of age as a lawyer. He was mature, thoughtful, and resourceful, and he had lived with the case for more than a decade.

Since two former witnesses to my character and reputation were dead and one was ill, additional witnesses had to be found. We presented the inimitable Julius Lucius Echeles as a witness this time (he had been absent from the first trial because the judge felt we ought not to call him). He gave an added dimension to our proof that I was not connected with the prosecution of Nuccio, conspiratorially or otherwise, and gave added dimension to a delineation of my character and reputation. Albert E. Jenner, Jr., was also called as a witness to my good name; he turned out to have tremendous value in other respects as well.

Undoubtedly the most important difference between the two trials was the appearance of Alan Stang, the author of the defamatory article, upon whom Stanley said he had relied. We had been unable to get Stang as a witness the first time because the defendant had been unwilling to produce him and the court had supported the position that the defendant had no control over him. Now Wayne had full scope to cross-examine him. Since Stang was a witness for the defense, we were not bound by what he said or hindered by any limiting rule as in the first trial. We could show the absurdity of the defendant's reliance upon Stang through his previous wild charges against presidents and public figures generally. My testimony also had a great bearing on the result. I could now cover a wider scope and introduce new areas of evidence.

I will emphasize here what was new and decisive in the retrial. Despite condensations and omissions, I hope to convey the general flavor of the event.

I cannot pretend to be completely fair to the defendant's attorney, Gerard C. Heldrich, Jr., but I don't think that he was fair to me either. Let me phrase it this way: We had a mutual antipathy. Heldrich seemed to believe that in defending his client's interests, he had to treat me with calculated disrespect. He had a gift for obfuscation, making complications out of simplicities, and he was tireless and amazingly resourceful in bouncing back after rebuffs. No sooner was one of his stratagems thwarted than he attempted substantially the same thing in slightly different form. As I have said, I had the feeling that he was trying to prolong the case beyond my life. He made no attempt at compromise, perhaps because his client would not permit it. In the end, I think that he offended the jury as well as me. Nothing seemed to daunt the judge, at least publicly, and Wayne too showed no sign of being offended until Heldrich accused him of being part of a "cabal."

Sitting at the counsel table with Heldrich was Gary R. Handy, house counsel of the John Birch Society. Tall and somewhat ungainly, largely silent and somber, he sat beside Heldrich, who said, somewhat bitingly, that the man was there to catch his errors. After a time, Handy's reserve vanished, and he talked in a friendly if not affable manner. We learned that he was a Utah Mormon with many children. Unlike Heldrich, he showed few signs of animosity. Attentive every moment, he showed great restraint in the in-chambers discussions and abstained completely in open court. Of course, we were not privy to what he said to Heldrich or to his principal in Belmont, Massachusetts.

In what seemed to us an almost mindless fashion, the defendant's attorney announced that he was going to introduce a large number of articles by or about me. Copies were submitted to us; we naturally objected to them. In the end, defense counsel attempted to offer only a few of the documents. Perhaps Heldrich was probing for weaknesses on our part or the court's. If so, he scarcely achieved this purpose through the largely irrelevant documents.

During most of the time that my suit was pending, I was on the faculty of the John Marshall Law School, in later years conducting seminars on civil rights and privacy. In the privacy seminars, we discussed such matters as obscenity, birth control, abortion, euthanasia, search and seizure, and defamation. The subjects were controversial, the students lively, the professor congenial. I required a paper, the equivalent of a law-review article, from each student, and some of them did surpassingly well. From time to time, students chose to write of my libel case or related matters, and I read each such paper with great interest.

Just before the retrial, there was an animated discussion in the privacy class about my case. One student inquired why it had been pending so long, why it had not been retried or settled. I gave a candid account of the situation, ending: "When you are dealing with zealots, as the John Birchers are, you don't get reasonable or even rational conduct. It would have been wise for them to settle long ago, as I would then have been very reasonable in my demands."

After the class was over, a bright young man came up to me. "Professor Gertz," he said, "I think that I have a conflict of interest." "What do you mean?" I inquired. He then told me that he was clerking for the opposing counsel, doing research on the issues in my case. I assured him that he need not be concerned. Thereafter, I observed Enrico Mirabelli closely. He was a good student, active in student government and in student divisions of various bar associations. He was the student representative for the Seventh Circuit at the American Bar Association. I was very pleased at the end of the semester when I could give him an A, which he fully deserved. He was thoroughly worn-out by his efforts in my case. After it was over, I discussed the case in class and asked Rico to give his views, which he did in a thoroughly honest and competent fashion. I am sure that one day he will be a great success in the practice of law.

One of the defendant's last-ditch efforts was a motion to file an affirmative defense, to limit certain testimony that I might give, and to strike the word *crime* from the complaint—all of these twelve years after the filing of the first complaint, when the case was finally ready for retrial. The proposed affirmative defense was that Stang, as a reporter, had the right to rely upon public documents and the statements of public employees and thus had a qualified privilege to use such material, which would be lost only by actual bad faith. The testimony to be excluded was that since the filing of suit, I had become a law-school professor. The reason for such exclusion was that members of the jury might think that I had a superior knowledge of the law and that this might prejudice them in my favor. The reason alleged for striking the word *crime* was that the *American Opinion* article referred only to *intelligence*, not *crime*.

Wayne argued persuasively against these maneuvers and was sustained by Judge Flaum, except for the defense of qualified privilege related to the defendant's use of government documents. This, said our opponents, was permitted under the doctrine of fair comment. On this claim, the court reserved judgment. Judge Flaum did not make a definitive ruling until the trial began. He then permitted the filing of the plea, which complicated the case greatly and filled us with foreboding.

While the date of the trial was approaching, a federal judge, George N. Leighton, and I were sent on a mission to the Soviet Union by the National Conference on Soviet Jewry. Our assignment was to call upon the "refuseniks," Jews who had been refused permission to leave the USSR on one pretext or another—or none. It was a visit packed with adventure and high emotional content. Upon our return, the Public Affairs Committee of the Jewish Federation of Metropolitan Chicago set up a press conference that was to take place during the lunch-hour recess of the court on the date of the trial. Heldrich professed to be troubled by the possibility of prejudicial publicity. Perhaps Heldrich and Handy were distressed by the visible proof that I was not a Communist dupe, as Stang had claimed, that I was in fact strongly opposed to the Soviet system. The judge rescheduled the case, but this was the last delaying tactic. The day of reckoning was at hand.

12 ■ A New Trial: A Resounding Victory

While we were selecting the jury in the second trial, I thought of Melvin Belli in the Jack Ruby case years earlier. Because he contemplated a complicated defense in that unfortunate case, he wanted a well-educated jury who would understand what the psychiatrists and other experts said. The result was that he got a collection of stiff-necked people who lacked sympathy for Ruby, a rough character who had killed the slayer of the president in circumstances that embarrassed an already discredited city. Almost inevitably, they brought in a verdict of death, which Wayne and I ultimately helped set aside.

In this trial, we were content to deal with ordinary men and women. The first chosen was Barry Brown, an unmarried student at a beautician school who had held odd jobs and had never been on a jury. The next, Gordon Parks, was from suburban Long Grove, a cash register salesman, married to a part-time secretary, the father of three children. Mrs. Betty Hallcraft was from suburban Oak Lawn, a housewife married to an insurance statistician. She had been a juror in a personal injury case fifteen years previously. Henry Martin was from Joliet, an engineer whose wife was a microbiologist. They had two children. He too had never been on a jury. Barbara Rosson, a first-time juror, worked in the personnel department of an insurance company and lived with her parents. The sixth regular member of the jury, John Burt, a Chicagoan, was unemployed but had been a maintenance worker for twenty-five years. His wife was a teacher in a Catholic school. They had four children. He had been in a lawsuit stemming from a traffic accident some years previously, which had been settled. The two alternates, who sat with the jury during the trial but were excused before deliberations began, were women — Corrine Clark, of Waukegan, and Lois Bloom, of Skokie, both married, one to a lawyer, the other to a Defense Department employee. In the second trial there were only six jurors, not twelve. Since the first trial, the Supreme Court had found a six-person jury permissible.

This was a representative group but heavy on suburbanites. Only one was black, accepted by defense counsel in order to excuse a member of the American Civil Liberties Union and the Independent Voters of Illinois. This was probably a bad exchange. Heldrich did not realize that we would make many points in cross-examination by showing the hostility of defense witnesses to Dr. Martin Luther King, Jr., whom they had characterized as a tool of the Communists. A civil-liberties absolutist would have been opposed to all recovery in libel actions, but it was unlikely that a black would forgive such an attack upon King.

On April 14, 1981, the jury having been selected, the attorneys for both sides gave their opening statements, necessarily brief and intended to give the jury an overall impression of what was at stake. Wayne told the jury that the jigsaw puzzle that is a lawsuit would be put together through the testimony of witnesses. He painted a quick picture of me as a lawyer and citizen who had earned a good reputation through more than fifty years in the practice of law and said that the monstrous lies about me in the *American Opinion* article had caused me great grief and impaired my reputation. He summarized what Alan Stang had said of me and declared that all of it was false and defamatory.

Heldrich responded. His aim was to show that 1968 was a year of "horrendous controversy"; "there were accusations, and counteraccusations, and commissions and countercommissions. And not only here in Chicago . . . but in the rest of the country there was chaos and turmoil." His theme was that I was involved in the controversy and therefore was fair game for Stang. Besides, he argued, I had suffered no injury.

We then called our first witness, Irving Kupcinet, known to Chicagoans as "Kup," a journalist and broadcaster. He had known me, he said, for thirty-five years, and he had also known many people who had known me. Thus he had come to be familiar with my reputation as an attorney, citizen, and patriot, and it was "impeccable." He had never heard me espouse communism.

On cross-examination, Heldrich observed that I, like Kupcinet, wrote articles and book reviews for the *Chicago Sun-Times*. Kup had no idea how many articles I had written for his newspaper. He acknowledged that my name often had been mentioned in the

Sun-Times. Obviously Heldrich was trying to make the jury believe that Kup must be predisposed in my favor because we wrote for the same newspaper—he regularly; I occasionally.

He inquired if the witness knew what organizations I had belonged to during the years he had known me.

Kup said that I belonged to many civil rights organizations. "I do not keep records of all of the organizations he belongs to. He is very active."

"In other words, Mr. Kupcinet, you don't know very much about Mr. Gertz?"

"I know a lot about Mr. Gertz," Kupcinet responded. "I don't know the organizations he belongs to, sir, but I know a lot about his character and who he is and what he stands for."

Heldrich was not tempted to question him further. Heldrich presumed a knowledge of the inner workings of everyone, including witnesses such as Kup. He wrote later: "Kup left the courtroom hurriedly as if he had never wanted to be there. I felt somewhat sorry for the aging journalist. He was just trying to help his old friend, but he wasn't much help. Gertz had imposed upon him unnecessarily."

Wayne Giampietro's wife, Mary, next took the stand, testifying substantially as in the original trial. A pamphlet was thrust upon her while she was shopping in the Lincoln Square area. Glancing at the pamphlet later, she was surprised to see my picture. She called her husband immediately: "Wayne, you are not going to believe what I just got." She then got into her car, drove to my office, and showed me the pamphlet.

Heldrich said that it was not "really pleasant cross-examining a colleague's wife." Mary quipped, "I will be kind." Heldrich tried to pin Mary down as to the date. How did I react to the pamphlet? "When Mr. Gertz saw it, he was quite surprised and started looking at it frantically." Thereupon Heldrich said to the judge: "Your honor, I may have to call Mrs. Giampietro back as an adverse witness." Wayne countered that he was quite willing to have Heldrich question his wife while she was still on the stand, even if he went beyond the scope of the direct examination. Heldrich said that he preferred calling her back. He never did.

Wayne then introduced into evidence the *American Opinion* article and the reprint of it. He told the judge that he wanted to pass out copies of the article to the jurors so that they might follow it while he read the full article to them. Heldrich was clearly disturbed, but Judge Flaum said that he would permit Wayne to distribute the copies; then they would go to the jury room and read it. Heldrich formally objected, but the court went ahead with the procedure. Earlier, Judge Flaum had refused to permit the use of an enlarged version of the article.

When the jury had read the article, they heard the reading of the deposition of Julius Lucius Echeles. We would have preferred Echeles in person, for he would have given sparkle to the proceedings, but he was out of the country, in the south of France and Monaco. Wayne proposed that his young associate, Kathryn Koenig, read the questions and he the answers.

Echeles testified that he had represented Richard Nuccio in his first trial on the charge of murdering Ronald Nelson. Nuccio had been convicted in a bench trial before Judge Richard Fitzgerald. He represented Nuccio in the appeal of the conviction to the Illinois Supreme Court and won a reversal. He had then represented Nuccio in the second trial, before a jury, where there was again a conviction. Nuccio had engaged other counsel for the second appeal, and Echeles was out of the case.

He had known me since 1947 or 1948. I had never had anything to do with the prosecution of Nuccio, nor had I ever made any public statements about the charges against Nuccio.

He had met Alan Stang when Nuccio asked if he would permit Stang to read the transcript of the trial. "I asked him for what purpose. He said that Mr. Stang was interested in helping Nuccio. I asked if Mr. Stang were a lawyer, and he advised me Mr. Stang was not a lawyer, but was associated with some magazine." This was after the first trial of Nuccio while he was preparing the brief, not yet filed.

There followed this colloquy between Wayne and Echeles:

A: I told you the entire meeting and relationship related to my introduction by Mr. Nuccio to Mr. Stang, and I made the transcript available to Mr. Stang in my library. I then went about my business working and had very little conversation, if any, with Mr. Stang.
Q: Were you in sole charge of the defense of Mr. Nuccio on those criminal charges at that time?
A: I was.

Wayne then asked about the charge that there had been a conspiracy against Nuccio:

Q: Did you become aware of any facts which would lead you to conclude that there was a conspiracy to frame Mr. Nuccio for the charge which had been placed against him?
A: I know of no such conspiracy to frame Mr. Nuccio. I was not then or am I now aware of any facts or circumstances by which it could be claimed that he, Mr. Nuccio, was the victim of a conspiracy. None came to my attention.
Q: And it is safe to assume, I take it, based upon your prior answers, that you had no discussion of any alleged conspiracy or frame-up with Mr. Stang?
A: None with him or anybody else.

Echeles testified that he knew of my "excellent reputation of the highest order for truth and veracity," of my reputation as a lawyer with the highest competence, highest regard for responsibility to clients, and the greatest integrity. "Mr. Gertz bore the reputation as a very loyal American, as a person who is dedicated to the principles of the Constitution, and who was then and is now a lawyer dedicated to the principles of our Constitution. He is a loyal and patriotic American." He had never known me to espouse any of the principles of communism. A lawyer called a Communist "would suffer amongst his clientele or possibly even future clientele."

Echeles said that we would have been amazed to learn that I had any connection with the prosecution of Nuccio. He had talked with people in the state attorney's office who were prosecuting Nuccio, and he could recall no reference by them to me.

A question came up about the B'nai B'rith. Echeles said, "It is a Jewish organization." Heldrich commented cryptically, "I understand. We have ours, too." It was not until later that I learned Heldrich's views with respect to Jews.

Echeles said in response to a question on cross-examination that the ACLU never espoused any of the doctrines of communism. Its purpose was to protect the civil liberties of individuals and organizations.

Wayne advised the court at this point that he had found Michael Kachigian, a character witness in the first trial who had been unlocatable. Also, he had concluded that he would not call another former character witness, Frank Greenberg, who had been handicapped by a stroke. He said that he would read the prior testimony of my departed friends Fink and Ligtenberg. Heldrich objected on the ground that the issues in the retrial were different from those in the original trial and that the jury could not observe the witnesses. The judge said that he would look at the transcripts of their testimony and then decide whether to permit the transcripts to be read into evidence.

As another witness on reputation, Wayne called Carol Bellows, former president of the Illinois State Bar Association, a charming, articulate woman. She attested to my excellent reputation in every respect. There was then a lively confrontation between the attorneys:

MR. GIAMPIETRO: Do you have an opinion as to whether calling an attorney a Communist would have any effect upon that person's reputation?
MR. HELDRICH: Objection to the answer, Your Honor. She is not qualified as an expert in that area. And what she may think of what an attorney is called is irrelevant.
THE COURT: That objection will be overruled.
THE WITNESS: Yes, I do.
MR. GIAMPIETRO: And what is that opinion?
THE WITNESS: My opinion is that calling an attorney in this country a Communist would be very detrimental and have a very negative effect.
MR. GIAMPIETRO: And why do you say that?
THE WITNESS: Because *communism* is a dirty word in this country. It is—someone who is called a Communist is thought to be anti-American and somebody who wants to tear down our system of government.

Winfield Scott Stanley, Jr., the managing editor of *American Opinion*, was called to the stand as an adverse witness. Stanley made a curious remark in view of his failure to check thoroughly the Stang article involved in this litigation:

A: Now, while I have been copyediting, I have been thinking about the piece. Sometimes there will be something in a piece that will make you uncomfortable as to—you just want to be sure of every detail. We have a rule at our shop that involves what I call checking the checkables. For example, my editorial assistants know that when we get to the galley stage, if there is a biblical quotation, they had better check it. They also checked literary quotations, poetry.

Q: My question is: When did you first send any of the manuscripts for that magazine to be set into type, if you can recall?
A: Sometime in—probably sometime around the eighth or tenth of February.
Q: And would that be typical for most issues of *American Opinion* magazine that you would start sending manuscripts to be set into type about a month before the magazine is to appear?
A: Yes, that is correct.

Wayne tried to get Stanley to be more specific about the article:

Q: Do you remember what the release date was for the April 1969 issue?
A: I do remember.
Q: And what was that release date?
A: It was the eighteenth day of February.
Q: So, I take it from what you tell me, that the article "Frame-Up" was first set into type the day before the release date?
A: Yes, we had—we had that manuscript in the house for twenty-four hours.

Stanley admitted that he endorsed what Stang said in the article and warranted its truth. About this time Stanley made a statement at variance to admissions in the defendant's pleadings, something he had failed to state in the first trial, although he had had ample opportunity to do so.

A: I presume you want to know if I checked anything with regard to Mr. Gertz.
Q: Did you?
A: Yes, I did.
Q: What did you check in regard to Mr. Gertz?
A: I reached to my right and pulled down a book called *Guide to Subversive Organizations and Publications*.
Q: All right. What else?
A: Appendix nine, which was within three feet of my right hand.
Q: Anything else?
A: In the page-proof stage, I went a step further. I went to the file and pulled the document called *National Lawyers' Guild, Foremost Legal Bulwark of the Communist Party*.
Q: Okay, anything else?
A: That is all I remember, Counselor.

The documents he now purported to have examined indicated that I had been the director of public relations for the Illinois Police Association. We felt that this should have alerted Stanley to the unlikelihood of my being involved in a conspiracy against a police officer. This did not seem to have occurred to him. He was interested only in adverse information, it seemed.

He stated time after time that his source for the various statements made about me in the article was Stang, whom he had found to be completely reliable. He was more vocal in dealing with the suits the Nelsons had filed against Nuccio:

A: Officer Nuccio had been convicted and stood in jeopardy of going to jail, leaving his family unsupported. He had three small children. He lived in a $100-a-month apartment that you entered through an alley. He was going to be taken to jail. And his family was going to be left to whatever Mrs. Nuccio could do for them, which apparently would be welfare. And a well-heeled prominent lawyer was bringing suits for substantial sums of money against this family.

It seems to me that a man who had been a police officer and whose previous job had been as a postal worker probably hadn't squirreled away $100,000 or $20,000 or $1,000. And that when you proceed in that way, especially with three suits, you are talking about harassment.

Q: Now, the same things might happen to the family of anyone who was convicted of murder, might they not?
A: They might be left destitute and without the father or the mother or whoever is the main support, that is correct. It could happen to anyone who has been—that's correct.
Q: All right.
A: But anyone wasn't being sued in three separate suits with—
Q: Did you ever see a copy of any of those suits at the time that you are editing the article?
A: No, I had relied upon the professional investigator I had sent to Chicago.
Q: You didn't know what those suits were about, did you?
A: I knew that the suits were for substantial sums of money.
Q: Against a person who had killed someone, correct?

After the luncheon break, Stanley was temporarily withdrawn so that Wayne might call Albert E. Jenner, Jr., as a witness. Jenner, the senior partner in one of Chicago's larger and better-known law firms, was one of the most prestigious attorneys in the nation. We were singularly fortunate in securing him as a witness. Jenner gave a long recitation of his remarkable qualifications, including drafting laws, membership in various legal conferences, authorship of various books, law-school professorships, presidencies of legal associations—just about every honor an attorney-citizen might win. Instead of conceding Jenner's qualifications, Heldrich let him go on and on for at least seven full pages in the transcript.

Jenner was impeccably dressed in expensive attire. His voice was well modulated. He had the self-confidence of one who has achieved far more than most mortals. It would have been surprising if the jury had not felt that a very considerable person was testifying in my behalf.

Jenner testified that we had been good friends since about 1932 and that we belonged to several professional organizations. He had joined the National Lawyers Guild in the 1930s when I was also a member, as well as Chief Justice Walter Schaefer and other distinguished lawyers. The Lawyers Guild had never espoused the tenets of communism "or I wouldn't have been a member." He testified to my reputation for truth and veracity as an attorney and as an American. "He is, if I may say, that he is as loyal to America as I am." He had never heard me advocate the violent overthrow of this country.

The cross-examination of Jenner began with an unexpected tribute by Heldrich that could have done me no harm, and probably much good: "Well, you certainly have had a very long and distinguished career, Mr. Jenner. I'm very pleased to meet you." Heldrich tried to pin Jenner down on my reputation in April 1969.

A: His reputation among his friends was the same as it has always been—a man of highest character and integrity.
Q: Do you know anything about his law practice, sir?
A: I haven't finished my answer.
Q: I'm sorry.
A: His reputation at that time among citizenry generally that I would meet at my wife's parties and that, at association meetings and so forth, there was a lot of talk about something that had been said about him in some magazine, or book, or I don't know what it was.
Q: You don't know what was said?
A: Something about communism, that is all.
Q: I see. But nevertheless, Mr. Jenner, was his reputation in your opinion at that time harmed?
A: Yes.

This testimony by Jenner was invaluable as direct proof of the harm suffered through publication of the Stang article. Wayne returned to the subject of communism in his redirect examination of Jenner:

Q: Mr. Jenner, would it cause harm to an attorney to have someone call him a Communist?
A: It certainly would.
Q: And what would that harm be?
A: First, that lawyer would lose respect among his colleagues. Those who were good close friends of his and knew him solidly would not lose respect. But the major portion of the bar who either did not know him or knew him slightly — he would lose some respect from them.
Q: And why would that be?
A: That would be because there are members of the bars of this and other states who regard being a Communist or a member of a Communist group as odious and that that person is disloyal to the United States of America, and that those persons should have nothing to do with them.

Heldrich foolishly returned to the fray:

Q: Did you ever hear of the Roger Baldwin Foundation?
A: Yes, sir. I am a member of it.

Heldrich having opened up the subject, Wayne returned to it in further redirect examination of Jenner:

Q: Mr. Jenner, what is the Roger Baldwin Foundation?
A: It is the foundation that really founded the American Civil Liberties Union. Mr. Baldwin was a great citizen of this city and of this state, and generated the founding of the — of that group, the American Civil Liberties Union. Started generating it here in Chicago, now centered in New York City.
   In honor of him, the Baldwin Foundation was established by contributions from lawyers and other citizens throughout the — especially in Illinois and also throughout the nation.
   And the Baldwin Foundation raises money to help the American Civil Liberties Union. It participates in the policy established by the governors of the American Civil Liberties Union.

Q: And what is the American Civil Liberties Union?
A: That is what some people call a liberal organization. I happen to be a member of it. If it's liberal, if it's meant as I judge it, and why I am a member, to see that the provisions of the Constitution of the United States, especially the Bill of Rights, are adhered to by the government and by the people themselves. Very active group.
Q: To your knowledge, is either the Roger Baldwin Foundation or the American Civil Liberties Union connected in any way with the Communist party, or is it a Communist front?
A: No way. It isn't now, and it never had been from the time it was generated.

We were satisfied indeed with Jenner's testimony. He had not only attested to my good reputation and the harm to it from charges of communism but had denied much that Stang had said in his article about the ACLU, the Roger Baldwin Foundation, and the National Lawyers Guild. He was persuasive in all he said. We felt that Heldrich had gravely erred in his handling of Jenner by giving him opportunities to contradict what Stang had written.

We were also pleased with the testimony of Jon R. Waltz, who followed Jenner on the stand. His credentials were highly impressive too, although not as exhaustive as Jenner's. He was a professor at Northwestern University School of Law, the author of legal books and articles. He had been a member of the Judge Advocate General's Corps of the U.S. Army, receiving a medal for the successful prosecution of a number of Soviet espionage cases. He had been in private practice as a trial lawyer, was active in various legal groups, and was then a member of the Illinois Judicial Inquiry Board, appointed by the governor to review the conduct of Illinois state judges.

He had known me since working on a book on the trial of Jack Ruby. Did he discuss me with other people, particularly lawyers? "Yes, people have a tendency to discuss Mr. Gertz." As a result, he learned that my reputation was "excellent, unblemished, the best." "Mr. Gertz is what is called an old-fashioned patriot."

Furthermore, it would be hurtful to any member of the legal profession to become known as a Communist. It would have impact on clients. There are really not very many clients, or at least clients of the sort lawyers are fond of having, who would be desirous of having a lawyer who is known to be a Communist. And of course I guess I have some tendency to think about his position as one who has been interested in teaching law and has been a professor of law. It would assuredly be hurtful to one who was a teacher of young law students to have it be suggested that he was a Communist.

Heldrich now asked some questions whose motivation seemed obscure:

Q: Now, the Chicago legal community is a rather closed community, is it not?
A: How do you mean, "closed"?
Q: Well, lawyers associate with lawyers.
A: You do have to be a lawyer.
Q: Is that correct?
A: I beg your pardon?
Q: Lawyers associate with lawyers, is that correct?
A: At least during the day.
Q: That's correct. Hopefully not after that anyway. After eight hours, we have enough of it, right?
A: I am with you on that.
Q: So, you are aware of Mr. Gertz's reputation among lawyers?
A: Yes.
Q: Are you aware of Mr. Gertz's reputation in 1969 among nonlawyers?
A: Not as well as I am familiar with it among lawyers.
Q: And to your opinion as to his reputation in 1969—was the reputation good or bad?
A: Good from my standpoint would be understatement.

Stanley was kept yet longer from resuming his testimony while Wayne questioned Michael Kachigian, who testified substantially as he had in the first trial: that he had been associated with Echeles in the defense of Nuccio; that I had no involvement in the prosecution of Nuccio and never made any comments about Nuccio; that the prosecutors had never mentioned me; that he knew of no one with a Communist background or connections that was involved in any way in the prosecution of Nuccio; that he was never approached by Alan Stang with questions about the Nuccio trial.

At last, Stanley was recalled to the stand for the continuation of his adverse examination. Later, Heldrich quoted Stanley as feeling that the prior Welch attorney was "totally unprepared" and "incompetent." He felt that he was made to look like "a bumbling idiot." Heldrich seemed to feel that Stanley was even more determined to vindicate himself than his employer.

Wayne took Stanley through each offending passage in the *American Opinion* article. Stanley admitted that his documents showed that I had been a member of the national executive board of the National Lawyers Guild through 1950—nineteen years prior to the publication of the article. They showed nothing about the subsequent years. Wayne went on to demonstrate Stanley's complete ignorance of me:

Q: I take it that your knowledge of whether Mr. Gertz was a Leninist is from the contents of the article, is that correct?
A: From the contents of the article and eight or nine years of experience with people who engage constantly in Communist-front activity.
Q: Now, you didn't know Mr. Gertz at the time this article was published, did you?
A: I did not.
Q: As a matter of fact, until his name was set forth in the article by Mr. Stang, you had never heard of him before, had you?
A: That is correct.

Wayne went into the commissioning of Stang to write the article. It was essential to show Stanley's editorial role in connection with the article.

Q: You told him at that time that Mr. Nuccio was being railroaded, didn't you?
A: No, I did not.
Q: You didn't tell him that?
A: I told him that we had reports from Chicago from readers who were concerned that Mr. Nuccio was being railroaded. That is quite a different thing, Counsel.

Stanley testified that Stang had been paid $450 and his expenses for the article, a small amount for the labor involved. Wayne asked Stanley about Stang's propensity for finding that subjects had Communist ties:

Q: Mr. Stang has found a great number of people to be Communist-affiliated, has he not?

A: Counsel, if you will look and spend the time researching government documents, you would find a great many people, indeed you would.

Wayne wanted to know what Stanley meant by "Communist," and Stanley obliged:

Q: Well, let me ask you this. When you talk of a Communist, what do you mean? What is your definition of a *Communist*?
A: I think it depends entirely on the context.
Q: Does the definition change?
A: Yes, it does. A communist, lowercase *c*, might be a communalist, someone who—lives with seven hippies and a goat.

A Communist, uppercase *C*, might be a member of the Communist Party U.S.A.

A Communist who is a Trotskyite might dislike the Communist Party U.S.A.

A Communist who is associated with the Peking group might think that they are all rather bad and ought to be shot in the morning.

There are people who call themselves Communists who are—who I might think are mild socialists.

There is a disagreement among Communists themselves and among radical socialists such that in the last eighty years, even they have not been able to agree on what that term means.
Q: Well, now you didn't make that differentiation when you edited "Frame-Up," did you?
A: Indeed I did.

We make references to Communist-front organizations, and we repeat that term *Communist front* again and again. There is no question but what we are talking about Communist fronts, which are officially cited, officially cited by committees of the United States government.
Q: Communist front with a capital *C*?
A: Well now, Counsel, we can uppercase it or lowercase it, as you like.
Q: Mr. Stanley, when you talk about communism, you are talking about a worldwide conspiracy to control the government of this country, are you not, as well as other countries?
A: That is assuredly one term. Another might be a communalist with a—communalist on the corner.

I listened with wonderment and disbelief to this strange exposition. Wayne now tried to particularize:

Q: When you refer to Communist and Communist front in this article, or when Mr. Stang referred to Communist and Communist front in the article, they all had upper-case *C*'s, did they not?

A: When he refers to Communist fronts in that article, he is referring to officially cited Communist fronts, which is—which means organizations which have been found by the United States government investigation to be adjuncts, avatars, or extensions of the activities to the Communist party U.S.A.

Q: And that party, the Communist party U.S.A., is connected with the worldwide conspiracy, if you will, to control every government it can get its hands on, isn't that right?

MR. HELDRICH: I object, Your Honor. It's not relevant in this case.

THE COURT: I will permit that question to stand. If Mr. Stanley wishes to disagree, to dissect that definition, you may.

THE WITNESS: I'm happy, Your Honor, to say that it's my opinion, and I think that opinion of everybody I know, that the purpose of the Communist party U.S.A. is to link with others to destroy the governments of the free world.

Wayne pinpointed further:

Q: And when you talk about a Communist front, you are talking about an organization that is doing the work of this worldwide conspiracy to control this government and any other government it can get its hands on, correct?

A: More specific than that, Counsel. When I'm talking about a Communist front, I am talking about a front for the Communist party U.S.A., which has been officially cited by the United States government to be a Communist front.

Q: But your definition is an organization which is working towards the overthrow of this government and the control of this government, isn't that right?

A: That is the purpose of the Communist party U.S.A., indeed it is.

Q: A Marxist revolutionary is working towards the same end, is he not, or she?

MR. HELDRICH: Objection, Your Honor. There is no definition here, no foundation laid for that.

THE COURT: Is that phrase contained within the body of the article or reference made in some fashion?
MR. GIAMPIETRO: Well, there is a reference to *Marxist*, Your Honor.
THE COURT: All right. I will let you explore on the term *Marxist*.

Stanley continued to spin his web of definition with a kind of assumed erudition. He was plainly uncomfortable, and Heldrich was even more so. I was amazed and amused.

Wayne tried to sum up for him:

A: These are carefully delineated terms being written for a sophisticated, conservative, and anti-Communist audience.
Q: So *Leninist* and *Marxist* and *Communist* all have many of the same vices in common, do they not?
A: Assuredly they do.

Wayne reminded him that Stang had called the Democratic party a Marxist organization. We were beginning to benefit from the fact that there was no order of limitation barring us from this kind of questioning. We would profit more from it as Stanley continued on the stand and especially later when Wayne cross-examined Stang. I suspect that Heldrich had not asked for an order of limitation because he hoped to get into evidence many documents that went far afield from the issues of the case as we saw them.

Wayne questioned Stanley about Stang's linking of Hubert Humphrey and Communists in an earlier *American Opinion* article. He pointed out that Stang in an *American Opinion* article had called the prime minister of Canada, Pierre Trudeau, "a Marxist revolutionary of such virulence that he has been denied admission to the United States."

Stanley defended Stang's findings: "Check your history on these things before you ask those questions." An amusing exchange followed:

Q: All I'm asking is if Mr. Stang had found all of these things, that is all I am asking, Mr. Stanley.
A: Not only did he find it; you can find it with forty minutes' work in a good library.
Q: The ones that are just to your right?
A: I beg your pardon?
MR. HELDRICH: Objection, Your Honor.

MR. GIAMPIETRO:	I will withdraw the question.
THE COURT:	The objection is sustained.
	Mr. Giampietro, you avoid editorial comments on the responses of Mr. Stanley.
	The jury will disregard that remark of Mr. Giampietro.

At this point, I wondered why the material was not to the left rather than the right. The direction would have been appropriate, regardless of the facts.

Wayne would not let go of the characterizations of Hubert Humphrey by Stang. He believed that their very absurdity and malice would indicate that the two were engaged in the same kind of mendacity in dealing with me. Stanley persisted in defending Stang: "Counselor, Mr. Stang has convictions. And men who have convictions, men of character, tend to stand by them in the same way that Mr. Gertz stands by his convictions."

This was an unexpected tribute to my persistence in my suit for a dozen years, despite every obstruction.

Wayne went on to an examination of Stang's 1965 book, *It's Very Simple*, published by a member of the Birch Society corporate group. Stanley was aware of this book and the views Stang expressed in it. The book designated Dr. Martin Luther King, Jr., a member of the Communist conspiracy in his struggle for civil rights: "I accuse the Reverend Dr. King of being in effect one of the country's most influential workers for communism and against the Negroes. I accuse President Kennedy and President Johnson of knowing this, but nevertheless not only closing their eyes to it, but lending a hand. I, therefore, accuse them both of having betrayed their oath of office."

Wayne continued his questioning of Stanley by asking about Stang's book *The Actor*, which stated: "Conservative Republican anti-communist John Foster Dulles not only was not a conservative or Republican or anti-communist, but a member and leader of the International Marxist conspiracy."

Stanley commented, and do did Wayne, and the court stepped into the imbroglio:

A:	My guess would be that that was—like the other case, after many hundreds of pages of detailed presentation of his argument, that Mr. Stang is a professional polemicist, who is accurate, in fact, to the nth degree, and then

draws opinion, always controversial, based upon the facts he has presented. That is what polemics is, and that is—I think it's fair to say that Mr. Stang is a polemicist.

Q: That's a guy that goes around calling people names—is that the definition of *polemicist*?

MR. HELDRICH: Object, Your Honor.

THE COURT: I will sustain the objection to the form of that question.

Wayne tried to drive home the meaning of what Stang habitually did:

Q: So you knew when you sent Mr. Stang out to write this article on Mr. Nuccio that Mr. Stang was good at finding Communists in different places, did you not?

A: I knew that he was a—that he was a professional reporter, who to my knowledge had never been found to be in error of fact. I will agree, and I think it's evident here, that he is a man who draws broad conclusions. And no question about it, I'm talking about his skills as a reporter to go and observe and report the facts. And if you have some errors of fact, rather than opinions with which you disagree, Counsel, I would like to hear them now.

Wayne could have told him that our complaint pointed out many errors on Stang's part, atrocious errors. Asked whether he or Stang had talked with me, Stanley responded:

A: The discussion with Mr. Gertz was not relevant.

Q: You didn't know—it wasn't relevant at all?

A: No, it was not relevant to this case, no.

I was astounded to learn that I was not relevant to an article that dealt with me.

Wayne probed further concerning Stang's relationship to the various Birch Society publications and entities. He finally elicited a clear response.

Q: So that Mr. Stang had an ongoing relationship with your corporate family and you so list him?

A: That is correct, yes.

Wayne brought out the continued distribution of the article and reprint:

Q: Did Robert Welch, Incorporated, continue to distribute reprints of "Frame-Up" and copies of the April 1969 issue after that lawsuit—this lawsuit was filed?
A: They did, against my advice.
Q: And they did continue to do so up—as a matter of fact, until the spring of the next year, 1970, did they not?
A: They did until 1970, that's correct.
Q: Almost a year after the lawsuit was filed?
A: This is correct.

Wayne concluded his questioning of Stanley with some simple questions that were answered directly:

Q: And when you say someone is a Communist or a Communist-fronter, you mean that they are doing things that are bad, do you not?
A: I do.
Q: That is what you meant when you said, "Mr. Gertz of the Red Guild harasses Nuccio," that he was doing something bad, did you not?
A: Yes, sir, I did.

Our having called Stanley as an adverse witness gave Heldrich a choice of responses. He could examine Stanley immediately to correct or soften the effect of anything that Stanley had said in response to Wayne's questioning. But this would give Wayne the opportunity to question Stanley again, a disadvantage to the defendant. Heldrich could choose to postpone all of his questioning of Stanley until it was time for the defendant to present its defense. This too would be followed by Wayne's cross-examination. Or Heldrich could examine Stanley both now and later, and this was what Heldrich chose. Since we felt that we had Stanley in a tight corner and wanted to push him further, we welcomed this choice by Heldrich.

Heldrich asked Stanley about the language of the caption under my picture. He had used the word *Red* as a substitute for *Communist front*. He had used the verb *harass* for another reason:

A: I knew that Officer Nuccio had been convicted in a trial and that he was up on appeal; that he might have to go to jail and leave a wife and family of three children. I knew that he was living in a hundred-dollar-a-month apartment that you enter through the alley. I

	knew that he had no employment, that he was working odd jobs just to put meat on the table for his family. Frankly, it seemed to me that when a big-time lawyer sues a man like that for hundreds of thousands of dollars—
MR. GIAMPIETRO:	Your Honor, at this time I'm going to object. I think the editorializing has gone just a little bit too far.
THE COURT:	I'm going to permit the witness to respond to what his thought processes were, and if it includes descriptions of the parties, Mr. Giampietro, I will let you examine on any definition you have or seek a definition of any of those terms that are used.

Stanley was asked about one of Stang's books. He was impressed by its thousand footnotes, which as far as he knew, had not been challenged: "I had found Mr. Stang to be one of the most scrupulously accurate reporters in contemporary political affairs." And he was asked about the pictures in the article, most of them furnished by Nuccio.

On redirect examination, Wayne asked Stanley if any of the books that Stang had written had any references to me, and he answered: "Not to my knowledge, Counselor." He had not checked any of the references in the footnotes of Stang's books, and he did not personally know whether they were accurate, but "no one had ever challenged them" as far as he knew. The publisher "made it very clear to all of us that there had never been... any such complaint."

He admitted that *American Opinion* had a particular viewpoint.

Q: And I think that you said when you select an author to write a particular subject, you try and get the right man for the job.
A: Yes, that's correct.
Q: And you got the right man for the job to write "Frame-Up" in this case, right?
A: Yes, sir, I hope I did. I think I did.

He was reminded that he had testified that he did not know of me until he had read Stang's article.

A: I was aware in the article that he was a big-time lawyer. And I think Mr. Stang more than made that clear.
Q: So that your knowledge about Mr. Gertz being a big-time lawyer was from the article itself, again?
A: ... Not only from Mr. Stang or from the article, Counselor, but I had checked on Mr. Gertz in Appendix nine of the House committee hearings and in five or six or seven government documents, which assuredly made him leader of national organizations and very prominent in all kinds of activities. Yes, sir, I would say I was well aware Mr. Gertz was a big-time lawyer.

The document, it should be remembered, also referred to me as having been director of public relations of the Illinois Police Association.

Wayne and Stanley sparred on the subject of the civil suits I had filed for the Nelsons. This concluded Stanley's testimony until he was recalled to the stand during the presentation of the defense.

The first-trial testimony of Eli Fink and of John Ligtenberg on my character and reputation was now read to the jury, Wayne and Kathryn Koenig doing the reading.

At last, I took the stand in my own behalf. Ralla Klepak's testimony remained, awaiting her recovery from surgery, but we had arranged that she could be called at any time, even in the midst of the defense's case. Heldrich later wrote of my testimony: "Old Elmer got up smiling like a fox who had entered the chicken coop. He wore a gray suit and had on a white shirt and a red colored tie. I thought that the tie was appropriate. He ascended the witness box and sat down with his wrinkled lady-like hands folded together across his lap. If he was ever a champion of the proletariat, at least one thing was certain: he didn't do any more manual labor than Marx or Lenin did."

I will not repeat testimony given in the first trial except when necessary but will concentrate on what was new. By reason of the Supreme Court opinion, certain new facets of the case had to be stressed.

Wayne took me through my career and connections for the obvious purpose of showing that I was a person of substance. My organizational ties had grown considerably since the first trial. Of course, I denied membership in the various groups that Stang had characterized as subversive, except for my earlier membership in the National Lawyers Guild and my continuing membership in the American Civil Liberties Union. I spoke of the ACLU, as Jenner had, with the utmost respect for its defense of the Bill of Rights. I told of my connection with the Sparling Commission:

> Dr. Edward J. Sparling, an old friend of mine, came to me and asked if I would serve as counsel of a commission that was being set up by the Roger Baldwin Foundation of the American Civil Liberties Union to make inquiry into what occurred in Chicago during the spring and summer of 1968, and determine the causes, and determine what, if any, lessons could be drawn from it, and how public officials and the public ought to react to it.

I stressed the fact that neither I nor any of the people on the Sparling Commission had any connection with the Chicago Peace Council. I told of the National Lawyers Guild in my day:

> The National Lawyers Guild was founded in a period when the usual bar group like the American Bar Association, Chicago Bar Association, did not admit blacks to membership. The National Lawyers Guild had no distinction of the race, color, creed, sex, or the like. It was more inclined than the ordinary bar group to be interested in constitutional rights, particularly the Bill of Rights. And most of the membership, I would say, were what you would call New Dealers; they believed in the social programs that Franklin D. Roosevelt inaugurated. And that differentiated it, I believe, from the other bar groups.

Wayne now entered into the more ticklish aspects of my membership in the National Lawyers Guild:

> Q: Did you ever know during the time you were a member of the National Lawyers Guild of any of its officers espousing Communist doctrine or of the organization being a Communist front or in any way affiliated with any Communist or communistic type of organization?
> A: No. If I had known of any such thing, I would have ceased belonging to it.
> Q: And you did in fact cease belonging to it at one point in time?
> A: Yes, but not because I believed it to be a Communist organization; for other reasons.
> Q: That was my question. Why did you stop your membership?

A: Really two reasons. First of all, the organization began being too preoccupied with foreign policy, the Korean War and other such situations. And I thought lawyers' groups should not be primarily interested in foreign policy.

It happened, at the time I left, it was in agreement with my views, supported our interest in Korea, for example.

I also felt that I could accomplish more in the fields in which I was interested through working with other organizations. I became very active in the Decalogue Society of Lawyers, for example. I became president of the American Jewish Congress. And I felt that I could be more usefully employed with those organizations, even though I belonged to many organizations, probably too many, that I don't have unlimited time and never did have unlimited time, and I had to be selective.

So the organization that I then thought was most dispensable from my viewpoint was the Lawyers' Guild, but it was not intended with any reflection upon them.

I told of my connection with the Illinois Police Association and representing police officers as individuals and groups. I told of my authorship of books and articles, of my representation of Jack Ruby on his appeal and other postconviction aspects of his case. I told of my attitude toward the House Un-American Activities Committee:

I joined with a group of one hundred constitutional lawyers, practically every professor of constitutional law at the leading American universities and many lawyers who were known in that field, and we urged the abolition of the committee. And ultimately the Congress of the United States failed to appropriate money for it, so it ceased to exist. I hope it was in part because so many of us were opposed to its unconstitutional efforts.

I disclaimed all connection with any communistic organization, cause, or ideology. I summed up my viewpoint: "I believe in individualism. I believe in the free-enterprise system. I believe in the utmost freedom for the individual."

Wayne questioned me closely about the *American Opinion* article. What reaction did I have when I first saw the article?

I was just shocked that anyone could publish such outrageous lies about me. I was deeply upset. I spent a lot of time away from other work looking into the matter to see what could be done for redress.

And I was very much worried about what the effect of the article is, knowing that many people believe charges, whether they are true or not, as long as they are made publicly.

What other reactions?

It knocked me out emotionally for a long period of time, and then later in July 1974, when I heard that Robert Welch had stated publicly that everything in the article was true, it started all over again, my being terribly upset and humiliated, embarrassed.

And then, more recently, I saw an article in which Stang refers to me as a Marxist revolutionary.

So that it has been almost a continuous process during the years of salt being put on wounds.

Wayne pressed further:

Q: Now, did your reading this article have any effect on your ability to carry out your practice of law at the time, that is, back in 1969?
A: I was obsessed with the article, deeply upset, knowing how people react to the charge of communism. It worried me that the charge was made. And I was fearful that some people might believe it.

I didn't think those that really knew me intimately would believe it, but I thought others might. And particularly where I was told by a member of the board of managers of the Chicago Bar—
MR. HELDRICH: Objection as to what he was told. Hearsay.
THE COURT: I will sustain the objection.

I wished that I could have told what had been said to me—that some bar-association members had thought, following the *American Opinion* article, that I might be a Communist. However, I felt that Jenner had brought out the same point more effectively because he was not personally involved.

I went through the article for the benefit of the court and jury, so that they would understand why the article was so offensive, defamatory, false, harmful. I considered the article as a whole, its general thrust: "Reading the whole article, I felt that the article as a whole, in addition to the specific passages which referred to me by name, made me out to be a part of a Communist conspiracy against the police in general and a conspiracy to frame Richard Nuccio for murder."

I was vehement about the charge that Chicago Police Intelligence had a file on me that "takes a big Irish cop to lift": "I knew of no such file. I knew of no reason why there should be any such file. I had never committed any crime, didn't contemplate any crime. I didn't know why the police should be interested."

The reference in the article that the *Communist Worker* mentioned my signing a petition to abolish the House Committee on Un-American Activities angered me:

I winced at the reference to the *Communist Worker* because my petition had been referred to in the *Christian Science Monitor*, the *New York Times*, the *Washington Post*, all of the Chicago papers, papers all over the country. And it seemed to me that this was deliberately an effort to connect me with communism again, which was completely unwarranted. I gave nothing to the *Worker*, and I don't know whether or not they had the article, why they would have it. Every other paper did, because it was news that a hundred authorities on constitutional law were in favor of the abolition of that committee.

I took apart the Stang article point by point, dealing with it as effectively as I could. Sometimes I had to struggle through Heldrich's objections and the court's comments. Whenever I seemed to hesitate, Wayne prodded me on. Between the two of us, we were depicting Stang's article in the most despicable light. We stressed that what I said and did, the organizations to which I belonged, my ideas, had nothing to do with the suits I filed against Nuccio on behalf of the Nelson family.

There was a series of questions about my conduct of the Nuccio suits. But Wayne wisely returned to the effects of the article:

Q: How long did you continue to have any effects from the publication and issuance of this article?
A: Continuously. Still. Just the other day, I read for the first time a reference by Mr. Stang to me as a Marxist revolutionary and Communist-fronter.
Q: And did that . . . upset . . . you . . . , did that have any physical manifestations?
A: I felt dreadful. I felt upset, physically ill at ease, emotionally ill at ease. Nobody likes to be called a Communist or anything like that.

Wayne also returned to the subject of communism, giving me the opportunity again and again to disclaim any belief in its precepts, and there his direct examination of me ended. It was now Heldrich's privilege to tear down my testimony if he could. Later, I read what he thought of me:

Having taken his pre-trial deposition, I knew that the aging advocate would be sly and slippery. He would be evasive if he could get away with it.

Despite Elmer's anticipated craftiness, I could not deviate from my game-plan. I had to establish that Stang was accurate and Elmer did in fact belong to the organizations reported. The only and best witness to prove it was through the witness himself.

I looked upon the cross-examination as a test of skills. I had to be careful to retain the jury's confidence and not to yield to anger or sarcasm. Heldrich was slow in getting to the heart of my direct examination. He suddenly began questioning me in detail about the report *Dissent and Disorder*, dealing with the troubles in Chicago in 1968. It was necessary for me to tell him repeatedly that I had not written the report, although I had been responsible for the gathering of much of the material in it. He persistently questioned me about persons whose names were suggested to him by something in the report—Rossen, Spiegel, and others I did not know.

He then asked me details of my membership in the National Lawyers Guild and meetings outside Chicago. I replied: "I remember attending a convention in Washington, D.C., where every top official of the United States government was present. I remember a meeting in Cleveland, where I went with Judge Gutknecht and with Arthur Goldberg, but I don't remember many of the national meetings. I am sure I attended some."

By this time, Wayne was restless and began to voice objections to some of the questions. Heldrich persisted and showed me a report by the House committee, dated September 17, 1950, characterizing the Lawyers Guild adversely. He then questioned me about the Abraham Lincoln School, of which I had no recollection. Somewhere, I was listed as a guest lecturer at that school along with the famous psychiatrist Alfred Adler and others known and unknown. Heldrich persisted:

Q: The point, Mr. Gertz, is that you were associated with the Abraham Lincoln School, weren't you?
A: No, I was not associated with it. It says I was a lecturer. I don't remember being a lecturer because I have lectured at innumerable places in virtually every major city of the United States, and practically every university.

He tried to make something of the letter I had sent to *American Opinion* under date of March 20, 1969, ordering extra copies of the reprint of the Stang article. Frankly, I could not tell what he had in mind. Somehow, he seemed to find a mystery in the date—why, I never understood, even when he became most exercised about it.

He tried to make points about my attending the inquest on Ronald Nelson:

Q: And there is no doubt that you attended the inquest of Ronald Nelson, correct?
A: I have testified to that fact. And the fact is I did attend.
Q: Didn't you say you asked a few questions?
A: Yes, I asked some questions.
Q: Then you did participate?
A: To the extent I asked questions, yes, sir.
Q: You weren't just a bystander, observing?
A: I didn't say I was a bystander. I said I asked questions.

Heldrich went into another aspect of my reaction to the article:

Q: Mr. Gertz, after you read this article "Frame-Up," did you ever demand a retraction?
A: No. From the tone of the article, I knew it was useless to demand a retraction. Anyone who would lie so outrageously wouldn't retract.
MR. HELDRICH: Move to strike the balance of the answer, Judge. I asked him if he demanded a retraction.
THE COURT: The objection will be sustained. The response "No" from Mr. Gertz will stand. The jury will disregard the comments after the response "No."

He inquired about the Chicago Police Intelligence file, the ACLU, again the report entitled *Dissent and Disorder*, and American Youth for Democracy. He tried to imply that I contemplated running for election as a delegate to the Illinois Constitutional

Convention at the time of the publication of the Stang article, and I assured him that at that time "I did not even think of becoming a candidate." He suggested that the article had no effect on my election. This led to his minimizing the injury I suffered:

Q: Mr. Gertz, as a result of the publication of the article, did you lose any clients in your practice of law?
A: I cannot be sure. I think I have.
Q: You can't name one, correct?
A: I cannot name one, but I think I have lost clients.
Q: But you cannot name one.
A: That's right.
Q: As a result of the publication of that article, did you have occasion to see a physician?
A: Because of that article?
Q: Yes.
A: I don't think so, but—
Q: Did you see a psychiatrist?
A: No, I didn't see a psychiatrist. Though I might recommend that to the author of the article.
MR. HELDRICH: Move to strike that last answer.
THE COURT: The jury will disregard the last comment of Mr. Gertz.
Q: Mr. Gertz, as a result of that publication of that article, did you lose any money in the practice of law?
A: Yes. I devoted and have devoted countless hours to trying to rehabilitate myself because of that. I imagine I devoted hundreds of hours in the effort to redeem my reputation.
Q: You are saying that you spent time on the lawsuit instead of practicing law—is that what you are saying?
A: The time I spent on the lawsuit, I couldn't practice law. I had to give undivided attention at many periods of time to try to seek redress for the great wrong done to me.
Q: Well, you filed a lawsuit, did you not?
A: That's right.
Q: And you worked on the preparation of the lawsuit, did you not?
A: That's right.
Q: Okay.
A: And doing all sorts of things in connection with this suit. It adds up to hundreds of hours, which could have been better spent practicing law or writing books or doing other things like that.

Q:	Are you telling me, Mr. Gertz, that subsequent to the publication of the article you wrote no more articles?
A:	No, I did not say that.
Q:	Okay. Did you write more articles?
A:	I might have written more, except for the loss of time and the agitation and upset due to the article.

He brought out—why, I do not know—that I had used tranquilizers. He questioned me at length about my income-tax returns, hoping to establish that the Stang article did not affect my income. I gave explanations for some of the entries, such as my contribution of personal papers to the Library of Congress, the receipt of a substantial fee that had been earned earlier, and my compensation as a delegate to the Illinois Constitutional Convention.

He now tried to show that Stang had not actually called me a Communist:

Q: Mr. Gertz, did he ever call you a Communist?
A: Yes, many times in the article.
Q: Mr. Gertz, didn't he call you a Marxist?
A: Yes, which is a Communist.
Q: Mr. Gertz, I'm talking about what it says in the article.
A: In the article he calls me a Communist, a Communist-fronter, a Marxist, a Leninist, and various other synonyms for *Communist*.
Q: It doesn't call you a Communist, though, does it, sir?
A: Yes, it does.

He returned again to the reference in the *Daily Worker* to my signing a petition to abolish the House Un-American Activities Committee. He tried to establish that John Rossen, who he claimed was a Communist, owned the building on West Madison Street that was the headquarters of certain organizations and tried, unsuccessfully, to connect them with me. He returned once more to the National Lawyers Guild, and with these questions, he concluded his examination.

Wayne then asked me a few more questions on redirect examination—about the fact that the Lawyers Guild had thousands of members in my day whom I did not know; that Roger Baldwin, Clarence Darrow, Morris Ernst, and Osmond Fraenkel were among the founders of the ACLU; that my contributions to the Library of Congress were reflected in my income tax returns.

Heldrich asked one further inconsequential question, and my turn on the witness stand was at an end. How I had done I could not be sure, but I felt comfortable. If Heldrich had harmed me, I did not know it. Was I like the man who did not realize he had been decapitated until he moved his head?

Wayne offered in evidence the copies of the payments to Stang for his airline fares, and his fee for writing the article, and the issue of the Birch Society *Review of the News* for January 8, 1969, showing that Stanley was the editor and Stang a contributing editor—these without objection.

Then Wayne tendered the balance sheet of Robert Welch, Inc., for 1969, and Heldrich took strong exception on the ground that it concerned no issues in the case and would only indicate to the jury "that there is a deep pocket to reach." Wayne responded that since we were seeking punitive damages, we could show the defendant's net worth and financial position, citing cases in support of his position. The court reserved ruling.

Wayne then wanted to read to the jury a paragraph in the defendant's amended answer to the complaint. It claimed that the defendant had relied wholly upon Stang in publishing the contested article, in seeming contradiction to Stanley's testimony in open court. Judge Flaum said he would deny the request for the moment but that Wayne might renew it after his cross-examination of Stanley when the defense called him as a witness.

Now Wayne wanted to introduce attorney James Boyle's statement to the jury in the first trial, a concession that I was not a Communist. Judge Flaum turned down the request. It seemed to us that he was following a policy of making few rulings that might be harmful to the defendant. Was this to reduce their chances on appeal if we should prevail?

Wayne now rested for the plaintiff, subject to the right to call Ralla Klepak when she became available. Heldrich, prodded by the judge, agreed to this. Heldrich observed later: "I looked over to the plaintiff's counsel table and fully expected to see Gertz thoroughly wrapped in Old Glory. I was reminded by the old adage that the last resort of a scoundrel was to wrap himself in the flag, but, of course, I never considered that Elmer was a scoundrel, just a joiner."

Heldrich called the much-battered Winfield Scott Stanley, Jr., to the stand again. Stanley told of his educational background and listings in several reference works such as *Who's Who in America*. He recounted his lecturing at various schools, his appearances on radio and television, and his connections with the John Birch Society publications and the distinguished persons of right-wing orientation who served on the editorial boards. He also now recited the merits of writers other than Stang who had contributed to *American Opinion*.

Then, to our surprise, Stanley was questioned about the deadlines for articles, which turned out to be from six months to a year, sometimes only two months. We could not help wondering why so little time had been allowed for checking the Stang article when obviously so much had been required. Did this not indicate reckless disregard of the truth?

He was asked specifically about the Nuccio article:

Q:	With respect to "Frame-Up," who conceived the story line?
A:	Well, I asked Mr. Stang to go to Chicago to verify some reports I had had in letters from our subscribers.
Q:	About what?
A:	About Officer Nuccio.
Q:	Was there anything in particular about Officer Nuccio, or was there some larger issue you had in mind?
A:	There was a much greater issue. This was in the winter of 1968. And in the winter of 1968, one of the most important issues of the day was the general attack on America's police departments.
MR. GIAMPIETRO:	Well, Your Honor, at this time I'm going to object to the witness testifying to what one of the most important issues of the day was.
THE COURT:	In his opinion. If it's qualified by Mr. Stanley as his opinion, certainly he may give it.
THE WITNESS:	Yes, Your Honor, it was my opinion that that was one of the most important issues of the day. In fact, my opinion was based upon knowledge of reading—the newspapers that I read and the periodicals that I read as a product of my normal professional duties. For example, I read every day the *New York Times*, the *Washington Post*, the *Chicago Tribune*, the *Richmond News Leader*, the *Manchester Union Leader*,

plus through the course of a week, maybe an additional twenty magazines or so to keep abreast of what is happening at large, plus the government documents in our specific field, which is political affairs, what is going on in Washington, and particularly what is going on of interest to conservatives in Washington. Our readers are primarily conservative.

What had he checked? He again referred to Appendix 9 in a government document, which referred to both the National Lawyers Guild and Elmer Gertz, the material dating back decades.

Stang had been recommended as a writer, and in 1963 Stanley began assigning him articles. Stanley was eager to discuss conversations and details, but Judge Flaum sustained Wayne's objections. Stanley told of Stang's work, probably fifty articles for *American Opinion* up to 1969. Stanley found Stang "to be scrupulously accurate as to detail and fact in every instance I encountered." Stang produced sources, sometimes confidential sources, for what he wrote.

Heldrich elicited further testimony about the strengths of Stang's articles:

Q: Did you ever have occasion to reject any articles written by Mr. Stang prior to April of 1969?
A: Never.
Q: Did you have an occasion prior to April of 1969 to receive any complaints at your offices about any work that you published of Alan Stang's?
A: We never had a complaint on anything that Alan Stang had ever written for *American Opinion* or for anything else we published.
Q: And did you have any occasion at all to publish any retraction on anything written by Alan Stang?
A: Absolutely not.

....

Q: Mr. Stanley, . . . after you received the article "Frame-Up" from Richard Nuccio, was there anything in that article that put you on any alert or notice of any kind?
A: No. To the contrary. Documents came with the article indicating that Mr. Stang had managed to develop sources within the Chicago Police Department Intelligence Squad.

Heldrich tried to make something ominous of the date of my letter to *American Opinion* and Mary Giampietro's testimony, to which Wayne made repeated objections, sustained by the court. Heldrich nonetheless persisted in trying to prove that copies of the reprint of the Stang article were not available until March 24, 1969, supposedly contradicting by a few days the testimony of my letter and Mary Giampietro. With this, Heldrich concluded his examination of Stanley, leaving him to Wayne's cross-examination.

Wayne established that Heldrich's documents pertaining to the sale and delivery of reprints were not complete. We regarded this as a minor point. Heldrich had only two weak witnesses to our eleven strong ones and was relying upon peripheral documents and any weaknesses inherent in our case.

The picture of me that appeared in the article had come from the *Chicago Tribune*.

Q: Did you inquire if the *Chicago Tribune* had any other information on Mr. Gertz?
A: You don't order information from the *Chicago Tribune*; you buy their paper.
Q: Mr. Stanley, would you please answer my question? And I think it can be answered in one of three ways: Yes, no, or I don't remember.
All right. Now, my question is did you inquire of the *Chicago Tribune* if it had other information about Mr. Gertz other than the photograph?
A: I did not.
Q: Now, you said, as I recall, that your research department gave Mr. Stang a package of material?
A: Yes.
Q: And I believe you also said that—
A: I said they sent him a package, Mr. Giampietro.
Q: All right. Okay.
A: Right.
Q: Do you remember what was in that package?
A: I asked our research director to put together what he developed on the theme of the attacks on the police, the general war on police. And I had a listing of that at one time, and I believe I gave it to you at the deposition.
Q: It had to do with Communist attacks on the police, didn't it?
A: Communist and other attacks, criminals and a broad range of persons, but primarily Communists, yes.
Q: And you told Mr. Stang what it was he was supposed to check out, didn't you?

A: I told him I wanted him to go to Chicago and evaluate the story and follow through on it if his evaluation justified it—yes, that's correct.
Q: And the story you wanted him to evaluate was the Communist frame-up of Officer Nuccio, isn't that right?
A: It was a frame-up of Officer Nuccio as part of a general war on police involving Communists and a lot of other groups who at that time were attacking our police, that's correct.

Wayne tried to pinpoint when Stanley had tried to check Stang's statements. Wayne was intent on showing that the check, such as it was, was done after I had filed suit rather than prior to the publication of the article.

Stanley agreed that none of the eminent people on the masthead of the magazine had had anything to do with the Stang article. None of them had seen the article before its publication. Stanley agreed that two thousand more copies than usual had been sold.

Heldrich offered the now notorious Appendix nine into evidence, and over Wayne's objection, it was received, the court reserving the right to determine which portions of it would later be shown to the jury.

Wayne persisted:

Certainly, I would think that the jury ought to be instructed at the very least, if it is going to go in, that it's not for the truth of the matters asserted.

THE COURT: I will certainly entertain any such instruction that you wish to submit in that regard, Mr. Giampietro.
　　　　While I am letting Appendix nine in, it's for the same reason that if Mr. Stanley testified he relied on the Boston telephone directory in making his examination. I'm just letting it go in as one of the documents he said he went through in the course of his "checking the checkables."
MR. HELDRICH: That's correct.
THE COURT: It's going in not for the contents, other than as how he testified to it. And if you have some concerns as to the need for a limiting instruction if the entire volume were to be submitted to the jury, I certainly would consider it from both counsel.

Heldrich offered in evidence my letter ordering copies of the reprint. Wayne commented: "Again, Your Honor, I don't know how that is relevant in any way to any of the issues in the case. I don't understand the purpose for which it is being offered."

Heldrich responded in a rather muddy fashion, concluding, to our amazement:

So it goes to the credibility of a cabal between the plaintiff, his counsel, and his counsel's wife.
I'm sorry to say this, but this is what the document shows.
MR. GIAMPIETRO: Well, I am really taken aback at that last statement.
Is Mr. Heldrich going to now take a position that would make me a witness in this case? Because if that is the case, then he has now placed me in a very untenable position as of this point in time.

After protracted argumentation on the times of distribution of the article and reprints of it and the numbers involved, Judge Flaum closed the matter: "Mr. Heldrich and Mr. Giampietro, I think that ends it, then. There will be no more concern, as far as this court is concerned, about attacks upon respective counsel's credibility or a suggestion of improper, unethical conduct in connection with the filing or defense or prosecution of this lawsuit; that is, as to that."

Heldrich now tried to introduce the total court files in connection with the civil suits Ralla Klepak and I had filed for the Nelsons against Nuccio. Wayne objected strenuously: "There has been no testimony that anyone at all connected with *American Opinion* magazine or Robert Welch, Incorporated, ever saw these exhibits or in any way, shape, or form relied upon them."

Judge Flaum, continuing his apparent policy of letting the defendant have as much leeway as possible, admitted the court files in evidence, saying, however: "I continue to reserve on what parts, if any, of them were to be displayed to the jury." Judge Flaum explained further what he had in mind:

I'm not going to let the jury be involved in documentation which would in some way either confuse or detract from the issues at hand here.
The fact that there were the various lawsuits filed by Mr. Gertz is of record, that this documentation supports the fact that they were for that purpose, I am admitting them. Whether or not I am going to allow any parts of the pleadings in those lawsuits to go in is an entirely different matter.

The court was advised that Heldrich, despite the claim about a "cabal," was not going to call Mary Giampietro to the stand. She was now free to remain in the courtroom, which she did from then on, joining my wife, sister, and several friends, who helped sustain our confidence by their delight in Wayne's efforts. The wholly fictional cabal had vanished completely without an explanation or apology by Heldrich.

So at last Alan Stang, author of the disputed article, was called to the stand on behalf of the defendant. Wayne had previously taken his deposition in Belmont, Massachusetts, and was prepared for what Stang would say. Stang was a rather unprepossessing fellow who wore a conspicuous Star of David around his neck. Over the last six or seven years, he had lived in California, New Hampshire, Massachusetts, and New Jersey. He had been educated in public schools in New York City where he had been born and raised. His grandfather had sent him to the Concourse Center of Israel to learn Hebrew. He then had gone to DeWitt Clinton High School and to City College of New York where he had received a bachelor of arts degree. From Columbia University he had received a master of arts degree. He had majored in English.

Stang had worked as an editor for Prentice-Hall Publishing Company where he had written the Bank of America newsletter. He went on to the National Broadcasting Company in New York, working with the once well known Tex McCrary on both radio and television. Then he went to work for Mike Wallace in connection with an interview show that preceded "60 Minutes." He left after a year and a half to write a novel, then a book on civil rights that sold many thousands of copies, and won an award from the American Academy of Public Affairs in Los Angeles. He also won an award from the Pennsylvania House of Representatives. His next book, *The Actor*, dealt with John Foster Dulles, President Eisenhower's secretary of state.

The extensive research he had done in connection with that book and other writings led to his association with Stanley and *American Opinion*. He traced the course of his relations with this editor and magazine, and told of his research in connection with the Nuccio article: "I spent about a week altogether. So, I spent a few days the second time, adding up altogether to about a week." Considering the length of the article, the time devoted to research was short. Of course, Stang did not interview me or others with knowledge of the facts.

Stang was shown some lengthy documents identified as Exhibits 11 through 17:

MR. HELDRICH: I'm going to ask him whether he was familiar with this material and what he learned from it.
THE COURT: I'm going to permit you to have him identify it and that he became familiar with it. And he may describe topically.
MR. HELDRICH: Topically, right.
THE COURT: That is, not in depth.
MR. HELDRICH: That is correct.
THE COURT: I am not going to go into an analysis of any or all of the documentation. I will certainly let Mr. Stang relate all of the research areas he touched upon.

After further discussion between the court and counsel, Judge Flaum said:

I don't want his assessment, editorial comment, on what is contained therein. And, again, Mr. Giampietro, as a labeling of what he read in anticipation of this writing of the article, I'm going to allow. Whether or not any of this documentation will be submitted to the jury for their perusal is an entirely different matter.

He is charged with having written the article. And I will let him say what he did in advance of it.

But I don't want any opinion elicited as to how important he thought this piece was versus another piece, Mr. Heldrich.

Wayne continued to object to the material:

They first want to disassociate themselves from Mr. Stang and say we are not bound by what he did because he is a freelance author.

Now, on the other hand, they are trying to have Mr. Stang testify to all kinds of things that he may or may not have done and get the benefit of it.

Now, it doesn't seem to me that it's proper.

Judge Flaum attempted to make his position clearer:

I'm trying to strike what I deem to be the appropriate balance to show that the witness actually touched, read, held some physical documents which he claims formed the basis of his opinion and yet preclude parts of any such documents from clouding the jury or diverting them from their mission in this case, and that is the question of determining whether any negligence existed.

There followed an indecisive discussion about a large number of other documents that Heldrich said he was going to identify as having been consulted by Stang. Judge Flaum ruled:

I'm going to let you identify any document that Mr. Stang said he used in his research or preparation of the article.
I caution all counsel, both on direct and cross, that I'm looking only for an identification....
And let's not have any dramatic representation of documentation.

Just what the judge meant by this is not wholly clear, but the judge said enough to indicate that he wanted no histrionics.

Stang categorized the various documents that Heldrich had identified. They pertained to what was claimed to be an attack on the police, not on Nuccio or any particular police officer but the police in general. None of them referred to me. He then told of the people he interviewed for the article: Mr. and Mrs. Nuccio; Mr. and Mrs. Ben Citron; several policemen, including Commander John Fahey, and Father Carl Lezak. He went to Echeles' office and read the voluminous transcript of the first Nuccio trial. He "took a look at the papers that had been filed in the civil suit against Richard." He then did "backup research in the various government documents" and examined various fliers put out by neighborhood organizations involved in the Nuccio controversy and other printed material. And he picked up a copy of *Dissent and Disorder*. He was attracted to this report because it was financed by the Roger Baldwin Foundation, because it defended the 1968 turmoil in Chicago, and because I was designated chief counsel of the committee.

Stang testified with respect to his acquiring an intelligence file:

While I waited downstairs from police headquarters in a coffee shop on the corner—a little kind of Franksville-type lunch counter—a police officer, Chicago police officer, who was part of what was colloquially known then as Red Squad, went upstairs into police headquarters and after a while, came down and gave me some notes that he had written.
Q: How do you know where he went?
A: I saw him go into police headquarters.

Q: Okay. You don't know where he went in police headquarters, do you?
A: No, sir. Once he went into the building, I don't know where he went.
Q: Did he meet you when he came out?
A: Yes, sir.
Q: And did he hand you anything?
A: Yes, sir.

Stang described the contents of the notes supposedly given to him by the police officer: "There was a single sheet which said on it Chicago Police Intelligence, as I recall, and some other things were listed on there."

Stang then recited the contents of the document, over Wayne's objection. Stang testified about a photocopy of his notes, not the original. At this point, the judge intervened:

THE COURT: Mr. Stang, other than what you have described such as the meeting you have described with some individual who gave you certain material, is there any other research you did connected with the investigation into the article surrounding Mr. Gertz?

THE WITNESS: Well, yes, sir. I looked Mr. Gertz up in the various indexes to see whether he was listed. For example, Appendix nine, which is the colloquial name of another government publication published by a committee of the United States Congress—I found him listed. And it said in that publication that, for example, Mr. Gertz was a lecturer at the Abraham Lincoln School. So I looked in the government reports to see what the Abraham Lincoln School was. And the government report said it was a Communist organization run by Communists.

Is that what you mean, Your Honor?

THE COURT: Yes. Anything else you have done in connection with the investigation?

THE WITNESS: Yes, I went to the Chicago Public Library and looked Mr. Gertz up in *Who's Who in Chicago and Illinois.*

He was questioned about his use of various government documents, including the *Guide to Subversive Organizations and Publications.*

Q: Did you use that guide in preparation for your article?
A: Yes, sir.

Q: Okay. Did Mr. Gertz's name appear in that guide?
A: No.

There followed much testimony in which Stang claimed that he derived the statements he made in his article from government documents that did not mention me by name. It was difficult to follow his reasoning in every instance, and I was glad when his direct testimony ended and Wayne took over.

(The cross-examination was interrupted by the delayed testimony of Ralla Klepak, now well enough to appear in court. She testified substantially as in the first trial. She had brought me into the Nelson litigation. She testified to my good character and reputation, and said that I had no involvement in the criminal prosecution of Nuccio. She was not aware of any public statements I had made about the Nuccio suits; neither she nor I had been involved in any conspiracy against Nuccio. She said that I had never espoused communism and that it would be detrimental to a person's professional reputation to be called a Communist.)

The cross-examination of Stang began. It went on for a long while, and it pleased me. It not only contributed substantially to our victory but demonstrated what passes for historical analysis in the mind of a confirmed Bircher. There is little point in giving every detail of the cross-examination. It is enough to set forth the high points and some typical passages.

Wayne first brought out that Stang was a member of the John Birch Society and that the publishers of his books and articles were in the corporate family. Thus, he was very much a part of the philosophical apparatus of the society. Wayne queried Stang with respect to the various exhibits that had been marked for identification. After much wrangling, Stang admitted that only one or two of them mentioned me in any way. Wayne brought out that the documents had been certified by governmental agencies after the article was written by Stang. He could not have used them when he prepared the article since he had testified that the documents were in the same condition as when he first received them.

Judge Flaum now intruded:

THE COURT: I am not speaking to the material contained there in the body and the language of it. That specific physical grouping of paper that you have before you—I'm asking you if

	you believe that to be either from your research files, or is there something that would suggest to you that that is the actual copy that you used; that is all I'm asking.
THE WITNESS:	I couldn't swear to that, Your Honor.
THE COURT:	Do you believe it to be?
THE WITNESS:	I believe it to be, but maybe — if you are asking me to swear to it —
THE COURT:	I'm asking you what is the basis of that belief. Are there any markings that it comes from any files you have?
THE WITNESS:	No. It is devoid of markings as far as I can tell, other than this document that is affixed to the cover of it.
THE COURT:	I want the record to be clear I'm now inquiring into whether or not you used that report in some form, either that copy or others, in the compilation of the article. The question is only whether that specific one that is actually on the table before you is the one used in the body of your research.
THE WITNESS:	I don't know, Your Honor. I guess that is the best answer I can give you.
THE COURT:	That is all we want, are the best answers.

Wayne drove home that Stang was not at all sure about his use of the various exhibits. Stang seemed quite confused, possibly intimidated and frightened. He expressed his feelings thus:

Well, you see, I can't recall, because you were not there at the time to tell me which files to keep where. Had you been there to advise me as to which files you would have wanted to see twelve years later here in this courtroom, why then you could have instructed me in your expert manner. But unfortunately we didn't have the benefit of your expertise at the time, and so I didn't know, not being an attorney, not having the benefit of your training, where I should keep particular files for examination twelve years late.

The court now tried again to clarify the matter, without success. One byplay was amusing, at least to me:

Q:	Okay. How about Exhibit seventeen — does that refer to Mr. Gertz in any way?
A:	I made a mistake on this one too; it has a piece of paper.
Q:	You made a lot of mistakes yesterday, didn't you?
MR. HELDRICH:	Object, Your Honor

THE COURT: The objection will be sustained. The jury will disregard Mr. Giampietro's remark about "you made a lot of mistakes."

So Wayne went on and on with the remaining exhibits, eliciting from Stang that nothing in them referred to me. Wayne summed up the evidence with the aid of the witness:

Q: Now, those are all documents that I think you said you referred to about the general background about the situation involving police and some plot to discredit them, is that right?
A: Yes, sir.
Q: None of those refer to Mr. Gertz in any way?
A: No, sir.
....
Q: You never talked to Mr. Gertz about his involvement with Officer Nuccio and Ronald Nelson before you wrote the article, did you?
A: No, sir.
Q: You didn't talk to Ralla Klepak either, did you?
A: No, sir.

Wayne called Stang's attention to an article he had written for the Birch Society *Review of the News* of May 7, 1969, and specifically to this statement: "Then there is Ralla Klepak, an attorney I haven't yet mentioned, who was collaborating with Marxist revolutionary Elmer Gertz of the Communist National Guild to sue Nuccio in the City of Chicago on behalf of the Nelsons."

Wayne pointed out various discrepancies between what Stang had said in his deposition and what he testified in court. Then he pressed home other lapses:

Q: Did you interview Mr. Echeles about the facts of the case?
A: No, Mr. Echeles told me that no attorney—
Q: Thank you. You have answered my question.
   Did you become aware of an attorney named Michael Kachigian?
A: No, sir.
Q: You didn't become aware of the fact that he was also an attorney representing Richard Nuccio? . . .
   You didn't, obviously, then talk to him about the facts of the Nuccio matter, did you?
A: No, sir.

Q: Now, you mentioned in the article "Frame-Up" a number of the people who were witnesses in the criminal case against Officer Nuccio, did you not?
A: Yes, sir.
Q: Noel Kitchen, and John Ahrens, and George Bish, and Trina Ciabay, and Judy Rankin, and Les Paul, I think. Did you ever talk to any of those people?
A: No, sir.
Q: You mentioned a Carol Whiting, who wrote something about the Nuccio case. Did you ever talk to her about the case or the facts of the case?
A: I can't even recall her name.
Q: And you talked about in your article Linda Scheel, and Steve Austill, and Joe Rodriguez, and Edward Ryan. Did you talk to any of those people?
A: No, sir.

Stang had talked with Thomas Tully and Matthew Walsh, the prosecutors of Nuccio. Neither of them had told him that I was involved in any way with the criminal prosecution.

Wayne turned to the alleged Communist attempt to frame Nuccio. He stressed that Stang did not really know firsthand the origin or credibility of the information he had allegedly received at the police station. He had simply assumed it was true because it supposedly came from a police source.

Why had he referred to the *Worker* and not other newspapers that mentioned my joining in a petition to abolish the HUAC?

Well, because once again, of course, the *Worker* being the official newspaper of the Communist party, when you see something being pushed in there, then you have a good idea of what the Communists are pushing, what they are for or what they are against—whom they like, whom they dislike.

When you read something like this in the *Worker*, it does have a certain added significance in my mind, yes.

Wayne questioned Stang about the terms *Communist*, *Communist-fronter*, and *Leninist*:

Q: So that when you wrote that Mr. Gertz was a Leninist, you meant that he was working for the things that Lenin believed in, isn't that right?

A: Well, we discussed this yesterday, remember, counselor?
Q: We didn't discuss it yesterday, Mr. Stang. I wasn't talking to you.
A: I discussed it yesterday. And just to repeat what I said yesterday, by the use of that word I simply mean since Lenin invented the technique of the Communist front, somebody today who gets involved with a lot of Communist fronts in my mind can fairly be called a Leninist because Lenin is the guy who invented this technique of using these fronts to advance his purpose.
Q: Well, in your mind, someone who is a Leninist might be even more valuable to the Communist movement than someone who belongs to the Communist party itself, isn't that right?
A: This isn't just in my mind. Many experts have said this.
Q: We are talking about an article that you wrote, Mr. Stang, and I'm just trying to get at what you were saying when you wrote the article.
   So that a Leninist is perhaps in your mind more dangerous than someone who is an openly avowed Communist, isn't that right?
A: Possibly.
Q: And again, Leninists, Communists, Marxists—they are all working for the total enslavement of every individual on earth, correct?
A: That is what the Communists have said from the beginning, and I believe them.

With prodding, Stang repeated his view that "John Foster Dulles was a man who applauded Marxism and communism, fascism— yes, in his own writing. He is a member and a leader of the international Marxist conspiracy." Furthermore, Stang said, Presidents Kennedy and Johnson knew that King was a part of the Communist setup and went along with him.

Q: Mr. Stang, you weren't here when that happened, were you?
A: I wasn't there when Moses wrote the Torah, but I believe he wrote it.
Q: I understand. And that is a matter of faith, and I wouldn't for the world interfere with anyone's faith.
A: Thank you, sir.
Q: But you take anything that someone says that is written down someplace just on faith anywhere, anytime?
A: Well, this is my profession as a journalist.

Stang said that anyone connected in any way with the Chicago Peace Council was a Communist or Communist fronter, and he was not deterred from this conclusion when Wayne reminded him that the Lutheran Action Council and the Episcopalian Peace Fellowship were members of the Peace Council.

Stang had never talked with anyone on the Sparling Commission nor with anyone who had anything to do with the writing of its report, *Dissent and Disorder*. He had not read the transcript of the inquest on the death of Ronald Nelson. He recalled no mention of me in the transcript of either the inquest or the criminal trial of Nuccio. What he had written came from Nuccio. Echeles never told him anything about me. Nuccio had not told him that I had anything to do with his criminal prosecution. He did not recall reading anything of mine before he wrote the article. Why had he said I had generated publicity against Nuccio?

> He filed lawsuits, and this of course generates publicity. Lawsuits against a guy who, if he lost, could only deliver his underwear to the victorious people in the suit. Because, remember, the guy is living in a hundred-dollar-a-month apartment. He lost his job. He has no grocery money. What can this guy hope to pay if he loses the suit except his underwear and his toothbrush? So why else was the suit filed if it were not for publicity or politics, other than getting money, if the guy has got no money to pay his rent?

Wayne tried to drive home that Stang really knew nothing about what, if anything, I had charged for filing the Nelson suits. He simply assumed that I was high-priced and was using the suits for my own purposes. It did not seem to occur to him that I might have a legitimate purpose.

Wayne reminded Stang of what he had said in his deposition, which was now contradicted by his court testimony:

Q: How did you get the idea of writing that article, "Frame-Up"?
A: Our Managing Editor, Scott Stanley, pursuant to our usual practice from the beginning, called me and asked whether I would go to Chicago to investigate.
Q: Tell me everything you can remember about what was said during that telephone conversation between yourself and Mr. Stanley.
A: Mr. Stanley told me, to the best of my recollection, that it appeared that in the Nuccio case there was another example in which a fine, dedicated, conscientious police officer was being railroaded as part

of the then vigorous campaign to discredit local police. He asked me whether I would go to Chicago to investigate.
Q: Do you remember giving that answer?
A: Yes.
Q: So that is the first thing you heard about this case?
A: Yes.

The first person Stang talked to in Chicago about the Nuccio case was Carol Woodward, a member of the John Birch Society.

Stang knew nothing of how the Sparling Commission had gathered material for its report. He had read none of the testimony or depositions. He had seen none of the photographs. He really knew nothing of the facts upon which the commission based its conclusions.

Finally he agreed that I had absolutely nothing to do with the prosecution of Nuccio. With that startling admission by Stang, Wayne closed his cross-examination of that now unhappy man. We felt confident the jury would not miss the revelation that Stang had no basis for charging me with framing a police officer for murder.

Heldrich conducted the redirect examination of Stang. Stang repeated his charge that the Chicago Peace Council was run by a man named Jack Spiegel who had been on the Communist party ticket. With respect to this characterization of what had occurred in Chicago in 1968, he relied upon some hearings conducted by a committee of the U.S. Congress. He had not talked with me because Echeles had told him that no attorney would talk with him about the Nuccio case. With this bare redirect, Heldrich closed his examination of Stang.

On recross-examination, Wayne brought out that Stang had talked with attorneys Tully and Walsh, the prosecutors of Nuccio, but never tried to talk with me, Ralla Klepak, or Michael Kachigian ("I'm not sure who this person is"). He had found out that I was a member of the National Lawyers Guild in 1944, but he could not find out if I was still a member in 1968. That was the end of Stang's testimony. The defendant rested.

Out of the presence of the jury, the court now considered Heldrich's motion for a directed verdict. Both attorneys argued briefly, almost as if neither considered the matter seriously. With similar brevity, Judge Flaum denied the motion.

A New Trial ■ 173

Still out of the presence of the jury, Judge Flaum stated for the record which proposed instructions to the jury he was going to give as submitted, which he was not going to give, and which he would revise. (These will be set forth in due course.) For the record, both attorneys preserved their objections to certain proposed instructions.

Judge Flaum indicated that he intended to ask us to prove that the defendant had acted with actual malice—that is, either knowing that its statements were false or recklessly disregarding their veracity. He was making this requirement, he said, because defendants had made a plea of *fair comment*; that is, they claimed a First Amendment right to call me a Leninist and so on as a fair comment on matters of public interest and because of the alleged government reports on which they relied.

Wayne argued at length about this instruction. He reminded the judge that the Supreme Court had said that we did not have to prove malice but only fault, held by the Illinois Supreme Court in the *Troman* case to be simple negligence. Heldrich, not realizing the box in which his client would be placed, said that he was not going to object to that instruction at all. As matters turned out, that instruction was a godsend to us.

Suddenly Heldrich popped up again, and a further dialogue ensued:

MR. HELDRICH: I forgot something, Judge. And that was that I intended, as you may recall yesterday, to make a motion as to the dismissal of Count Two, which is the count for malice, because it hasn't been shown here that Mr. Stanley knew that the article was inaccurate or had any high degree of awareness that it was inaccurate. There has been absolutely no showing to that effect.
THE COURT: Mr. Giampietro.
MR. GIAMPIETRO: I think there is more than enough showing that it was Mr. Stanley who came up with the idea in the first place and sent the author out to say exactly what he did say without having knowledge of the facts at all, and that is a fabricated article that came from the brain of Mr. Stanley.

And under the law, that is enough to show actual malice, so I think clearly that the motion ought to be denied in that regard.
THE COURT: The motion will be denied as to the second count.

174 ■ *Gertz v. Robert Welch, Inc.*

It was now apparent that the court was holding with the defendant on evidentiary and procedural matters but with us on the more basic issues, except for requiring us to prove malice to overcome the defense of fair comment.

Heldrich had more to say in objection to some of the proposed instructions; Wayne, less. Essentially, Heldrich was arguing about the words used in the article. His contention was that they did not characterize me as a Communist and were therefore not defamatory.

The court made it clear that the jury was not to make findings as to the meaning of any of the allegations in the article. The court was determining that as a matter of law, it is libelous to be called Leninist, Marxist, or Communist-fronter, as such language tends to prejudice or injure one in his profession, subject only to whether a conditional privilege existed. The court made it clear once more that truth was not an issue in the case because he had found summarily that the article's charges against me were false.

Despite his holding that we had to prove malice because of the claimed conditional privilege, Judge Flaum insisted that this was still a negligence case. It was not easy to understand his distinction. Essentially, he was saying that we had to prove both negligence and malice.

The court refused Heldrich's request that special interrogatories be propounded to the jury so that the jury could answer yes or no in response to specific questions. For this we were grateful since such interrogatories or any "special verdicts" could only confuse the issues. Furthermore, if they appeared to contradict the verdict, as is often the case, the verdict would not stand. In such event, there would be a judgment notwithstanding the verdict or a new trial. At my age, however youthful I felt, this would have been too much.

When the jury reassembled, the two alternate jurors were excused so that only six would decide the case. Judge Flaum gave the excused alternates permission to remain and hear the arguments of counsel.

Wayne made an extraordinarily good closing argument. I thought at the time that it was the best I had ever heard. He told the jury that I had been a lawyer since 1930:

> Over that period of time, Mr. Gertz has very diligently and very carefully attempted to nurture a reputation; a reputation, number one, as an attorney; a reputation, number two, as a truthful and honest citi-

zen; a reputation, number three, as a good, loyal, patriotic citizen of this country.

A reputation is a very fragile thing. It is something that you build up over a long period of time by your actions day by day by day. Something that just doesn't arrive some day. It isn't because of any one thing you might do today or you might do tomorrow. It's something that only accrues over a long, long period of time, after you have been around a long time, after a lot of people have come to know you, and they in their various ways have formed an assessment....

You have heard from a number of witnesses in this case—Irv Kupcinet, Albert Jenner, John Waltz, Carol Bellows, Julius Echeles, Ralla Klepak—that Mr. Gertz had an excellent reputation that he laboriously built up over many, many years of practice here and other places in the country. There has been no dispute about that, and I don't think there can be any dispute about that reputation.

Then he dwelt upon the *American Opinion* article:

And the whole central thesis and the theme that we have talked about here, and we have talked about over the last two weeks, is that Elmer Gertz is not and was not in 1968, and was not in 1969, and is not now entitled to that trust by his clients or by anyone because they say that he is part of this evil conspiracy not just to frame Police Officer Richard Nuccio but to do something much more serious, to destroy our very government under which we live....

That is what Elmer Gertz is accused of in this article. In addition to being accused of having a part in sending an innocent man to jail, a man who was convicted in a court after due process of law, with an opportunity to be heard, to present his witnesses and his defense.

That system which gave Officer Nuccio a trial, that system which brings us here today to this courtroom, is what Elmer Gertz is being charged with trying to destroy. That is what this case is all about.

He told eloquently of the harm that such allegations did to me at the time of publication of the article and the continuing harm.

The issue is, was Robert Welch, Incorporated, the defendant in this case, guilty of negligence for publishing the article; was it guilty of actual malice in publishing this article and saying these things about Elmer Gertz.

. . . .
. . . Whose idea was it in the first place of the kind of article that Alan Stang ought to write? It was Scott Stanley's idea. The first thing he said

when he called up Alan Stang and said, "Hey, I've got this article that I want you to write; there is this fine upstanding police officer that is being railroaded, as part of this big Communist war. And I want you to go out there and find the evidence. And I want you to write an article about this."

He picked the right man for this hatchet job on the plaintiff in this case. Because he knew before he called Alan Stang what Alan Stang was going to write and what he was going to find. Because every time he sends Alan Stang out to write an article, Alan Stang finds a Communist, or a Communist plot, or a Communist conspiracy. All Alan Stang writes about is how everybody is a Communist: U Thant, secretary-general of the United Nations; John F. Kennedy; Hubert Humphrey; everybody he writes about.

Elmer Gertz filed this libel suit in June of 1969, a couple of months after the article came out.

Scott Stanley says normally when that happens the publisher will withdraw or at least stop distributing any more copies of the magazine. "And I told my bosses, 'Boy, that is what we had better do in this case, because now they have put us on notice there is something wrong.... Stop.'" But they didn't. They went right ahead and kept printing and publishing and disseminating to the public at large their venom in violation of what Mr. Stanley himself says are the standards of the industry.

Now you will get all of these exhibits. How many of these exhibits talk about Elmer Gertz or refer to him in any way, shape, or form? Four of them.

The report on the National Lawyers Guild—it has got Elmer Gertz's name in it as a vice president of the National Lawyers Guild in 1950, eighteen years before.

Now, Mr. Stang didn't care whether Mr. Gertz was still connected with the National Lawyers Guild. He didn't ever try and find out. Mr. Gertz wasn't, as it turns out.

This man, who Mr. Stang is trying to paint as being this Communist, warring on police, was affiliated with and acting on behalf of the Illinois Police Association. And he found that out, but he didn't think that was important to talk about.

Wayne had fun dealing with the alleged police file on me:

> The file on Elmer Gertz in Chicago Police Intelligence takes a big Irish cop to lift.
>
> Well, I am not a cop. And I am not Irish. And I'm not even very big. I don't have any trouble lifting it.

Wayne held up the couple of sheets that had been transformed to a huge file by Stang. The jury must have seen the absurdity of Stang's invention, and it could only suggest similar inventions.

Wayne showed how little research Stang had done. He did not talk to Nuccio's own attorneys, to me, to anybody who would give him anything other than what he wanted to hear.

Wayne showed, item by item, the falsity of what Stang had written. He pointed out that in the end, when he was being cross-examined, Stang admitted that I had nothing to do with the prosecution of Nuccio, despite the charge in the article that I had conspired to frame Nuccio for murder, that I was the very architect of the conspiracy.

He dwelt upon the anguish that I suffered, the humiliation, the embarrassment—that I was knocked out emotionally. How do you compensate for this in dollars? he asked. He suggested that a dollar a minute for one year would undervalue the injuries. He thought I should get $500,000 for compensatory damages and $1 million in punitive damages:

> I submit to you that the plaintiff has proved each and everything we told you at the beginning of this case. Defendants [sic] were negligent, reckless, intentionally harming Elmer Gertz in a way that they [sic] knew would be most hurtful to him, to damage that reputation that took so many years for him to build up in a way that he would have to live with the rest of his life.
>
> I submit to you, when you consider the evidence, you will have no alternative but to grant judgment in favor of the plaintiff in this case.

Wayne's closing argument was a hard act to follow. Would Heldrich be equal to it? It soon became apparent that he was not. He referred to my "parade of seven witnesses": "Consider, if you will, where those witnesses came from. I am an attorney. Mr. Giampietro is an attorney. I know Mr. Gertz. Most of the lawyers in our closed Chicago legal community know Mr. Gertz. It's a closed shop."

Warming to his theme, Heldrich went on:

And almost universally, down the line, they said Mr. Gertz is a great guy, but we don't know anything about him other than the bar associations and the professional committees which he was involved with. . . .

Well, if they didn't know anything about him, then they didn't bother to check his record.

Mr. Stang found out more about Elmer Gertz in one week than seven witnesses knew about Elmer Gertz in forty years.

At what point—at what point are we, as lawyers, to involve ourselves in political controversy under the cloak of our profession and not be free to have comments made upon us?

Heldrich was gambling that jurors dislike layers. Perhaps he was taking too seriously the remark of a ruffian in Shakespeare's *Henry VI*: "The first thing we do, let's kill all the lawyers."

He scanned the allegations of the article lightly: "We are not here, Mr. Giampietro and I, Judge Flaum, to try Richard Nuccio again or the House Un-American Activities Committee. We are here to prove that an editor has a right, sitting in Belmont, Massachusetts, to rely on an author who had a good track record."

He considered organizations that I was charged with belonging to. He talked of what Stang had done while in Chicago gathering information for his article. He interviewed witnesses. He didn't interview lawyers. He focused on the suits I had filed for the Nelsons:

But Alan Stang came in here, and you heard him say that Nuccio told him that he was being sued by a prominent big-time downtown Loop attorney for well over a half-million dollars. And Stang said that he had seen Nuccio's apartment where Nuccio lived, a hundred dollars a month—it's in the article. And the only thing that anyone could possibly get from Officer Nuccio was his underwear and his toothbrush.

Why? Why? That is what put Alan Stang on the trail of Mr. Gertz. Found out Gertz was involved in this matter. Found out he was involved in *Dissent and Disorder*. Found a long trail, long trail that his own witnesses never knew about.

Heldrich suggested that I had suffered no damages, that only lawyers thought I had been damaged. He gave a Birch-eye view of American culture:

But the point I'm getting at, ladies and gentlemen—it's as American as apple pie, the right to use labels, to call people names, to go to the ballpark and say "kill the ump" or to listen to somebody speak and say

A New Trial ■ 179

he is a jerk, or even maybe worse, which I can't use in a courtroom. It's as American as apple pie. You have a right to call names and use labels.

It seems to me that if you swim with ducks and you walk with ducks and you talk with ducks and you are associated with ducks, then you have every right to call a man a duck.

And we have every right to call Mr. Gertz what we called him, and that isn't actionable, and it's not compensatory.

Thus he ended his argument.

Wayne responded to Heldrich's argument. He disposed of much of Heldrich's argument forcibly by reminding the jury of what *American Opinion* had said of me:

And just calling it name-calling doesn't change it from what it is. It is a false statement of fact, and that is not mere name-calling.

The defendant even now goes on with its guilt-by-association tactics, saying since one person once upon a time was a member of the ACLU and he was a Communist, that makes everybody that ever joined the organization a Communist.

He warmed to his theme:

Guilt by association, I thought, went out years and years ago. And indeed, if maybe we were back in the fifties when Joe McCarthy and all of the people like him were finding a Communist under every bed and around every corner, maybe you could even excuse the defendant for just sort of jumping on the bandwagon and doing what a lot of other people were doing.

But this article was written in 1969, long after that was all over. Yet they continued to perpetuate garbage from 1944, 1950. They won't leave it alone.

He stated the essence of our case:

Stang said he was writing about what happened to Richard Nuccio in the criminal case. And he set out all of the names of the witnesses that testified in that criminal case. He didn't talk to one of them. He didn't talk to any of the people. I read him the whole list and said, "Did you talk to any of these people that knew about the case?" No. They weren't important.

Scott Stanley said it's not important to talk about Elmer Gertz or talk to Elmer Gertz to find out what he has got to say; it's irrelevant. Sure it's irrelevant because as they say on the inside front cover of their magazine, "We use almost no articles except those written to order to fit our specific needs."

You want to talk about a track that somebody leaves, look at Alan Stang's track record. Everybody that he sees, writes about, or talks about is a Communist: John Foster Dulles, President Eisenhower, President Kennedy, President Nixon, Hubert Humphrey—anybody and everybody.

He declared that neither Stanley nor Stang had read one word of the many I had written. About Stang:

He didn't care what Elmer Gertz stood for. He didn't care what he said. He didn't care what he had written because that would have gotten in the way of his hatchet job. He didn't interview the Nelsons. Certainly, they might have had something to say about this. It was their son who was shot in the back. And yet they say, "Well, Elmer Gertz shouldn't represent those people. I mean, after all, their son had a criminal record. He had been arrested before." So I guess that means it's okay to shoot him in the back and everybody should just forget about him.

He concluded fervently:

In our free society, along with freedom goes responsibility. And if you abuse one of those freedoms that we have here, you have got to pay. And it's time for Robert Welch, Incorporated, to pay for what they have done and what they continue to do to Elmer Gertz.

I submit to you that when you look at all of the evidence in this case, you will have no other recourse but to find for the plaintiff for the damages that he continues to suffer today and will continue to suffer every minute of every hour that he is fortunate enough to remain on this earth.

It was now time for Judge Flaum to instruct the jury members on the law that they were to apply to the facts as found by them. We assume that the jury will heed these instructions, but it is probably more true to say that it forms a gut reaction to what it hears in the courtroom and decides accordingly. Still, if the instructions are wrong, this may be grounds for an appeal and reversal.

Most of the instructions were the usual cautionary ones, a brief treatise on how to consider and decide a case. The critical instructions were these:

In reading defendant's articles, the articles must be read as a whole and the words given their natural and obvious meaning. The headlines, subheadlines, pictures, and captions in the articles must be construed in the context of the articles when read as a whole.

The plaintiff has filed suit seeking compensatory and punitive damages on account of an alleged libel, in the form of a magazine article and reprint published by the defendant of and concerning him.

The plaintiff's claim consists of four essential elements:

First, that the defendant published a magazine article of and concerning the plaintiff which was libelous;

Second, that the defendant was *negligent*, as that term is explained in these instructions;

Third, that the libelous statements were read by persons other than the plaintiff, namely, members of the general public; and

Fourth, that the libelous statements were published with *actual malice*, as that term is explained in these instructions.

The burden is on the plaintiff to prove the first three of these elements by a preponderance of the evidence.

The burden is stricter with regard to the fourth element—the element of actual malice. The plaintiff has the burden of establishing by clear and convincing evidence that the publication was made with actual malice.

If you find that the plaintiff has established these four elements by the standards here explained, you may find for the plaintiff. If you find that he has failed to establish any element, then it is your duty to find for the defendant.

As has been said, the burden of proof of each element is upon the plaintiff. The defendant is not obliged to call any witnesses or to introduce any evidence.

Statements about the plaintiff which describe him as a Communist-fronter, Leninist, and Marxist tend to prejudice or injure him in his profession and are therefore libelous.

When I use the word *negligence* in these instructions, I mean the failure to do something which a reasonably careful person would do, under circumstances similar to those shown by the evidence. The law does not say how a reasonably careful person would act under those circumstances. That is for you to decide.

A publication is made with *actual malice* as that term is used in these instructions if it is made with knowledge that it is false or with reckless disregard of whether it is false or not.

Other important instructions included definitions of *recklessness*, *negligence*, *contributory negligence*, and *conditional privilege*. Judge Flaum then dealt with damages:

If you find that the plaintiff has established the essential elements of his claim as explained in these instructions, he is entitled to compensatory damages, and you should award him such amount as you find will fairly and adequately compensate him for his actual injuries. Only actual injuries which are the direct and material result of the libel may be recovered as compensatory damages. Actual injury is not limited to out-of-pocket loss and includes impairment of reputation and standing in the community, personal humiliation, and mental anguish and suffering.

He told of the necessity for reasonableness and avoiding speculation. Then the judge discussed punitive damages:

If you find that the plaintiff has established the essential elements of his claim as explained in these instructions, then you may award the plaintiff punitive or exemplary damages in addition to the compensatory damages assessed. Punitive damages are designed to punish the offender and serve as an example to others. Whether or not to award such damages, and the amount thereof, are matters confined to you for your decision.

The jury was told about selecting a foreperson and the forms of verdict. Then the oath was solemnly administered to them. The alternates left, and the marshal escorted the jury to its chamber. After a few more formalities, the court stood in recess to await the jury's verdict.

Somehow, I had a feeling of unease about the jury, from the moment of its selection through the trial. It was not that I felt it was hostile; indeed, I thought that certain members of the panel were friendly. It was simply that I did not register any warmth, acceptance, deep interest. I pride myself on having a sensitivity to the reactions of judges and jurors. This time I felt comfortable with the judge, despite some of his adverse rulings, but uncomfortable with the jury, although it had indicated nothing about its attitudes.

About 3:00 P.M., the jury retired for its deliberations. Judge Flaum told us to be back in the courtroom at 5:00 P.M. when we would decide whether to keep the jurors segregated for the night or permit them to go home.

Suddenly, at about 4:00 P.M., we were called by Judge Flaum's clerk: The jury verdict was ready. Wayne, his assistant Kathryn Krueger, his wife, Mary, and I walked briskly to the Dirksen Federal Building courtroom. Just before reaching the entrance to the building, I turned to Wayne and said with the confidence that can come only with a kind of extrasensory communication: "The jury verdict will be in my favor. They will award me one hundred thousand dollars in compensatory damages, five hundred thousand in punitive damages." Wayne looked at me, startled, but said not a word. In the courtroom, the defendant's attorney walked over to our table and said, "Congratulations, you have won." "How do you know?" we inquired. "I don't know how much," he responded, "but I am sure that you have won." In moments, the jury confirmed my vision of what they had done, except for the punitive damages (although we learned later that some had contemplated my higher figure):

THE COURT: Mr. Heldrich, Mr. Giampietro, the marshal has informed me that the jury has announced to him that they have reached a verdict in this case. That's correct, Mr. Marshal?
THE MARSHAL: Yes, Your Honor.
THE COURT: All right. Will you please bring in the jury?

The following proceedings took place in open court in the presence and hearing of the jury:

THE COURT: Please be seated. The foreperson is Mr. Brown?
JUROR BROWN: Yes.
THE COURT: Mr. Brown, has the jury reached a verdict in this case?
JUROR BROWN: Yes, we have, Your Honor.
THE COURT: Would you hand it to the marshal, please? Mr. Fulbright, you may read and announce the verdict.
THE CLERK: "We, the jury, find in favor of the plaintiff and against defendant. We assess plaintiff's damages in the sum of $100,000 compensatory damages and $300,000 punitive damages."
....
THE COURT: Gentlemen, the court will enter judgment on the verdict, and both sides may have ten days in which to file any posttrial motions. I commend you both for your able advocacy in the case.

Then the court stood in recess. Twelve years of struggle had reached a new climactic moment.

Rob Warden, the author of the best account of the trial, which appeared in *Chicago Lawyer* (May 1981), quoted the jury foreman, Barry Brown, as saying the jurors were "in complete agreement" from the first that *American Opinion* had been malicious in publishing its article calling me a Leninist and Communist-fronter. "It's not that I necessarily wanted to give four hundred thousand dollars to Elmer Gertz," the twenty-five-year-old foreman said to Warden outside the courtroom after the verdict was returned. "I was looking at it like I really wanted to punish the John Birch Society. Freedom of the press is fine, but to call someone a Communist can really hurt him. The Birch Society was totally out of line. It showed complete disregard for the public and for the truth."

Wayne Giampietro had asked the jury to award $500,000 compensatory damages—"a dollar a minute for all the time Elmer Gertz has had to suffer in one year"—and "at least twice as much" in punitive damages. The jury foreman told Warden that the jury thought Giampietro had asked for a total of too much money but that his suggested 2:1 ratio of punitive to compensatory damages was too low. "That's why we raised it," said Brown.

The verdicts in defamation cases in Illinois have always been relatively modest (the original verdict in my case, it will be remembered, had been only $50,000). This may have been one reason (my age another) for the failure of the Birch Society people to attempt settlement of the case.

It may also have been the judge. In the federal courts in the Northern District of Illinois, the judges fell into two categories in this respect. Some, like Judges Hubert Will and Abraham Lincoln Marovitz, always tried to settle litigation, often succeeding and seldom disqualifying themselves from further activity in the case if they failed. Others, like Judge John Grady, did not initiate settlement efforts because they felt that the consequence of their failure might be prejudice. In perhaps the most famous of all libel cases in our century, a court gave Henry Ford only six cents when he defeated the *Chicago Tribune* for calling him an anarchist and ignoramus. There was the possibility, I suppose, that the jury in my case might have accepted the argument that since communism is not illegal in this country, there is no harm in making such charge.

"We believe we had the law, and the court did not follow the law," Heldrich said to Rob Warden. He contended that Judge Flaum had erred in denying a motion for a directed verdict in favor of the defendant under the innocent-construction rule applicable in Illinois.

The rule requires that if it is reasonably possible to construe offensive language innocently, it must be construed that way by the trial judge. In a memorandum supporting his motion (one of many memorandums he filed), Heldrich cited various Illinois cases in which epithets such as "rip-off speculator," "arrogant nigger," "member of crime syndicate," and "political hack" have been held to be innocent under the rule.

"Are 'Leninist' and 'Communist-fronter' any worse than those?" Heldrich asked Warden. He added, "Because the Gertz case has been to the Supreme Court, there was no way that the judge wasn't going to let it go the jury."

In his *Chicago Lawyer* article, Rob Warden summed up the postverdict situation:

> Attorneys on both sides of the Gertz retrial assumed that, while to collect punitive damages Gertz had to meet the *New York Times* standard, the controlling principle for compensatory damages in Illinois was simple negligence, as set forth by the Illinois Supreme Court in *Troman v. Wood*, 62 Ill. 2d 184, 34 N.E.2d 292 (1975). "[I]n a suit brought by a private individual to recover actual damages for a defamatory publication whose substantial danger to reputation is apparent, recovery may be had upon proof that the publication was false, and that the defendant either knew it to be false, or, believing it to be true, lacked reasonable grounds for that belief."
>
> But Flaum did not share the assumption of counsel. Over Giampietro's objection, the judge instructed the jury that the publisher had a conditional privilege—to publish a libel, if it is published in good faith, if it concerns subject matter in which the publisher has an interest and if it is communicated to persons having a corresponding interest. Therefore, Flaum instructed the jury that to award even compensatory damages it had to find that *American Opinion* had abused the conditional privilege. He said the jury had to apply the *New York Times* standard across the board—to actual as well as punitive damages.
>
> Ironically, Gertz's long battle through the Supreme Court thus was rendered a purely academic exercise—at least as far as the trial of his own case before this judge and jury was concerned.

"We're right back where we started 12 years ago," Giampietro grumbled.

But Flaum's adverse ruling soon appeared to be a blessing in disguise for Gertz. When the jury, after deliberating only an hour, found that Gertz had proved malice and awarded the $400,000, what moments earlier had been the defendant's First Amendment insurance policy suddenly was the plaintiff's insurance policy against reversal.

Defendant's counsel got extensions of time to file its posttrial motions. Finally, it filed such motions, a supplement to them, what it called a summary of testimony and comments, and a memorandum. These documents rehashed arguments already made, misstated facts, and misconstrued documents. They seemed to be gestures of desperation. We realized, however, that it was not our views that governed but the judge's.

I must confess that I was not worried about the rulings that might be made by the court, except for a possible *remittitur*, a reduction in the amount of the judgment. Wayne was not worried, even as to the latter point. Meanwhile, interest at the statutory rate was running on the judgment and would continue to run unless Judge Flaum should decide, as Judge Decker had done more than a decade earlier, to grant judgment notwithstanding the verdict. This seemed inconceivable to us.

In its amended posttrial motion, the defendant set forth its revised reasons for urging the court to enter judgment for the defendant notwithstanding the verdict of the jury and to grant a remittitur of the compensatory and punitive damages assessed by the jury. As this motion was the basis of any appeal, it is necessary to examine its grounds.

Again Heldrich stated that as a matter of law, the court was required to construe innocently the allegedly libelous language and failed to do so.

But Judge Flaum, like Judge Decker and the Supreme Court before him, construed the language as libelous and not innocent. They could not have done otherwise in view of the nature of the language, charging me with committing a crime—framing Nuccio for murder—and with being a Communist (as both Stang and Stanley testified, being designated a Leninist and Communist-fronter was tantamount to being called a Communist).

Again Heldrich stated that the standard of negligence is not the substantive law of Illinois in defamation actions.

But this is directly contrary to what the Illinois Supreme Court said in *Troman v. Wood* and what other Illinois cases had said. Besides, we were held not simply to proof of negligence but malice as well—the highest possible standard, despite what the Supreme Court had said. This was due to the largesse of Judge Flaum in permitting the defendant to file a plea of fair comment at the last moment (after Judge Decker had stricken such a plea).

Heldrich contended that we had failed to sustain our burden of proof by clear and convincing evidence, that there was no evidence of malice on the part of the defendant, and that the plaintiff had failed to prove actual damages.

Such contentions were clearly contrary to our evidence that directly or circumstantially established the defendant's negligence, its knowledge of the defamatory falsehood in its publication, its reckless disregard of that falsehood.

Again and again Heldrich contended that we had not proved any injury. Heldrich seemed to believe that one was not injured unless one collapsed physically or emotionally. He would have been on sounder ground if he had argued the extent of the injuries rather than their existence. He misconstrued the nature of punitive damages and argued that the punitive damages exceeded the net worth of the defendant. However, he offered no proof of that contention. We had not offered the defendant's financial statement in evidence, nor had he.

Again he argued that the court erred in entering summary judgment on the issue of truth, thereby barring the defendant from proving truth.

In fact, virtually all of the defendant's evidence amounted to an unsuccessful attempt to prove that I was a Communist-fronter and Leninist. Its own witness Stang admitted that there was no evidence that I was involved in any way with the trial and conviction of Nuccio.

Heldrich attempted to make much of Wayne's argument to the jury as somehow in violation of the judge's ruling. Although he had made no objection at the time of the argument, he still smarted over the attempted use of graphic blowups and the jury's reading of the very article that was the heart of our case. He was still troubled (although he had entered no formal objection) that one of the jurors had taken notes at the outset of the trial until stopped by the court. He made something of a claimed failure of proof on the issue of contributory negligence, although there was not the slightest evidence of contributory negligence. At the time of my trial, the Illinois Supreme Court had adopted a standard of *comparative negligence*, and doubt had been cast, in any event, upon the necessity of proving absence of contributory negligence.

If we had had any sympathy for the defendant or its counsel, it vanished as we read the reply to our memorandum opposing the Welch motion. Ironically, Heldrich complained in the very first sentences about the manner of our response: "One can not easily ignore the usual vitriolic inflamatory rhetoric the defendant has come to expect from the plaintiff. It occurs in print as it occurred in closing argument." This from a party that had not hesitated to impugn my character in the most extreme fashion and had charged me with the commission of a crime.

He then went on to repeat, in effect, the very libels about which we had complained:

> This Court should bear in mind that in the first trial, the first appeal and in the Supreme Court case, it was *assumed* but never proven that the article was false. This Court assumed the same when it denied truth as a defense.
>
> How can it now be denied, after thirty-five (35) exhibits, that Elmer Gertz *was not* [sic] involved with numerous organizations deemed Communist Fronts by our governmental leaders?
>
> Whether this Court or this attorney, looking backwards, believe such reports today were either accurate or fair today is not important. What is important is that we must have faith that at the time our representatives were motivated by the good of the people and would not have intentionally published falsehoods.
>
> It is not defamatory to call a black man an "arrogant nigger," why is it defamatory to call Elmer Gertz a Marxist?
>
> It is not defamatory to call a police officer a "pimp," why is it defamatory to call Elmer Gertz a Leninist?
>
> It is not defamatory to say that a "physician maltreats" his patients, why is it defamatory to call Elmer Gertz a Communist-fronter, especially when a communist can not be defined . . . and when being a Communist Fronter is not, nor ever has been, a crime. . . .
>
> Perhaps it is because the plaintiff is Elmer Gertz, the Elmer Gertz that every Chicago lawyer and judge seem to know. The Elmer Gertz who knows Irv Kupcinet and the Irv Kupcinet who knows other persons of position and influence. The Elmer Gertz who knows Albert Jenner and the Albert Jenner who knows more people of power and influence.

These very same people can not believe that this kindly looking grandfatherly figure could have used the mantle of his profession all these years to engage in political activity.

These very same people can not and will not believe, even when documents are placed before their very eyes, that Elmer Gertz was involved with the doctrine of destruction. But, you see, he was, he really, truly was....

The defendant repeats and reiterates that it was not, is not, and can not be actionably libel to call a person a Marxist, Leninist or Communist-Fronter—even a lawyer—even Elmer Gertz—a person evidently on the endangered species list.

If we are at the point where defamation is weighed solely by one's occupation we as a people are in trouble indeed.

For a court, this Court, to so declare, is error, serious, serious, reversible error. Once having so declared, this Court, fallibility has directed, in effect, the jury to find for the plaintiff.

He then disputed that we had proved that I was actually injured by the defendant's defamations:

But, as the defendant has proven and pointed out to this Court in its post-trial motion, Elmer Gertz merely proved through his colleagues that his reputation *could have been damaged*, but in fact *never was*.

He was never sick, never lost a day's work, never lost a client, was elected to public office and made more money. No actual damages, not one dime!

Gertz did not prove any damages actual or punitive.

Finally he set forth a conclusion:

It seems to this journeyman that from the onset to this very moment, that no one reads, nor listens to the defendant.

It was assumed, but never proven, that labeling an attorney politically is libelous.

There can be no doubt from the countless documents admitted into evidence that Elmer Gertz was involved in countless organizations deemed Communist-Fronts.

Associating with one front could be innocent, as with Albert Jenner, and many other distinguished Americans. Association with two fronts may also be innocent, but less so. But, as the number of fronts joined increases, one could reach the same justified conclusion as did Alan Stang, the author.

Scott Stanley, the editor, was never proven negligent to the degree required by the law.

Elmer Gertz never proved any damage.

Reporters have a right to rely upon history. Accurate reporting of facts upon which an ideological opinion is made is not defamatory.

The defendant's Post Trial Motion should and ought to be granted.

Heldrich awaited the court's determination of the matter. He had asked for oral argument on his motion. It was not granted. Judge Flaum lost no time in deciding against the defendant. He did not bother to file an explanatory memorandum but simply ruled in one sentence: "Defendant's motion for judgment for defendant notwithstanding the verdict of the jury and for a remittitur of the compensatory and punitive damages assessed, found and determined by the jury, is denied."

Congratulatory letters and calls poured in following the extensive publicity of the jury verdict. If some were critical of the result, they remained largely silent; none wrote to me. Those who applauded the result expressed themselves with varying degrees of enthusiasm. A friend of my youth, Leo Rosten, thought the verdict "simply marvelous." "It's a great country!" he concluded. He urged me to use "the entire sum on self-indulgence." Dr. Edward J. Sparling, whose name graced the commission that Alan Stang had regarded as part of a Communist conspiracy against the police, regarded my victory as "important." "It has been great to know and to see the kind of law you have practiced from the beginning to your career," he wrote. Another old friend wrote: "Wow! It's wonderful — it's fantastic — it's the only heartening news I have had in months."

Anthony Lewis, the much-quoted columnist and Supreme Court reporter whose book *Gideon's Trumpet* is a classic in narrating a case in understandable terms, had been calling me from time to time during the long years of delay to learn the latest developments in my case. "You did it for many others besides yourself," he wrote. "Your perseverance and dedication in the libel suit is a lesson for us all — don't give up," declared Julius Lucius Echeles. I took great joy in the letters that I received from students, clients, lawyers, secretaries, and friends from whom I had not heard in years.

Certainly because of Carol Burnett's victory, possibly because of mine, the Libel Defense Resource Center was established. As of April 15, 1981, the supporting organizations included the American Newspaper Publishers Association, American Society of Newspaper Editors, Association of American University Presses, Association of American Publishers, Authors League of America (I had long been, and still am, a member of this oganization), Magazine Publishers Association, National Association of Broadcasters, National Newspaper Association, publishers, insurance companies, and others. It was an imposing group.

A brochure describing the organization stated that "libel litigation undeniably remains a major deterrent to freedom of speech and freedom of the press." It contended that the largest and most careful publisher lives in fear of the "boxcar awards and so coordinated and sustained (defense) action is needed." Thus, voluntary funding for several months of operation had been secured, a general counsel retained, a staff coordinator hired, committees set up, a brief and pleading "bank" developed, systems for monitoring cases established, bulletins and studies projected.

Under date of July 31, 1981, I received the first bulletin of the Libel Defense Resource Center (LDRC) and discovered that I was a potential menace. One section of the bulletin advised that briefs were being sought on *Gertz* standards. It began with a summary of the situation:

> One of the most notable developments in libel law over the past several years, of course, is the state by state redefinition of the appropriate fault standard to be applied pursuant to the constitutional guidelines defined in *Gertz v. Robert Welch, Inc.*, 418 U.S. 323 (1974). For better or worse a substantial number of jurisdictions have already definitively ruled on the matter, with the majority of those jurisdictions adopting the minimal standard of mere negligence. Nevertheless, at last count some twenty-five states had still not yet definitively adopted a *Gertz* standard. Therefore, in many states the issue is still a very live one and the LDRC wishes to be actively involved in assisting local defendants in making the most effective possible argument for the most favorable possible legal standard in private-figure actions.

For this reason, LDRC sought briefs "for standards more protective than mere negligence," so that it might develop a "'model' brief on the issue that could be widely disseminated."

I wondered why the publishers and their colleagues were so concerned in view of other material that appeared in this first issue. For example, one study indicated that plaintiffs prevailed in only 7 percent of the libel cases. The awards in the few successful cases were relatively small. The difficulty may have been that cases tried under the *New York Times* standard were successfully defended more often than in *Gertz*. Ergo, they advocated the *New York Times* standard for private persons as well as public.

A few days after the verdict, on April 27, 1981, the *St. Louis Post-Dispatch* published a provocative editorial under the heading "What Penalties for Libel?" Although I disagreed with its conclusion, I believed it reflected media views generally:

> As a result of Supreme Court approval of more relaxed standards for the recovery of libel damages, juries seem to be more inclined to assess heavy penalties in such cases. Recently a Los Angeles jury awarded actress Carol Burnett $1.6 million in compensatory and punitive damages against the *National Enquirer* for its report that she had been involved in a boisterous encounter in a Washington restaurant with then Secretary of State Kissinger and other diners. The high judgment was awarded despite the facts that the paper published a retraction and that Ms. Burnett's reputation was probably not hurt.
>
> Now a federal jury in Chicago has awarded attorney Elmer Gertz a $400,000 libel judgment against the John Birch Society magazine, *American Opinion*, for an article accusing him of being a "Communist fronter" and "Marxist-Leninist." The 12-year-old case was recently retried (Mr. Gertz lost the first time) after the U.S. Supreme Court ruled that Mr. Gertz is not a "public figure." That being the case, he is not required, as proof of libel, to show that the alleged defamatory statement was published with reckless disregard for its truth or falsehood.
>
> Mr. Gertz, a respected Chicago lawyer, was understandably outraged by the magazine's report about him and was entitled to an apology and some damages. There is reason to doubt whether he was injured to the extent of $100,000 in actual damages, or whether the magazine should be penalized to the extent of $300,000 in punitive damages. We certainly have no admiration for the kind of journalism engaged in by *American Opinion* or the *National Enquirer*. But freedom of the press, which can be severely hampered by heavy libel judgments, is not guaranteed just for popular publications.

A bit later, in its June 6 issue, the *Nation* had a front-page article under the heading "Suing Free Speech—Libel as a Political Weapon" and a supporting editorial. The article, by Eve Pell, mentioned Carol Burnett's suit and mine, and added, "But a very different, generally less publicized sort of libel suit is proliferating throughout the nation these days. In these cases people using the political process to redress grievances or bring about change are being socked with huge damage suits by the interests they have offended." In the accompanying editorial, the *Nation* declared: "Libel suits can indeed cast a chill on freedom of speech and the press, but liberals who advocate abandoning this recourse completely are under an obligation to come up with alternative means for salvaging damaged reputations."

My wife, Mamie, coupled the Burnett victory and mine in an intensely personal way. On July 7, 1981, she wrote to Burnett:

Dear Carol Burnett,

I am enclosing an account of a fantastic victory in a libel case in which my husband, Elmer Gertz, was the plaintiff.

We felt the great joy of your victory and feel that we must share that feeling of our own experience with you.

My husband is too modest to make the move but I feel that the momentum of the moment must not be lost. Since my husband brought suit against the John Birch Society 12 years ago, his case known as *Gertz v. Robert Welch, Inc.* changed the law of libel. His case probably figured a great deal in handling the legal technicalities of your case. So you see we are sort of kin-in-law.

If you ever get to Chicago, we would love to get together for coffee or whatever to share a "victory" hug.

Sincerely,
Mamie Gertz
(Mrs. Elmer)

Burnett replied on August 18:

Dear Mamie:

Thank you for taking the time to write, and for sending along the issue of "CHICAGO LAWYER" in which your husband's libel suit against Robert Welch, Inc. was written up.

I am delighted to learn of the outcome of your twelve year fight against those who libeled him, and want to extend my "congratulations" to you both. I know it has been a trying twelve years.

I didn't get into things like this with my own attorney, but I am sure he knew of your case and that it helped in sorting out legal technicalities in mine. We all thank you for being a 'front runner' against unscrupulous publishers who don't care a whit for the importance of truthful reporting. Maybe now they will!

Congratulations to us all!!!

Sincerely,
Carol Burnett

On September 4, 1981, more than four months after the judgment in my favor was entered, Heldrich delivered to Wayne's office a notice of appeal "from the order denying Defendant's motion for judgment for defendant notwithstanding the verdict of the jury and for a remittitur of the compensatory and punitive damages assessed." On the face of it, there seemed to be some defects in this notice of appeal, but we were looking to the substance rather than technicalities to decide the appeal.

The notice was signed by Heldrich and added another firm as defendant's attorneys: Pierson, Ball and Dowd, through David Machanic and Michael Minnis of Oklahoma City. The late General Watts had also come from Oklahoma City. With the notice was a motion to admit Machanic and Minnis to practice in the Northern District for the limited purpose of the case. An accompanying document told something about the new counsel in the case. They had been admitted to practice in Oklahoma, Virginia, and the District of Columbia, and Minnis also in California.

Heldrich said that he had no desire to be a part of the appeal because he thought that a group of appellate specialists, taking a fresh look, would do better. But he believed in the end that the "silk-stocking" appellate specialists called in by the defendant did not do well—that their briefs and argument were poor.

Now the usual procedure would unfold—the filing of a surety bond or other assurance that the judgment, interest, and costs would be paid if the appeal failed; the record; the briefs; the oral argument before a panel of the court of appeals; then the court's decision. And there was still the possibility of an appeal to the U.S. Supreme Court. These things would consume precious months; we hoped not years. I fervently wished that the trip around the world that Mamie and I had promised ourselves out of the proceeds of the judgment would take place closer to my seventy-fifth birthday than my eightieth.

The objective considerations were favorable. The *Media Law Reporter* stated that lawyers were concerned over the Supreme

Court's reluctance during the 1980–81 term to review libel issues. The Court had had before it during the term over twenty petitions for the review of libel decisions and had turned them all down. Observers declared that this was part of the continuing trend since my case was decided in 1974—to consider libel cases, if at all, on a very narrow basis. The Court seemed to want to encourage the development of state law in that area, as suggested by *Gertz*.

But what was the situation in the U.S. courts of appeal, particularly in the Seventh Circuit? In due course, we and the appellant-defendant would learn.

13 ■ An Interminable Case Is Terminated

There were moments when I felt that the case would never end, but I seldom despaired. Some well-meaning persons thought that I might win the case but would never succeed in collecting a judgment. They seemed puzzled by the effort I put into the case for so many years.

I have an enormous store of self-confidence, akin to religious faith. For example, shortly after I filed suit against Robert Welch, Inc., I ran for election as a delegate to the Illinois Constitutional Convention at the urging of my friend Seymour Simon, later a justice of the Illinois Supreme Court. I learned later that my family and friends, perhaps even Simon, thought that I would lose, that the opposition of both Republicans and Democrats would be too much for me, an independent. But from the first moment, I thought that I would win, even when I was fourth in the primary and only two could win in the election. I was first in the election. So it was with my suit against the Birchers.

Naturally, I was eager to learn how the new defense attorneys would pursue the formidable task of overcoming the judgment in my favor. In November 1981 they filed their brief in the U.S. Court of Appeals for the Seventh Circuit. Fresh thinking went into it, although the line taken was simple enough. They thought the district court had erred in allowing the jury to find that the defendant had published the article with "actual malice" when the district court, the court of appeals, and the Supreme Court had each held after the first trial that the defendant did not publish with actual malice. Their other major point was that the district court erred in ruling that the plaintiff had produced sufficient evidence to support the jury's verdict. Their statement of the case was admirably set forth, considering the difficulties they had to contend with. There was nothing shrill or offensive. All had the aura of reasonableness.

Counsel recognized that if the defendant was to prevail upon appeal, they had to persuade the court of appeals that it was bound by the doctrine of *the law of the case* to find in their favor, as it had done before reversing the district court. According to this doctrine, once there has been an adjudication of an issue by the reviewing court, it cannot be relitigated, in the interests of judicial economy and general fairness. Although we had differed from the court in each instance, it is true that in connection with the first trial, all three levels that had considered the case—the district court, the court of appeals, and the Supreme Court—had found that I had not established actual malice on the part of the defendant. True, I had not been permitted to offer such evidence, but was I not bound by the adverse determination nonetheless?

Counsel also contended that there had been no proof that I had suffered any injury that would warrant compensatory damages. They claimed that it was legally prejudicial to submit to the jury the matter of compensatory damages when the matter was irreparably tainted by improperly submitting the issue of punitive damages as well.

The responding brief was submitted by Wayne and his associate Mildred F. Hagerty. They questioned whether the defendant could raise the doctrine of the law of the case for the first time on appeal when they had not done so on retrial. They pointed out that without objection by the defendant, I had filed an amended complaint in the district court after remand of the case by the Supreme Court and in it had set forth in detail no less than nine elements that in our judgment showed actual malice. And we had presented proof in support of the elements of actual malice, and more. We summed up the situation in this manner:

> At no time in the District Court had Defendant objected to Plaintiff introducing evidence of actual malice on its part, either by way of motion *in limine* [that is, a motion to preclude the introduction of such evidence] or by objection at the trial, or in any other manner.
>
> . . . .
>
> Neither in their Motion for Summary Judgment, nor in any other motion or action either prior to or during the trial of this cause, did Defendant contend that Plaintiff was foreclosed from proving actual malice on the part of Defendant at this second trial. Nor did Defendant raise the issue in its post-trial motion. Indeed, during the trial, the Defendant urged that Plaintiff was required to prove actual malice through evidence at the trial and expressly urged the Court to instruct the jury that Plaintiff was required to so prove.

My attorneys summed up the evidence with great particularity. They pointed out that defendant had admitted that the statements made about me were basically false and that all the courts that had considered the case had so found. For this reason, Judge Flaum had precluded the defendant from attempting to prove that the allegations of the *American Opinion* article were true. He confined the defendant to proof that it acted without fault and without actual malice, and that I had suffered no injuries.

Wayne and his associates also presented telling arguments on the legal doctrines that bore on the case. Our opponents had argued that the doctrine of the law of the case precluded relitigation of the issue of actual malice. That issue, they said, had been foreclosed by the first trial court. However, my attorneys showed that it was not the intention of the Supreme Court to preclude the offering of additional evidence in support of our position and that, if anything, the Court was inclined to find in my favor on the basic situation.

They admirably summed up the evidence regarding the injuries I had suffered. They also questioned the court's ruling that we needed to prove actual malice. Such proof was supposed to overcome the plea of fair comment that had been granted late in the case. However, Judge Decker had earlier denied permission to file such a plea. Besides, they contended, no basis for this First Amendment privilege could be found in the public record claimed by defendant.

Closely analyzing all the evidence, they contended quite persuasively that we had proved both fault and actual malice and that the jury could not reasonably have found otherwise. Particularly damning to the defendant was Stang's last-minute confession that there was no evidence to establish that I had had anything to do with the criminal case against Nuccio—that I was not the architect of any conspiracy, Communist or otherwise, against that unfortunate police officer.

The brief concluded forcibly:

The record in this case shows a flagrant and malicious defamation of a private attorney. The subject matter of the article involved herein was wholly concocted by Defendant, who sent its agent, not to get the facts, but to get misstatements, twisted and distorted in a manner so as to fit respondent's preconceived attitude. That there was actual malice here cannot be open to question.

Publishers are granted wide leeway under our Constitution to write and publish on virtually anything they wish. However, along with that freedom goes the duty to act in a responsible manner. There can be no license to drag the name of innocent bystanders in the mud by making utterly false and highly damaging charges against them in the most irresponsible manner where truth is readily available and could easily have been ascertained. At no time during the long history of this case has Defendant ever attempted to prove the truth of the statements concerning plaintiff. Almost from the start, they admitted that they were untrue. The jury has found actual malice, with more than sufficient justification.

The Defendant's last-ditch attempt to argue that Plaintiff was foreclosed from proving actual malice is of no avail. There is absolutely no foundation for that argument.

The jury's verdict is more than substantiated by this record. The judgment of the District Court must be affirmed in all respects.

In view of what followed in the court of appeals, it is sufficient here to repeat what defendant's counsel contended in the conclusion of their reply brief:

The plaintiff has failed to meet his burden of proving by clear and convincing evidence that the defendant published with actual malice.

It is unnecessary for the defendant to defend any opinion of Stang in order to disprove actual malice.

The plaintiff's brief reveals that he feels that actual malice has been established because he disagrees with the political philosophy of the defendant and the author of the article as expressed on other occasions. Apparently he believes that because of that disagreement he is entitled to ignore the prior decisions of the district court, this Court, and the United States Supreme Court on the critical issue in this case.

The First Amendment does not allow damages based upon such differentiation among beliefs. Because the plaintiff can justify his claim of actual malice only on the basis of such an attack upon political beliefs, we submit that the jury's verdict cannot stand. Therefore, it is respectfully requested that the judgement below be reversed.

Then came the oral argument before the court of appeals, with a different panel of three judges. The positions of the parties were now reversed. I had been the appellant earlier; now I was the respondent, a position that I greatly welcomed. The argument for the defendant was made by a different attorney than earlier—David Machanic, of the Washington law firm of Pierson, Ball and

Dowd. Only Wayne and I were veterans of earlier stages of the case. He was now a seasoned advocate of forty and I a white-haired veteran of seventy-five. I sat at the counsel table with Wayne, but I could say nothing except to pass notes or whisper to him. He required no guidance from me.

Judge Richard A. Posner, a former University of Chicago law professor, was the most persistent interrogator of Machanic. Joseph R. Tybor, of the *National Law Journal*, caught the flavor of the argument, and I paraphrase what he wrote:

> In his briefs, Machanic had attempted to convince the panel that because the initial trial judge, an earlier panel of the Seventh Circuit, and the Supreme Court had found that Gertz had failed to prove actual malice at the first trial, he was prohibited from introducing evidence of actual malice at the retrial.
>
> Judge Posner was skeptical.
>
> He asked Machanic to point out in the transcript of the retrial where that argument was made and preserved for appeal.
>
> When Machanic replied that he felt the argument was "implicit" in motions made in connection with the case, Judge Posner responded, "I don't think it was made at all."
>
> Referring to the Supreme Court's statement that Gertz had failed to show actual malice at the first trial, Judge Posner asked Machanic, "So you think every sentence in a Supreme Court opinion is a mandate?"
>
> Machanic replied rather sheepishly, "I do not," and then attempted to show that evidence of actual malice presented at the retrial was insufficient to support an award of punitive damages.
>
> Judge Posner pursued him with more questions, referring to Stang's prior writings in which he applied a Communist or Marxist tag to Hubert Humphrey, Pierre Trudeau, Richard Nixon, John Foster Dulles, and U Thant.
>
> Machanic insisted there was not "actual knowledge" that the Communist charge against Gertz was false and that, nonetheless, Stang's assertions were opinions that merited First Amendment protection.
>
> Judge Posner continued: "If Stang told Stanley [the managing editor of *American Opinion*] that J. Edgar Hoover was a member of the Communist Party, . . . is it a fact or an opinion?
>
> "If I say Ike was a member of the Communist party, is that an opinion or an assertion of fact?"
>
> Machanic persisted that unless one has actual knowledge of its falsity, "whether a person is impressed with the doctrine of communism [is] an opinion" entitled to protection.

Senior Judge Dudley B. Bonsal, sitting by designation from the U.S. district court in New York, asked Machanic if in light of Stang's prior statements, Stanley was not required to investigate whether the Communist charge against Gertz was false.

"He relied on Stang," Machanic replied.

"And he could rely, no matter how fantastic Mr. Stang's beliefs?" Judge Posner asked.

He persisted. Might not a jury infer falsity from such an outlandish statement as "I have discovered unicorns on the dark side of the moon?" he asked.

"... I believe that every member of Congress is a homosexual," the judge postulated again. "I want to write a story about Elmer Gertz, who is also a homosexual...."

"Could a jury infer that the statement about Elmer Gertz is probably false ... that Stang had a bee in his bonnet?"

"Could a jury have found that Stang's assertions about Nixon ... were as fantastic as saying that every member of Congress was a homosexual?"

"I don't think so," replied Machanic gravely. "The evidence in this case was insufficient to show actual malice."

Few questions were put to Wayne by the panel, probably a good omen. Wayne felt encouraged to take less than his allotted thirty minutes. He reminded the panel that at the first trial we were not allowed to put into evidence Stang's prior writings, which exhibited his gross tendency to call everyone a Communist. In the retrial, we had been permitted to offer these strange writings, and we could cross-examine Stang and draw all sorts of concessions from him, including an admission that I had nothing to do with Nuccio's trial. Wayne concluded:

> If there were not obvious reasons to doubt the veracity of Alan Stang, never is there going to be any reason to doubt the veracity of anyone.
>
> The man made the most outlandish statements time after time again. We are trying to punish them not for their opinions but [because] they had malice aforethought ... in making irresponsible, knowingly false accusations.

Judge Robert Sprecher, who ultimately wrote the court's opinion, said very little, but he listened to everything intently.

The oral argument over, we now had the ordeal of awaiting the court's decision. We felt more assured than the last time, perhaps because we had grown accustomed to the ups and downs of the case. The case was argued on February 8, 1982, and decided on June 16, 1982—a markedly shorter period than for the other decisions. Now further delay would have no legal effect on the "survival" of the judgment.

In the conclusion of the court-of-appeals case, however, there was great sadness. Judge Robert A. Sprecher died before the opinion was officially released. He was only sixty-four and had been hospitalized for eight weeks. He wrote the opinion in the hospital. "His ability to keep current in writing the decisions assigned to him was the envy of all the judges of the court of appeals," Senior Judge Thomas Fairchild said. "Scholarly effort and thoughtfulness were uniform hallmarks of his writing."

Later, a memorial meeting was held for Judge Sprecher in the main courtroom of the Seventh Circuit, and I was invited to attend. Supreme Court Justice John Paul Stevens, who had written the first court of appeals decision against me, presided and spoke. Chief Circuit Judge Walter J. Cummings talked of his late colleague in eloquent terms. I was startled and moved when Judge Cummings said suddenly, "I am glad that Elmer Gertz is here, because Bob Sprecher's opinion in the *Gertz* case will stand as his monument." Later, Judge Joel Flaum, who had presided so ably at the retrial, was named to the court of appeals where he now sits with distinction.

At the bottom of the first page of the opinion was this sad footnote: "Judge Sprecher's untimely death occurred between the preparation of his opinion for the court and the voting on that opinion by the judges on the appeal." Also on the first page was the notation that the case had been argued on February 8, 1982, and decided on June 16, 1982—a week longer than four months. The whole process of winding up the case was speeding up appreciably after the long delay between the Supreme Court opinion in 1974 and the retrial of the case almost seven years later.

With admirable brevity, all things considered, Judge Sprecher summed up the stance of the case and the situation from which it arose. He also summarized what had occurred in the initial trial and subsequent appeals:

> The assertion that Gertz was a Communist or part of a Communist conspiracy was false. Many of the other statements concerning his membership in particular organizations also were false. When Gertz

learned of the article, he filed this diversity suit for defamation in the Northern District of Illinois. In a pre-trial ruling, the trial court held that the libelous words published by the defendant constituted libel *per se. Gertz v. Robert Welch, Inc.*, 306 F. Supp. 310 (N.D. Ill. 1969). Because of this ruling, injury was presumed, and upon proof of the falsity of the statements in the article, the court submitted only the issue of damages to the jury. The jury returned a verdict in favor of Gertz and awarded damages of $50,000. The trial court, however, granted judgment notwithstanding the verdict on the basis that the subject matter of the article was of "public interest" and therefore required a showing of actual malice under the standard announced in *New York Times v. Sullivan*, 376 U.S. 254 (1964). *Gertz v. Robert Welch, Inc.*, 322 F. Supp. 997 (N.D. Ill. 1970). Because the court found that actual malice had not been established, the jury's verdict could not stand. On appeal, this court affirmed. *Gertz v. Robert Welch, Inc.*, 471 F.2d 801 (7th Cir. 1972).

The Supreme Court granted certiorari and reversed *Gertz v. Robert Welch, Inc.*, 418 U.S. 323 (1974). The Court disavowed the "public interest" doctrine as a basis for requiring that actual malice be shown in suits involving defamation of private individuals. The Court further held that states could set their own standards of liability for defamation of private individuals as long as they did not impose liability without fault. Damages could not be awarded without proof of injury, however, and punitive damages required a showing of actual malice. The case was remanded for a new trial consistent with these guidelines.

On remand, Gertz amended his complaint to allege both negligence and actual malice by Welch, and requested compensatory and punitive damages. On cross-motions for summary judgment, the trial court held that, based on the law of the case, Gertz was not a public figure, but otherwise denied the motions of both parties. Shortly before trial, Welch was permitted to file an affirmative defense of conditional privilege based on the assertion that the article merely repeated statements in government publications.

After a six-day trial, the jury found in favor of Gertz and awarded compensatory damages of $100,000 and punitive damages of $300,000. It is from this judgment that Welch appeals.

A clear statement of the issues before the reviewing court followed:

Welch's final argument is that the issue of actual malice was erroneously submitted to the jury in the second trial because the law of the case doctrine precluded the relitigation of that issue. Welch bases this argument on the first trial court's finding, subsequently upheld by this court and the Supreme Court, that actual malice in publication of the article had not been proved. The issue of actual malice thus was foreclosed from being a basis for either liability or punitive damages. Welch would then read the Supreme Court's mandate remanding the case for a new trial as limited to the issues of whether liability existed and whether compensatory damages could be awarded predicated on a negligence theory. Because the trial court on remand determined that Welch was entitled to a conditional privilege which could only be overcome by a showing of actual malice, Welch argues that the trial court should have directed a verdict in its favor once the privilege was established.

The court then entered into a lengthy and learned discussion of the law-of-the-case doctrine. The doctrine, Judge Sprecher said, "is a self-imposed prudential limitation rather than a recognition of a limitation of the Court's power." For this reason it is not "an immutable rule, but rather a way to foreclose continued appeals for reconsideration of prior rulings of law." It is thus not like res judicata, which is a binding rule of law and not merely discretionary.

The court considered the circumstances in which the doctrine would be applied and when not. This led readily to a decision not to apply the doctrine in my case:

Applying these well established principles to the case before us, we find no basis for the position that the issue of actual malice was determined and foreclosed from reconsideration by the Supreme Court's mandate. The primary issue in *Gertz* was "Whether a newspaper or broadcaster that publishes defamatory falsehoods about an individual who is neither a public official nor a public figure may claim a constitutional privilege against liability for the injury inflicted by those statements." 418 U.S. 323, 332 (1974). The Court answered this question in the negative. The Court also expressly rejected a constitutional privilege for defamatory statements contained in an article on a subject of "public interest." Rather, the Court held that "so long as they do not impose liability without fault, the States may define for themselves the appropriate standard of liability." *Id.* at 347. The Court further stated that the states could only permit compensation for actual injury, and that a showing of actual malice was required to support presumed injury or punitive damages. *Id.* at 349. Finally, the Court ruled that Gertz was not a public figure. *Id.* at 352. The Court had no difficulty in agreeing with the trial court that Gertz's legal and community activities were not equivalent to "general fame or notoriety," nor had Gertz "thrust himself" into public view in the course of his involvement in the Nelson case so as to make him a public figure.

Thus, the law of the case in *Gertz*, as defined by the issues before the Court, consisted of the Court's guidelines on liability for defamation of private individuals by the media and the Court's further refinement of the public figure standard. Whether or not actual malice had been proved below simply was not an issue before the Court. The Court did not establish as a matter of law that actual malice had not and could not be proved. To the contrary, the Court's position on liability opened the door to a different standard for the second trial.

Judge Sprecher then took up the issue of whether I had proved negligence and actual malice, as required by Judge Flaum's instructions to the jury. This required that he consider the question of the privilege asserted by the defendant. Unlike earlier cases where the privilege was applied, this case involved reports of congressional committees published in the 1940s and 1950s rather than relatively contemporaneous newspapers or magazines. The Illinois cases, he said, were silent on this distinction. He concluded:

Even assuming the privilege was properly invoked in this case, we find that the district court's application of the privilege was overbroad. First, the court appeared to extend the privilege for *reporting on* government proceedings to cover articles *relying on* reports of government proceedings. We have found no Illinois case to support such an interpretation of the privilege. Where a publisher merely reports a statement, states it fairly, and does not modify or misstate the statement, the privilege is applicable, provided there is no actual malice. Where, on the other hand, a statement in the record of public proceeding is merely part of one's research, and is used to support an assertion not made in the public document, the privilege does not apply. Rather, in the latter situation, whether there is liability for the republication of the statement should be judged by the reasonableness of reliance upon the public document.

The only statement about me in any of the documents cited by Stang, he said, indicated that I was a member of the National Lawyers Guild from the 1930s to 1950:

Other than that "fact," which Stang may not have reported accurately, there were no other statements about Gertz in these government reports. Thus, Stang *relied* on those reports to characterize as Communist the organizations which he claimed that Gertz belonged to, which claim was, in turn, based on Stang's *reliance* on material from the police intelligence file. The same three documents identified by Stang were the only documents used by Stanley when he "checked the checkables." Again, only Gertz's past membership in the National Lawyers' Guild could be verified in those documents. Otherwise, Stanley testified, he relied on Stang. Thus, government documents were primarily relied upon, not reported on, for this article.

This led the judge to conclude that

any application of the privilege should have been limited to those statements about Gertz that were actually checked against these documents. Instead, the trial court applied the privilege to the entire article. This might have been appropriate had the focus of the article, or even a substantial section of the article, been upon the congressional committee proceedings which were the basis of the public reports. Application of the privilege to the entire article was not appropriate here, however, where the reports were used only to verify certain statements.

Now the issue of actual malice had to be considered:

In summary, Stanley conceived of a story line; solicited Stang, a writer with a known and unreasonable propensity to label persons or organizations as Communist, to write the article; and after the article was submitted, made virtually no effort to check the validity of statements that were defamatory *per se* of Gertz and in fact added further defamatory material based on Stang's "facts." There was more than enough evidence for the jury to conclude that this article was published with utter disregard for the truth or falsity of the statements contained in the article about Gertz.

The remaining issues raised by the defendant pertained to damages, compensatory and punitive. Judge Sprecher found that Judge Flaum had given clear and explicit instructions to the jury on damages. The defendant had argued that there was no proof of actual injury. "The short answer to this contention," Judge Sprecher said, "is that because there was evidence of actual malice in the publication of the defamatory statements, which were libel *per se*, Illinois law would permit, and the constitution would not prohibit, presumed damages."

Nonetheless, Gertz has proved actual injury in this case. Gertz testified to the severe mental distress, anxiety and embarrassment which he suffered as a result of the article. Several attorneys testified at trial that calling a lawyer a Communist would be highly injurious to professional reputation. One witness, Albert Jenner, testified that he had heard the defamatory statements about Gertz repeated.

Besides, I had clearly met the standards set forth by the Supreme Court for proof of actual injuries "not solely measured by out-of-pocket economic loss."

It was a wholly satisfying opinion. In some respects, it was superior to the 1974 Supreme Court ruling.

After the court of appeals ruled in our favor, the defendant petitioned for a rehearing and suggested that the case be reheard by the entire court (*en banc*) rather than by the original panel of three judges. Its counsel contended that the opinion misapplied the law-of-the-case doctrine, because the issue of actual malice had been fully litigated previously and was a necessary part of prior decisions by the district court, the court of appeals, and the Supreme Court. The Supreme Court had no need to remand the case for retrial unless it found that actual malice had not been proved at the first trial. The opinion of the court of appeals, it claimed, was directly contrary to the law regarding what constitutes actual malice.

The petition was eloquent in its appeal for caution:

In its earlier opinion this Court recognized the dangers to free speech which can arise when a court allows disagreement with political philosophy to influence its decision making. Here the panel has used its obvious distaste for the political opinions of Stang as the basis for its holding that Stanley had a subjective awareness of the falsity of an article which did not even contain those opinions. Special caution should be used by this Court in considering this Petition for Rehearing, with Suggesion for Rehearing *En Banc*. For, as was stated previously, "[w]hether we are moved to applaud or to despise what is said, our duty to defend the right to speak remains the same." 471 F2d at 808.

No oral argument is heard in connection with such a petition, and only on rare occasions does the court grant one. It was not surprising, therefore, that the court handed down an adverse ruling on September 15, 1982: "On June 30, 1982, Robert Welch, Inc., filed a petition for rehearing with suggestion for rehearing *en banc*. All of the judges of the original panel have voted to deny the petition, and none of the active members of the court has requested a vote on the petition. The petition is therefore DENIED."

Defendant was confronted with a potentially disastrous situation when judgment was rendered against it by the court of appeals on June 21, 1982. While it clearly had the right to appeal to the Supreme Court, the judgment was in full force and effect unless it was stayed (suspended) by posting of the required bond or by court order, and I could proceed in any lawful manner to collect what was owing to me. I could seize property, garnishee, issue citations, and do all of the usual things to learn what assets of the defendant were available and to obtain them or their proceeds.

After we had taken various steps to collect the judgment, the defendant moved for a stay of execution. It contended that the appeal involved substantial issues, was not frivolous, and was not intended for the purpose of delaying payment of the judgment. It filed an affidavit to indicate that its only substantial property was located in Massachusetts where the law permitted a stay until affirmance. Meanwhile, we asked Judge Flaum to set an appeal bond for the defendant. We had learned that the defendant owned paintings valued by it at $79,268; that substantial sums were owing to it by various parties, including no less than $1,287,585 from the John Birch Society; and that there were funds in its banking account. We said that defendant's assets should be turned over to us; we would deposit all sums so received in an interest-bearing account until the determination of the appeal or further order of the court.

Almost frantically, the defendant responded to our petition for a turn-over order, and we replied to it as we did not want to chance that the fruits of our efforts to slip away from us. Judge Flaum gave his usual careful consideration to the matter and filed a carefully wrought opinion in which he held that regardless of where the defendant's property might be located or the law in such locations, the court had jurisdiction over the defendant and could order a turnover. He therefore instructed us to submit to him an appropriate order.

By this time, the defendant was prepared to agree to such an order if some of its harshness was modified. It agreed to put up a deed of conveyance granting legal title to its real estate in Massachusetts, free and clear of all liens and encumbrances. This deed would be deposited with the clerk of our district court, together with the sum of $5,000, to be held by him until final decision upon the appeal was rendered or the court issued a further order. The defendant would not encumber the property in any way, and it would pay all taxes and assessments. It would then have ninety days after an upholding of our judgment to pay in full; otherwise, the deed could be registered, the property sold, and the proceeds applied to discharge the judgment. It was not a perfect arrangement but was fair in the circumstances since we felt that the real estate was sufficient to satisfy our judgment.

So the defendant's last route of escape was filing an appeal in the Supreme Court of the United States. This it did under date of December 14, 1982. It must have realized that its chances of prevailing were slight. The highest court does not grant many such writs, and the odds of its taking any case it has previously considered are slim indeed. But David Machanic and his associates were persistent and resourceful, and they had nothing else to do unless they were to surrender to us and pay our judgment, with costs and interest.

In the very first paragraph of its petition, defendant summed up the issue, as it had to do if it was to prevail:

The Court of Appeals concluded that the editor of petitioner's journal of conservative political opinion acted with reckless disregard of the truth because objectively he must have had "obvious reasons" to doubt the accuracy of the disputed article, which was authored by a freelance writer, and therefore should have investigated the article further. The "obvious reasons" which the Court of Appeals found to require further investigation were what is called the "unreasonable" political views of the freelance writer. The Court of Appeals imposed this duty of investigation even though subjectively the editor had confidence in the freelance writer and agreed with his views.

Stated more succinctly, the defendant complained that in direct conflict with the Supreme Court's prior decisions, the courts below had used an objective rather than a subjective standard in determining the existence of actual malice. It contended that to call a person a Marxist, Leninist, or Communist-fronter in the circumstances of this case, was to express a constitutionally protected opinion rather than to state a fact. It also contended that damage to my reputation had not been proved. In essence, it was saying that in 1974 the Supreme Court had remanded the case to give us the opportunity to prove negligence and actual injury. Thus, the issue of actual malice could no longer be considered; the doctrine of the law of the case precluded our doing so.

Wayne came at once to the basic conflict, pointing out that virtually none of the questions the petitioner said had been presented had been raised in the courts below. Furthermore, he continued, the questions presented by the petitioner were not based upon the record below but upon distorted views of the evidence and the opinion of the court of appeals.

Then Wayne stated one basic issue with the utmost clarity:

Whether the self-serving statements of a defendant may insulate it from liability in a defamation case where the objective evidence shows that any person would have had reason to doubt the veracity of the damaging and harmful statements made by a publisher in undue haste after having conceived the story line itself, carefully selected an author known for his propensity to label persons as Communists or Communist-fronters and then furnishing the author with information to be used as the basis for the story.

He then summed up what the case was about and how it had proceeded. Wayne simply stated objectively what had been determined.

The defendant's reply memorandum repeated more briefly what it had said in its original petition and downplayed what we had contended. We could not afford to be cocksure, but we felt that the defendant was unlikely to undermine our judgment.

We were not disappointed. The Supreme Court denied the appeal rather promptly, and our long travail was at an end. The supreme irony was that my earlier defeat had ultimately meant a greater victory: an award eight times greater than the original judgment. All the delay, expense, uncertainty, heartache, and agony were mercifully forgotten as we rejoiced.

In my home there is a picture of two broadly smiling men — the older, myself; the younger, Wayne B. Giampietro. We are holding a check just received from Robert Welch, Inc., in the sum due on my judgment. Lest there be any remaining doubt, we placed a photostat of the check under the picture, legible enough for all to read. Now and then I look at the picture and check, and many who come to my home do so. Much of the money is now spent, but the satisfaction lingers.

When the check was sent to Wayne, the Welch people wrote to say they wished they could have paid the judgment in pennies. Perhaps they wished the judgment had been as small as the six cents awarded to Henry Ford in his famous libel suit against the *Chicago Tribune* a generation before. Perhaps they wished we had had to count thousands of coins. Perhaps they were simply trying to be funny. We never inquired.

As my case neared its conclusion, the Birch Society underwent basic changes in leadership. Robert Welch, who had founded the society a quarter of a century earlier, resigned the presidency and became chairman emeritus. During Welch's declining years, the society maintained a lower profile than in its heyday. It was criticized even by many conservatives, including President Reagan, whom Welch had described in characteristic fashion as a "lackey" of Communist conspirators.

Less than two years later, Welch was dead. He was succeeded in the leadership of the society by Lawrence P. McDonald of Georgia, a tireless proselytizer for the cause. His wife had divorced him, she said, because she was weary of the thousands who traipsed through their home in suburban Atlanta to hear her husband, a urologist and politician, talk about the society and its causes. Not long afterward, McDonald was a passenger on Korea Airlines Flight 007, which was shot down by a Soviet fighter. "The reason the aircraft was shot down," said McDonald's aide, "was because Congressman McDonald was a passenger." This explanation did not win general acceptance, but it seems characteristic of Bircher thinking.

According to Heldrich, I was paid chiefly from contributions by Birch Society members. In any event, publication of *American Opinion* ceased, its headquarters in Belmont, Massachusetts, was closed, and Stanley obtained employment with another conservative group.

The Birch Society did not disappear. It is now stationed in Appleton, Wisconsin, an implied tribute to red-baiting Senator

Joseph McCarthy whose home base was Appleton. It claims to have more supporters than in decades. It says it has thirty employees in its home office and forty-five field representatives across the country. It publishes advertisements in newspapers such as the *Chicago Sun-Times*, advancing its views. While much of the rest of our nation and the world applauds Gorbachev and Mandela, it still describes the Soviet leader as "an international criminal with the blood of millions on his hands" and calls Mandela "a heathen criminal terrorist." Thus, my victory did not silence the organization.

Perhaps nothing written about my final victory pleased me more than an editorial in the *Chicago Sun-Times* for March 3, 1983. I relished every word:

PERSISTENCE PAYS

It took 14 years, two trips to the Supreme Court and a landmark decision, but Chicago lawyer Elmer Gertz finally has the vindication he sought. We join in the cheers.

Long a champion of civil liberties, Gertz took exception to being labeled a "communist fronter," a "Marxist" and a "Leninist" in a 1969 article in American Opinion, the John Birch Society magazine. His initial libel suit resulted in a finding against the magazine and a $50,000 damage award. When the verdict was overturned, Gertz went to the Supreme Court, where he made some new law and won a new trial.

The 1981 retrial produced the same verdict and a bigger award of $400,000. Last week, the Supreme Court refused to hear an appeal by Robert Welch Inc., the publisher. Perhaps because of Elmer Gertz, our public discourse is a bit more civil.

It is extraordinary indeed for one of the media to applaud a victory in a libel case.

Later, when I collected the judgment from the defendant and decided to use part of the proceeds to finance a cruise around the world, the *Sun-Times* published the articles I forwarded from each major port. During succeeding years, I made other lengthy cruises and wrote additional travel articles for the *Sun-Times*. In the first article, I dwelt at length upon the legal victory as the source of financing for the journey. It was the source of much more.

14 ■ The Meaning of a Landmark Decision

Decided the same day as *Gertz*, another First Amendment case, *Miami Herald Publishing Co. v. Tornillo*, 418 U.S. 241, seemed to fly in the face of the reasoning implicit in my case. The issue was whether a state statute granting a political candidate a right to equal space to reply to criticism and attacks on his record by a newspaper violates the guarantee of a free press. Chief Justice Burger, delivering the opinion of the Court, declared:

> Even if a newspaper would face no additional costs to comply with a compulsory access law and would not be forced to forego publication of news or opinion by the inclusion of a reply, the Florida statute fails to clear the barriers of the First Amendment because of its intrusion into the function of editors.

"It has yet to be demonstrated," he continued, "how governmental regulation of this crucial [editorial] process can be exercised consistent with First Amendment guarantees of a free press as they have evolved up to this time."

While Justice White concurred this time in the Court's judgment, he had misgivings that were apparent in his dissenting opinion in *Gertz*. In *Tornillo* he said:

> Reaffirming the rule that the press cannot be forced to print an answer to a personal attack made of it, however, throws into stark relief the consequences of the new balance forged by the Court in the companion case also announced today. *Gertz v. Robert Welch, Inc.* . . . goes far toward eviscerating the effectiveness of the ordinary libel action, which has long been the only potent response available to the private citizen libeled by the press. Under *Gertz*, the burden of proving liability is immeasurably increased, proving damages is made exceedingly more difficult and vindicating reputation by merely proving falsehood and winning a judgment to that effect are wholly foreclosed. Needlessly, in my view, the Court trivializes and denigrates the interest in repu-

tation by removing virtually all the protection the law has always afforded.

Of course, these two decisions do not mean that because government may not dictate what the press is to print, neither can it afford a remedy for libel in any form. *Gertz* itself leaves a putative remedy for libel intact, albeit in severely emaciated form; and the press certainly remains liable for knowing or reckless falsehood under *New York Times Co. v. Sullivan* . . . and its progeny, however improper an injunction against publication might be.

Then he took a stronger line on the matter, which might be taken as an indication of what he might do in other situations involving the press:

To me it is a near absurdity to so deprecate individual dignity, as the Court does in *Gertz*, and to leave the people at the complete mercy of the press, at least in this stage of our history when the press, as the majority in this case so well documents, is steadily becoming more powerful and much less likely to be deterred by threats of libel suits.

Of course, such sentiments did not make Justice White popular with the press.

Another case was argued in tandem with *Gertz*. In *Old Dominion Branch No. 496 v. Austin*, 418 U.S. 264, the Supreme Court was more protective of harsh diatribes than in *Gertz*. In that case, three letter carriers who had refused to join a union were called "scabs, traitors, and men of low character and rotten principles." The Virginia courts had found these words actionable and awarded damages, but the U.S. Supreme Court reversed, holding that unions have the right to publish the names of "scabs" and to criticize them vehemently. Thus, the Court may still have been adding instability to an uncertain balance in the area of defamation.

Of course, the Supreme Court in my case did not answer all the questions that might arise in a libel action brought by a private person. One persistent question was whether the truth is always a defense, constitutionally speaking. It will be remembered that the constitution of Illinois declares truth a defense only when there are good faith and justifiable motives. In one of my cases, *Farnsworth v. Tribune Company*, the Illinois Supreme Court had declared this provision of the Illinois Constitution of 1870 federally unconstitutional because of *New York Times* and its progeny. But the convention that produced the constitution of 1970 had persisted in retaining this provision. Apparently, it would take a clear pronouncement of the U.S. Supreme Court to stifle the concept.

That Court has not yet explicitly made such a pronouncement, but Justice Powell, who wrote the Court's opinion in my case, wrote a concurring opinion in the important privacy case of *Cox Broadcasting Corp. v. Cohn*, 420 U.S. 469 (1975), in which he stated that my case had disposed of the matter, even though the Court had identified "as an 'open' question the issue of 'whether the First and Fourteenth Amendments require that truth be recognized as a defense in a defamation action brought by a private person as distinguished from a public official or a public figure.'" He went on to say:

> In some instances state actions that are denominated actions in defamation may in fact seek to protect citizens from injuries that are quite different from the wrongful damage to reputation flowing from false statements of fact. In such cases, the Constitution may permit a different balance to be struck. And, as today's opinion properly recognizes, causes of action grounded in a State's desire to protect privacy generally implicate interests that are distinct from those protected by defamation actions. But in cases in which the interests sought to be protected are similar to those considered in *Gertz* I view that opinion as requiring that the truth be recognized as a complete defense.

Until the Court by majority opinion says so, we cannot be as sure as Justice Powell is that truth constitutes a complete defense constitutionally.

Other questions were left unanswered by *Gertz*. Did it apply only to "publishers and broadcasters"—the media? Was there a different constitutional rule applicable to other publishers of defamatory material? Was a corporate plaintiff bound by *Gertz*? The Supreme Court has not spoken on these questions, but the state tribunals and lower federal courts have done so, with varying results. The tendency seems to be to extend the effects of my case to as many litigants as possible. This is seen especially in the basic issue of the case: Who is a private person, constitutionally speaking? The Supreme Court spoke clearly on this issue, despite the many law review notes, commentaries, and articles that questioned my designation as a private person. Ralph Otwell, then editor of the *Chicago Sun-Times*, spoke for many when he said that I was the most famous private person he had ever known. No one seems to remember that Justice Brennan, while dissenting generally, agreed with the majority of the Court that I was at the time of publication a private person. It may be that my case, because of the interest it aroused, did make me a public figure in some quarters. The academic and media views of this aspect of the case will be discussed later. Now it is clear that to the Court the concept of private person is fairly fixed. In only the rarest instance will the ordinary person be declared a public figure or public official.

The Court made this certain in a series of cases that followed mine. The first in time, and perhaps in importance, is *Time, Inc. v. Firestone*, 424 U.S. 448, decided in 1976, less than two years after my case was decided. Mary Alice Firestone and her husband had been involved in a sensational divorce case in which the trial judge had said that "neither party is domesticated." The judge had said that the marriage should be dissolved and had awarded Mrs. Firestone support. On the basis of newspaper and wire-service reports and information from a bureau chief and a "stringer," *Time* had said, briefly, that the husband had been granted a divorce "on the grounds of extreme cruelty and adultery." Mrs. Firestone asked for a retraction, and this was refused; thereupon, she brought a libel action and obtained a judgment for damages, affirmed by the Florida Supreme Court. *Time* carried the case to the U.S. Supreme Court.

Justice Rehnquist delivered the opinion of the Court:

Respondent did not assume any role of especial prominence in the affairs of society, other than perhaps Palm Beach society, and she did not thrust herself to the forefront of any particular public controversy in order to influence the resolution of the issues involved in it.

Petitioner contends that because the Firestone divorce was characterized by the Florida Supreme Court as a "cause célèbre," it must have been a public controversy and respondent must be considered a public figure. But in so doing petitioner seeks to equate "public controversy" with all controversies of interest to the public. Were we to accept this reasoning, we would reinstate the doctrine advanced in the plurality opinion in *Rosenbloom v. Metromedia, Inc.*, 403 U.S. 29 (1971), which concluded that the *New York Times* privilege should be extended to falsehoods defamatory of private persons whenever the statements concern matters of general or public interest. In *Gertz*, however, the Court repudiated this position, stating that "extension of the *New York Times* test proposed by the *Rosenbloom* plurality would abridge (a) legitimate state interest to a degree that we find unacceptable." 418 U.S. at 346.

Dissolution of a marriage through judicial proceedings is not the sort of "public controversy" referred to in *Gertz*, even though the marital difficulties of extremely wealthy individuals may be of interest to some portion of the reading public. Nor did respondent freely choose to publicize issues as to the propriety of her married life. She was compelled to go to court by the State in order to obtain legal release from the bonds of matrimony.

We hold respondent was not a "public figure" for the purpose of determining the constitutional protection afforded petitioner's report of the factual and legal basis for her divorce.

Rehnquist asserted that the details of most courtroom battles would add very little to the "uninhibited debate of public issues" that the First Amendment is designed to advance. And while a few participants may be legitimate public figures, most will have been drawn into the limelight against their will. Such individuals should not be made to give up their ordinary protections against defamation, he contended. He added, "We think *Gertz* provides an adequate safeguard for the constitutionally protected interests of the press and affords it a tolerable margin for error by requiring some type of fault."

Time had argued that the divorce decree was ambiguous. To this, Justice Rehnquist replied:

Petitioner may well argue that the meaning of the trial court's decree was unclear, but this does not license it to choose from among several conceivable interpretations the one most damaging to respondent. Having chosen to follow this tack petitioner must be able to establish not merely that the item reported was a conceivable or plausible interpretation of the decree, but that the item was factually correct.

The Court returned the case to the lower court for consideration of the issues of fault and damages.

It was notable that Mrs. Firestone had held press conferences and that there was much publicity about the case but that this did not destroy her status as a private person. Justice Marshall, who had gone along with the designation of me as a private person, dissented in this case because he considered Mrs. Firestone a public figure within the holding of my case as well as *Curtis Publishing Co. v. Butts*. He expressed his disagreement with the majority with considerable plausibility:

> We must assume that it was by choice that Mrs. Firestone became an active member of the "sporting set"—a social group with "especial prominence in the affairs of society," . . . whose lives receive constant media attention. Certainly there is nothing in the record to indicate otherwise, and Mrs. Firestone's subscription to a press clipping service suggests that she was not altogether uninterested in the publicity she received. Having placed herself in a position in which her activities were of interest to a significant segment of the public, Mrs. Firestone chose to initiate a lawsuit for separate maintenance, and most significantly, held several press conferences in the course of that lawsuit. If these actions for some reason fail to establish as a certainty that Mrs. Firestone "voluntarily exposed [herself] to increased risk of injury from defamatory falsehood," surely they are sufficient to entitle the press to act on the assumption that she did. Accordingly, Mrs. Firestone would appear to be a public figure under *Gertz*.
>
> The Court resists this result by concluding that the subject matter of the alleged defamation was not a "public controversy" as that term was used in *Gertz*. In part, the Court's conclusion rests on what I view as an understatement of the degree to which Mrs. Firestone can be said to have voluntarily acted in a manner that invited public attention.

The issue was further addressed in *Wolston v. Reader's Digest Association, Inc.*, 443 U.S. 157 (1979). Writing for the Court, Justice Rehnquist made it increasingly clear that normally plaintiffs in defamation suits would be regarded as private persons in the *Gertz* sense. Wolston had been involved peripherally in investigations of espionage and had been adjudged guilty of criminal contempt. These events were reported in the press, but gradually the publicity subsided, and Wolston largely returned to private life. Then, in 1974, *Reader's Digest* published excerpts from a book charging Wolston with having been a "Soviet agent in the U.S." Wolston sued for defamation, but the district court granted the defendant's motion for summary judgment on the ground that Wolston was a public figure involved in matters of public interest and could not establish malice on the part of the defendant. The Supreme Court, reversing the lower court, held that under *Gertz*,

Wolston was not a public figure but a private person whose technical offense did not have any effect on any issue of public concern. The Court said further that a person who engages in criminal conduct does not automatically become a public figure; to hold otherwise would create an "open season" for all who sought to defame persons convicted of a crime. This time, Justice Marshall concurred in the Court's opinion.

In *Hutchinson v. Proxmire*, 443 U.S. 111 (1979), a case decided the same day as *Wolston*, the Supreme Court again showed in the most forcible manner that it was adhering to the *Gertz* concept of a private person. In some respects, this case was an even more extreme example of how far the Court would go in departing from the older concepts of public figures and public officials. Dr. Hutchinson received research grants from various governmental agencies for investigation of the emotional behavior of certain animals. Senator William Proxmire, famous for his exposes of wasteful government spending, gave Hutchinson his Golden Fleece of the Month Award. Since the announcement was made on the floor of the Senate, it was constitutionally privileged speech. Then the senator mailed newsletters, appeared in a television interview program, and engaged in telephone calls on the subject. When Hutchinson sued for defamation, the district court granted summary judgment for the defendant and was affirmed by the court of appeals. The Supreme Court reversed and remanded, holding that the speech or debate clause of the Constitution does not protect transmittal of information by individual members of Congress by press release and newspapers and that Hutchinson was a private person, not a public figure, and therefore did not have to prove malice.

Chief Justice Burger delivered the opinion of the Court. He stated the issues: "The petition for certiorari raised three questions. One involves the scope of the Speech or Debate Clause; another involves First Amendment claims; a third concerns the appropriateness of summary judgment, embracing both a constitutional issue and a state-law issue." We need not go into every aspect of the Court's reasoning but will state the conclusion regarding the alleged constitutional grant of congressional privilege: "We are unable to discern any 'conscious choice' to grant immunity for defamatory statements scattered far and wide by mail, press, and the electronic media."

On the public- or private-figure aspect of the case, the chief justice was clear:

> It is not contended that Hutchinson attained such prominence that he is a public figure for all purposes. Instead, respondents have argued that the District Court and the Court of Appeals were correct in holding that Hutchinson is a public figure for the limited purpose of comment on his receipt of federal funds for research projects. That conclusion was based upon two factors: first, Hutchinson's successful application for federal funds and the reports in local newspapers of the federal grants; second, Hutchinson's access to the media, as demonstrated by the fact that some newspapers and wire services reported his response to the announcement of the Golden Fleece Award. Neither of those factors demonstrates that Hutchinson was a public figure prior to the controversy engendered by the Golden Fleece Award; his access, such as it was, came after the alleged libel.

Hutchinson's activities were similar to those of "countless members of his profession," who cannot all be classified as public figures. Also, he "did not thrust himself or his views into public controversy to influence others." In fact, no particular controversy was identified. Rather, the issue had to do with public expenditures—surely a broadly based concern. "The 'use of such subject-matter classifications to determine the extent of constitutional protection afforded defamatory falsehoods may too often result in an improper balance between the competing interests in this area.' *Time, Inc. v. Firestone, supra,* at 456." Hutchinson attained public prominence only as a result of the Golden Fleece award, and "clearly, those charged with defamation cannot, by their own conduct, create their own defense by making the claimant a public figure."

In a footnote, the chief justice observed that inquiry into a defendant's state of mind to obtain proof of actual malice "does not readily lend itself to summary judgment." This was possibly a fatal blow to the practice of too readily awarding summary judgments in defamation cases to defendants, for the most part media people—the same people who had succeeded in imposing the innocent-construction rule in Illinois.

Clearly, my case gave breathing space to both the press and defamed individuals. However, as far as I know, there has not been any proliferation of libel litigation. It is simply that the individual whose reputation has been defamed has a fighting chance to prevail. He still has a great burden, and the odds are still in favor of the defamer. The media have perhaps exercised a greater degree of care. I see no harm in that. Responsibility never hurt anyone, including the press.

When I speak to journalism students and practitioners, as I often do, I give a simple example to illustrate my viewpoint. "Let us assume," I say, "that word has just come in to one of our great newspapers of an earthshaking event. It pushes the story through the presses and onto its delivery trucks. The drivers are so eager to get the story to the public that they rush through the streets, breaking all speed records and ignoring other traffic rules. As a result, they hit and kill a gifted child. Should they be permitted to defend on the grounds of the freedom of the press and the public's need to know? Of course not. Like all persons, they have to exercise due care. This is not an infringement of the freedom of the press. It is the necessary exercise of the kind of restraint and responsibility that all of us must exercise."

I then drive home the moral: "Reputations and privacy must be protected by the press. The First Amendment is not a license for riding roughshod on the streets or elsewhere."

This brings us at last to the case of *Herbert v. Lando*. Lieutenant Colonel Anthony Herbert, a military hero, sued CBS, those connected with its "60 Minutes" program, and the *Atlantic Monthly*. He charged that they had defamed him by making serious and false charges impugning his veracity, integrity, and military record. He accepted the burden of being a public figure and set out to prove actual malice through extensive pretrial discovery. He got a good deal of material that way, but the defendants objected to answering questions relating to the editorial or mental processes by which they arrived at the conclusions expressed in the program and the magazine article, the conclusions alleged to be defamatory. Herbert wanted this information because he believed it would show the reasoning behind their charges to be so frivolous and insubstantial as to constitute reckless disregard of the truth—actual malice. The defendants claimed that their First Amendment rights would be violated if they had to answer.

The trial court sided with Herbert. A divided Second Circuit reversed in favor of the defendants, Judge Irving Kaufman writing the sort of First Amendment sanctification in which the media delight. A strong-willed Herbert appealed, and the Supreme Court took the case.

It was clear that the press feared what the Court might do. Since *Gertz*, the majority of the Court had expressed itself on occasion as not impressed by the claim of the press for extraordinary status. The chief justice, particularly, seemed to show hostility. In one case, the court said that the media had no greater right than a private individual to pry into prison conditions. In *Houchins v. KQED* (1978), Chief Justice Burger wrote somewhat caustically: "Inmates in jails, prisons or mental institutions retain certain fundamental rights of privacy; they are not like animals in a zoo to be filmed and photographed at will by the public or the media reporters, however 'educational' the process may be for others." In *Zurcher v. Stanford Daily*, decided during the same term, the Court declared that newspaper offices may be searched and material seized under a warrant issued on probable cause and that the First Amendment does not require the issuance of a subpoena rather than a warrant. In this same period, the courts decided that neither Farber, a reporter, nor his employer, the *New York Times*, had the constitutional right to withhold sources in connection with a criminal trial and might be held in contempt for so doing. The Supreme Court refused to grant a review in this situation, purportedly to the loudly expressed delight of the chief justice.

Justice White wrote the opinion for the *Herbert* majority. "The evidentiary burden Herbert must carry to prove at least reckless disregard for the truth is substantial indeed," said White, "and we are unconvinced that his chances of winning an undeserved verdict are such that any inquiry into what Lando learned or said during the editorial process must be foreclosed." The opinion analyzed the First Amendment in the context of these heavy requirements of proof in a defamation action by a public figure and concluded that like every other defendant or witness in similar circumstances, those connected with the media must respond to appropriate questioning.

Thus, the harshness of the earlier rulings of the Court in this area has been mitigated, and the Court has taken another step in reinstating reputational rights, regardless of the status of the defamer or the defamed. Despite some editorial outcries, the Court has achieved a just and beneficial result. We ought not to decry what it has done because it is the Burger rather than the Warren

Court. The pendulum, having swung too far in one direction, is now moderating its position, as happens in all institutions.

After my case was decided, the various jurisdictions had to decide what standard of fault to adopt. It became apparent that most would choose simple negligence. As of this writing, thirty-three jurisdictions now have this standard; more are likely in future reckonings, for such is the direction of the law. Others stood by the *Rosenbloom* standard in which matters of general interest require proof of malice—Alaska, Colorado, Indiana, and Michigan. New York chose a standard between negligence and actual malice—"gross negligence." The others could be classified as undecided but showing a tendency to require less than actual malice; these include Alabama, Connecticut, Georgia, Iowa, Louisiana, and Montana. It is always possible that some of the courts may flip-flop, but the general direction is clear. In order to prevail in defamation suits, private persons, generously defined, will have to prove only negligence—and actual injuries.

On November 25, 1975, the Illinois Supreme Court handed down its ruling on the standard of care required of publishers in defamation cases involving private persons in *Troman v. Wood*, 340 N.E.2d 292, involving a reporter for the *Chicago Sun-Times* and Field Enterprises, Inc., its publisher. The defendant's motion to dismiss the complaint was granted in the lower court, and the appeal by the plaintiff was transferred to the Illinois Supreme Court from the intermediate appellate court, as is done in more important cases, especially when constitutional issues are involved.

The article had described the plaintiff's home as headquarters for a burglary gang. A photograph of the house had a caption that might have indicated that the plaintiff was connected with the gang. Justice Walter V. Schaefer wrote the opinion of the court, from which there was no dissent: "The central issue on this appeal concerns the standard of liability which should be imposed for libel in the light of the recent decision of the Supreme Court of the United States in *Gertz v. Robert Welch, Inc.* The court went through the by now familiar analysis of the law since *New York Times*. It then went on to say:

In the present case the trial court assumed for the purpose of its decision that the plaintiff was a private individual rather than a public figure. Nevertheless it held, notwithstanding *Gertz*, that actual malice had to be alleged and proved because the article in question concerned a matter of general public interest. For reasons that will be discussed, we do not agree.

Here a rather unusual situation was presented:

The complaint in the present case was cast in the language of strict liability. It did not allege actual malice, negligence or any other ground of liability. The complaint as drawn was therefore legally insufficient, whether the *New York Times* or some other standard is to govern. In such a situation we would ordinarily affirm the judgment of dismissal regardless of our disagreement with the views expressed by the trial court. In this case, however, the plaintiff's attorney had informed the trial judge of his willingness to amend the complaint to allege grounds of liability short of actual malice, but the trial judge dismissed the complaint because the plaintiff would not allege the *New York Times* standard of "actual malice"—that is, with knowledge of its falsity or with reckless disregard of whether it was false or not. (376 U.S. at 279-80, 84 S. Ct. at 726.) It has been stipulated before this court that the complaint is to be treated as though it had been amended to allege in the alternative "negligence, gross negligence or malpractice" on the part of the defendant, and on that basis we proceed.

This was indicative of the court's desire to fix the standard of fault in Illinois as soon as possible.

The court stated the position of the defendant publisher critically:

The defendant concedes that the Federal Constitution does not require Illinois to apply the *New York Times* standard. Nevertheless the defendant urges that we should now adopt that standard as a matter of State policy. The arguments in support of that position lean heavily on the adverse effect on freedom of the press which would supposedly follow in the absence of the actual malice standard. But the extent to which liability for defamation adversely affects freedom of speech and press is a Federal constitutional question, and it has been authoritatively determined by the Supreme Court that a standard of liability less rigorous than that of actual malice will not impermissibly abridge that freedom. In deciding what standard of liability shall now apply to defamatory publications, our function is not to make an independent reappraisal of the requirements of the first amendment, but rather to ascertain whether there is any basis in Illinois law which would prevent the application here of the general principle that a person is responsible for damage that he intentionally or negligently inflicts upon another.

Here and throughout the opinion, the court ignored *Farnsworth v. Tribune Co.*, not even mentioning it, as if that case, earlier lost by me, did not afford a basis to arrive at the proper standard. It should also have noted that the attorney for the plaintiff in *Wood* would have settled for a standard higher than simple negligence but less than malice. The court, it will be seen, gave him and other private persons a bonus, so to speak.

The court went through the relevant provisions in the present and past constitutions of Illinois and concluded that the state had from the outset recognized as fundamental the rights of enjoying and defending reputation. (Why, then, *Farnsworth*?) With his usual persuasiveness, Justice Schaefer summed up the situation as the court saw it:

The constitutionally recognized interest of the individual in his reputation is not and cannot be measured solely in terms of monetary compensation. At the least, the individual has an interest in preserving and restoring his reputation through an authoritative and publicly known determination that an injurious statement about him is in fact false. To foreclose or restrict the availability of the judicial process as a means of securing such a determination prevents the individual from obtaining the effective vindication to which he is entitled.

Justice Schaefer then answered and rejected the arguments of the defendant in the light of Illinois constitutional policy. It is clear that his sympathies, and the court's, favored the defamed private person. One paragraph disposed of what the plaintiff had been willing to concede:

It is suggested that, in lieu of ordinary negligence, liability should be limited to instances of either gross negligence or willful and wanton misconduct. We do not believe that this limitation is either necessary or appropriate. The law of defamation is already complex and multi-faceted, and it would not profit by the introduction of a distinction based upon differing degrees of fault. See Prosser, Law of Torts, pp. 180-185 (4th ed. 1971).

He also rejected Justice Harlan's notion of "journalistic malpractice," shrewdly observing that it might lead toward a progressive depreciation of the standard of care.

> We hold, therefore, that in a suit brought by a private individual to recover actual damages for a defamatory publication whose substantial danger to reputation is apparent, recovery may be had upon proof that the publication was false, and that the defendant either knew it to be false, or, believing it to be true, lacked reasonable grounds for that belief. We hold further that negligence may form the basis of liability regardless of whether or not the publication in question related to a matter of public or general interest. Our holding in the present case is, of course, not intended to remove any of the absolute or qualified privileges which have heretofore been recognized in this State to the extent that the facts may warrant their application.

So Illinois aligned itself with the majority regarding the requisite degree of fault, repudiating *Farnsworth* without mentioning it. I had won a belated victory in that unfortunate case without directly reaping the benefit of it, nor was there any gain for my client Dr. Farnsworth.

One of the greatest names in the history of Illinois jurisprudence is Walter V. Schaefer, long a justice of the Illinois Supreme Court and for several years its chief justice. More than any other member of the court, he helped elevate it from the disregard in which it was held by such scholars as Dean Wigmore, who once declared that the Alabama and Illinois supreme courts were the worst in the nation. As we have seen, Justice Schaefer wrote the opinion in *Troman*. He delivered the distinguished Coen Lecture at the University of Colorado on April 19, 1980, which was published as the lead article in the *University of Colorado Law Review* (Fall 1980, vol. 52, issue 1) under the title "Defamation and the First Amendment." This is a very important statement, chiefly for Illinois lawyers and litigants but for others as well. After a careful analysis of the case law, Justice Schaefer reached a conclusion sharply differing from that of many other enlightened students.

His first suggestion "would be to return the law of defamation to its *pre-Times* condition. This would put an end to the depreciation and disparagement of the citizen's right to his reputation that has resulted from the Supreme Court's recent construction of the first amendment." This line of opinions had hampered "the participation of individual citizens in public discussions and public affairs." It had eroded "the right of the public to know whether the statements that have been published about the character of their public officials and public figures are true or false." If public persons could ever effectively counteract defamation through superior access to the media, that access had been substantially impaired by *Tornillo*.

Schaefer also urged that punitive damages be eliminated. But recognizing that obstacles to this approach might have become insurmountable, he had an alternative suggestion: "If it proves impossible to eradicate the *Times* line of cases, a declaratory judgment as to the falsity of a defamatory statement should be available."

Currently a maligned person could not be vindicated unless he could also make a case strong enough to collect damages. Schaefer argued that there should be a remedy that did not involve monetary compensation but simply set forth the truth to clear a clouded reputation. Of course, he continued, "a favorable declaratory judgment, buried in the files of the clerk of the court, is scant comfort to one whose reputation has been falsely attacked. But it is vindication for the victim, and certainly it is far better than the misleading judgment for the defendant which must now follow in the absence of a declaration of falsity."

In any discussion of Illinois commentary on *Gertz*, Wayne B. Giampietro's article must be given a special place. "The Constitutional Rules of Defamation" won second place in the 1975 Lincoln Award legal writing contest sponsored by the Young Lawyers Section of the Illinois State Bar Association. It was published in the *Illinois Bar Journal* (September 1975, vol. 64, no. 1). The article begins with one of the most persuasive expositions of the difficulties and virtues of defamation cases that I have ever read:

> Few areas of the law give rise to more unusual fact situations and problems than the field of defamation. Such suits, be they libel or slander, are perhaps the most difficult to appraise in terms of whether to commence suit, whether to settle, and for what amount.
> The difficulties in dealing with such suits arise from the nature of the rights sought to be vindicated. In such cases there is no tangible

physical damage which may be demonstrated by photographs or paid bills. Yet, a broken arm will mend, a lost contract may be replaced. A destroyed reputation may never be repaired. The results of damage to a good name are never-ending, but difficult to pin down. The grapevine has many far-reaching tendrils. What is the value of a lost friend, a missed job opportunity? The ramifications are many, varied and incalculable, each case depending upon the individual and his unique place in time and station.

Wayne then presented an analytical history of defamation, particularly since *New York Times*, culminating in an account of my case in which I figure as an unnamed attorney:

> It will be noted that while the Supreme Court has stated what states cannot do in the way of compensating victims of defamatory statements, it has not set down any guidelines as to what they must do....
>
> As noted above, for the most part, the rules applicable to defamation in the United States are judicially created, rather than statutory. While it is too early to tell exactly what the various courts will do in evolving the new rules applicable to defamation, the decisions of the past give us a reasonable basis for prediction. The courts have developed a series of degrees of fault, through the establishment of various privileges for various defendants, abuse of which must be shown by the plaintiff in order to obtain recovery. It would appear that the new rules of the future will evolve out of these prior decisions.

His eyes on our case, he said:

> Proof of fault, be it negligence, or willful and wanton conduct, should present little problem. The courts have dealt with these definitions in numerous types of cases. The kinds of factors to be considered will be such things as, what was the source of the information, did the defendant make any attempt to verify the information, and what kind of effort, and did the defendant continue to repeat the statements after receiving notice that the statements were false.
>
> Certainly, actions for defamation are far from impossible to bring successfully under these rulings.... The amount is still left, in large part, to the discretion of the jury. So long as the damage award is not egregiously out of keeping with the statements made of and concerning the plaintiff, any such award is likely to be upheld.

His conclusion, while reasonable, is not accepted everywhere:

It should be noted, however, that the rules set down in *Gertz v. Welch* apply to those situations involving the press and the broadcast media. They do not necessarily apply to all alleged defamation situations. There is still a considerable area in which the traditional rules of defamation apply, and are not subject to the limitations first set down in *New York Times*. The entire thrust of the *New York Times* rationale was toward a free press, including the broadcast media. Other areas are not affected by the decisions. Purely private communications between individuals are not covered. Nor are matters which fall within a business context, such as credit reports. As to these areas, the traditional rules apply and have not been changed.

It should be noted that Wayne wrote his article years before the *Greenmoss* case, and he highlighted much that the later case was to emphasize, as we shall see later.

Comments on the case by the Illinois law journals are especially important since the case arose there. *Northwestern University Law Review* published a lengthy comment in its January–February 1975 issue (vol. 69, no. 6), under the expansive title "Defamation Law in the Wake of Gertz v. Robert Welch, Inc.: The Impact on State Law and the First Amendment." The article is well written, well thought out, but its basic conclusion is demonstrably false. The authors opine that "it would seem that *Gertz* diminishes rather than enhances the possibility for a plaintiff to prosecute a successful libel action." The subsequent history of *Gertz* and libel litigation would indicate otherwise.

Loyola University of Chicago Law Journal, in its comment on *Gertz* (Winter 1975, vol. 6, no. 1), expressed the thought that the Court might be using "the substantial danger to reputation terminology to qualify what they mean by liability without fault." It believed also that "by allowing recovery for emotional damage as actual damage," the character of the tort of defamation had been changed. By way of conclusion, the author of the comment, Steven Michael Levin, agreed with my libel opponent and friend Don Reuben that the *Gertz* decision is like a mongrel pup: "You don't know what it is going to be like until it grows up."

Professor Richard C. Turkington, writing in the *DePaul Law Review* (Winter 1975, vol. 24, no. 2), believed that the Supreme Court decision in my case would result, within a reasonably short time, in significant increases in private defamation suits. He thought the decision would "significantly undermine freedom of the press."

My initial opponent in the *Zeinfeld* libel case, Robert F. Hanley, wrote about my case in the July–August 1975 (vol. 57, no. 1) issue of *Chicago Bar Record* under the suggestive subtitle "Radical Changes in the Law of Libel." In his view, the decision obliterated the Illinois distinction between libel per se (damages assumed) and per quod (extrinsic proof required), since all libel now required proof of injury. With negligence as a standard, he asked, would there be a place for *res ipsa loquitur* ("the facts speak for themselves") and for contributory negligence? The latter question seems to have been answered affirmatively; the former is not yet definitively answered.

The John Marshall Journal of Practice and Procedure, published by the law school at which I teach, had articles on my case in two issues—a student casenote (Spring 1975, vol. 8, no. 3) and an article by Professor Michael J. Pelelle (Winter 1977–78, vol. 11, no. 2). The earlier casenote, by Daniel A. Weiler, stated that the *Gertz* opinion "may easily be misinterpreted" and that the issues "may be far from settled." On the whole, he thought, the *Gertz* opinion swung the scales in favor of the defamed private individual. Professor Pelelle's article, "The Unconstitutionality of the Qualified Truth Defense to Libel Actions," was largely based on my case and *New York Times*. It invites far more study than my comment here.

It is important to point out regarding all such commentary that the validity of the observations and conclusions depends largely upon when the material was published. The first comments are less likely to be valid than later ones, which had the benefit of the ensuing cases in the Supreme Court and the lower courts and the lengthier contemplation of legal scholars.

After the Illinois Supreme Court handed down its decision in *Troman v. Wood*, in which it found that simple negligence suffices to establish liability in defamation cases involving private persons, some of the Illinois law journals took a second look at *Gertz* while assessing the effect of *Troman*. Notable in this respect were *The University of Illinois Law Forum* (vol. 1977, no. 1) and the *Chicago Bar Record* (September–October 1976, vol. 58, no. 2). The latter journal is published by the Chicago Bar Association. John C. McMullen, a prominent practitioner, concluded that the problem of libel was "well resolved by the *Gertz* majority opinion." The court decided that there was no overriding public policy recognized in Illinois requiring a standard of malice or gross negligence in defamation cases involving private persons. This position, said McMullen, "has solid support in the tradition of the common law." The Illinois law, traditionally "complex and multifaceted," was made more so by the U.S. Supreme Court until *Gertz* and *Troman* clarified the situation. The *Illinois Law Forum* note, by Joffrey R. Tone, continued to see *Gertz*, and consequently *Troman*, as inhibiting the press yet simultaneously limiting the chances of recovery by plaintiffs. I have said, half seriously, that I know less about my case than I once did since reading the many contradictory articles about it.

The *Southern Illinois University Law Journal* (vol. 1979, no. 1) had a surprising article, "The Impact of *Gertz* in the Law of Libel in Illinois," by Professors Harry W. Stonecipher and Robert Trager, coauthors of *The Mass Media and the Law in Illinois* (1976). The authors considered the limiting effect of *Gertz* on the constitutional privilege of the media and, as the title suggests, the impact of the decision on Illinois libel law. They contended that the decision had had only a slight impact on Illinois libel law and found the need for some clarification. They examined more than forty-five reported defamation cases in the Illinois courts since the *Gertz* holding in 1974 and concluded that the common law was far from dead, largely because these cases involved nonmedia defendants and because of Illinois's peculiar innocent-construction rule.

I took great joy when *Student Lawyer*, the organ of the student division of the American Bar Association, asked me to do a feature article on my case not long after the Supreme Court handed down its opinion. The article appeared in the October 1975 issue (vol. 4, no. 2). This is the article that I began with "As I tell my law students, I am no longer a mere person. I am a legal landmark. The metamorphosis occurred in this fashion." The editors told me that this was the most provocative beginning of an article they had ever seen. Of course, I had to be circumspect because the case was still pending. The defense counsel did complain, unconvincingly, about this article and another that *Student Lawyer* published five years later in September 1980 (vol. 9, no. 1). This lead article, by Grant Pick, was entitled "He's Earned a Moral Fortune." I take special pride in two passages:

The *Welch* decision came a few years before Gertz abandoned full-time practice, but it marked for him a kind of capstone to his reputation. It is, after all, a precedent-setting case that lawyers may be relying on when the names of Ruby and Leopold have evaporated to mere historical footnotes. "*Welch* is the last word on the defamation of public figures and excuses for libel," attests University of Chicago law professor Philip Kurland. "Gertz regards himself now as a kind of maker of libel law as a result of that decision," observes law professor Jon Waltz of Northwestern University, "and it *is* an important case."

Waltz, as it turned out, was one of the star witnesses in the retrial of my case.

The other passage:

Gertz's forte, both in and out of court, always has been preparation. He *knows*. "One of the things my success indicates," he says, "is that you don't win cases on brilliance, but because you are thoroughly prepared and interested. Usually, it's just hard work." His skills earn him high marks from those who aren't usually wont to give them. "Elmer has always been an able, dedicated, tenacious opponent who has my highest respect and affection," gushes Chicago lawyer Don Reuben, against whom Gertz fought a slew of libel cases and who himself is known as a legal barracuda.

Shortly after John Paul Stevens was named by President Gerald Ford to fill the vacancy on the Supreme Court caused by the retirement of Justice William O. Douglas, Illinois governor Dan Walker tendered a dinner in Stevens's honor. It was to be expected that there would be such a dinner as the new justice was a member of a distinguished Chicago family, had graduated from the University of Chicago and the Law School of Northwestern University, had practiced law with a well-regarded Chicago firm, and had served as a respected member of the U.S. Court of Appeals for the Seventh Circuit in Chicago. President Ford had been praised for selecting a moderate like Stevens rather than an ideologue, as some had expected in view of Ford's previous efforts to have Douglas impeached. The choice was readily confirmed by the Senate.

I was delighted when the governor invited my wife and me, and I joined the many others who were seeking to congratulate the new justice. When he saw me, he smiled broadly. As he shook my hand, he said, "You are the only attorney who has reversed me in the Supreme Court." He then added: "We decided your case as we did because we thought that was the direction the law was going in defamation cases." A few days later, I got a letter from Justice Stevens to the same effect, with the semihumorous addition "You must have been pretty good to have reversed me."

This episode caused me to ponder other justices of the highest court. Justice Douglas, who dissented in our case, I had met on several occasions, especially noteworthy being the time when I presided at a dinner in honor of former president Truman and Douglas had been one of the speakers. I had known Justice Marshall when we were both young lawyers. He had joined with the majority in my case. I had met Chief Justice Warren, who had retired from the court years previously. I was not sure how he would have voted in the case, but I am reasonably certain that my old and cherished friend Arthur J. Goldberg would have dissented, with much personal sorrow, because he and Justices Douglas, Black, and Brennan were generally opposed to libel cases as an infringement on the essential freedom of the press. They felt that a completely free press was essential to a free society.

Not too long after the Supreme Court had ruled in my favor, I attended a convention of the First Amendment Lawyers' Association in Atlanta. A radio station asked me to be interviewed by their talk-show host. In the reception room I was confronted by Scott Stanley, Jr., still the managing editor of *American Opinion*. Despite the pummeling we had given him, we greeted each other pleasantly enough. He was interviewed before I was; we were not public opponents on the program, although certainly the views we expressed were opposed. Stanley remarked, "When the case is over, I would love to talk with you." I am still awaiting that choice opportunity, although Stanley was belabored even more in the second trial than in the first. During a recess toward the end of the later trial, Stanley turned to me in a surprisingly friendly fashion and said, "My daughter is a student of Professor Peter Viereck at Mount Holyoke College and likes him very much." He then asked me about my book dealing with Peter's once notorious father, George Sylvester Viereck, a poet, propagandist, and personality of a forgotten era. I thought of the parallels between the elder Viereck, Stang, and Stanley. All three were quick to see the menace of communism, regardless of whether it existed in the particular situation of which they wrote. I felt that what differentiated

Viereck from Stang or Stanley was that while Viereck could be the spokesman for a Communist Germany just as readily as he had been a propagandist for the kaiser's Germany, the Weimar Republic, and Hitler's Third Reich, I could not imagine Stang or Stanley defending communism or Communists in any circumstances.

Gertz, together with extensive commentary on it, is included in all law-school casebooks and treatises on torts, constitutional law, media law, professional responsibility, and various other areas. Virtually every reported defamation case since *Gertz* has referred to it, sometimes at length. State and regional examinations for admission to the bar contain questions and problems arising from *Gertz*, as do law-school examinations. It is the subject of moot-court and appellate competitions in the law schools, discussed in legal and media seminars and meetings. In the *Ten-Year Supplement* (1976–77) to *Freedom of the Press*, a bibliocyclopedia edited by Dr. Ralph E. McCoy, there are many references to *Gertz*, consisting largely of articles in media and legal publications. Since then, of course, many other articles have appeared.

The case has also affected my personal life. I have been invited to speak on the case and on media matters at all the Chicago law schools, Princeton, Wisconsin, Florida State, St. Louis, Washington, Ball State, and elsewhere. Years ago, strangers used to ask how my client was getting along; they meant Nathan Leopold, whom I had helped free from a long imprisonment. Now they ask me about *Gertz*. Virtually all seem to rejoice with me in the result.

The Practicing Law Institute (PLI), the organization that schools lawyers and laymen in contemporary legal problems, held a seminar on communications law in November 1975. A substantial segment of the handbook was devoted to post-*Gertz* libel law, discussed by Carleton G. Eldridge, Sr., of Coudert Brothers. Another segment was devoted to post-*Gertz* libel practice and tactics, discussed by Robert W. Meserve, former president of the American Bar Association. The post-*Gertz* libel-law portion of the program dealt with my case, the post-*Gertz* decisions, the treatment of *Gertz* in the *Restatement* of the law, and libel insurance.

Then, late in 1980, PLI published a lengthy treatise, *Libel, Slander and Related Problems*, by Robert D. Sack, a distinguished specialist in press law who had participated in each annual PLI communications-law program since the inception of the series in 1973. Here, of course, an enormous space is devoted to *Gertz*. It becomes clear from this treatise that the law of defamation is dominated in our day by *New York Times* and *Gertz*.

For over forty years, the foremost legal scholars, under the aegis of the American Law Institute (ALI), have sought to express the best views of the prevailing American law in various areas in the *Restatements*. They have struggled with the field of torts, in which defamation is a troublesome part. In 1977, *Restatement (Second) of Torts*, Volume 3, was published, thirteen years after the publication of the first two volumes. The time base was an indication, of the ferment and struggle induced first by *New York Times* and then by *Gertz*.

Here is a paraphrase of the *Restatement*'s conclusions about the impact of the First Amendment on defamation law:

1. Section 580A provides that in case of a defamatory communication published about a person in his capacity as a public official or public figure, the plaintiff must prove with convincing clarity that the defendant published the matter with knowledge or in reckless disregard of its falsity and its defamatory character, and that a finding of knowledge or reckless disregard involves the application of a constitutional standard subject to appellate review to determine whether the evidence is constitutionally adequate to sustaining the finding.

2. Section 580B provides that a private person cannot prevail in an action for defamation unless he proves that the defendant was at least negligent regarding the falsity and defamatory character of the communication.

3. Section 600 provides that a conditional privilege is lost through abuse, not by negligence regarding the truth or falsity of the communication but knowledge or reckless disregard of its falsity. (See the Special Note immediately preceding Section 593 on the relationship of conditional privileges to Section 580B.)

4. Section 621 provides that recoverable damages are limited to "compensation for actual injury" and treats the meaning of *actual injury*.

5. Section 566 provides that there can be no recovery for a mere expression of opinion that does not carry by implication an expression of defamatory facts and explains that as a result of this rule, the privilege of fair comment has become obsolete.

And here is a distillation, derived from *Gertz*, regarding the defamation of a private person:

One who publishes a false and defamatory communication concerning a private person—or concerning a public official or public figure in relation to a purely private matter not affecting his conduct, fitness, or role in his public capacity—is subject to liability, if, but only if, he
(a) knows that the statement is false and that it defames the other,
(b) acts in reckless disregard of these matters, or
(c) acts negligently in failing to ascertain them.

It should be observed that this is the prevailing rule as a result of *Gertz*. It prescribes the minimum in the standard of fault. But a few jurisdictions have opted for the higher standard set forth in *Rosenbloom*.

Professor George C. Christie wrote two articles on the reputational problems arising from *Gertz* and its progeny for the *Michigan Law Review*, the first in November 1976 (vol. 75, no. 1), the second in August 1977 (vol. 75, no. 8). In the first article, "Injury to Reputation and the Constitution: Confusion Amid Conflicting Approaches," Christie says: "The apparent orderliness that had characterized the principles enunciated in *Sullivan* was at least partially destroyed by *Gertz*." He believes "the difficulties opened up by *Gertz* are apparent." He lists some of these difficulties, several of which have not eventuated. He concludes:

The law in the area of injury to reputation is on the verge of chaos. Attempts by the Court to eliminate confusion have almost invariably increased it. The underlying reasons for these difficulties is likely traced to the fundamental assumption in *Sullivan* that it is possible to have different standards of liability depending on who is involved or, as the later cases have demonstrated, on what is involved. . . . The only way to accommodate all the conflicting interests in a manner that is socially acceptable . . . will be to generalize the *Gertz* negligence and actual damage solution.

In his second article, Professor Christie makes a detailed analysis of how the *Restatement* was rephrased in the light of *Gertz*. Christie considers only one important aspect of the ALI's work—whether opinion, including ridicule, can by itself be the basis of an action for defamation.

Over the objection of some scholars, the ALI had persisted in regarding opinions as the basis for a defamation action. It was so stated in the first proposed draft of the *Restatement (Second) of*

Torts. It resisted attempts to retreat from this position as late as May 1974 when it overwhelmingly rejected an effort to delete the provision. Then, on June 25, 1974, the Supreme Court handed down the decision in *Gertz*, declaring that "under the First Amendment there is no such thing as a false idea. However pernicious an opinion may seem, we depend for its correction not on the conscience of judges and juries but on the competition of other ideas."

The *Gertz* view of opinion was strengthened by the Court's decision in *Old Dominion Branch No. 496, National Association of Letter Carriers v. Austin*, handed down the same day as *Gertz*. It will be remembered that the latter case had been set for oral argument by the Court in tandem with *Gertz*. Despite this, the ALI did not at first accept the *Gertz* dictum. It still sought to make an opinion actionable if it "expresses, or implies the assertion of, a false and defamatory fact." The whole story is told by Christie with details and explanations for which there is insufficient space here.

The most prestigious of law journals, the *Harvard Law Review*, dealt with *Gertz* in its authoritative analysis of the Supreme Court decisions of the 1973 term in its November 1974 issue (vol. 88, no. 1). The conclusions were surprising indeed but might be discounted as a first view untested by the later cases and more analysis:

> Because *Gertz's* "public figure" test is unclear, and because the effects of the new rules of negligence and damages are uncertain, it is difficult to determine the overall impact of the decision. If judges are able to control jury prejudice, and if a liberal interpretation is given to the "public figure" standard, it is possible that the result of *Gertz* will be to make the media more free of the law of libel than they have ever been before. Insofar as juries can exercise uncontrolled discretion in assessing damages, and a more restricted test for the higher degree of privilege is applied, the decision will provide markedly less protection than *Rosenbloom* did.
>
> Justice Blackmun claimed that with *Gertz* the law had "come to rest in the defamation area." That claim is more hope than reality.

Most of the cases and commentary cited here date from the first several years after *Gertz* was handed down. Opinion jelled in the earlier years, but commentators continued to find new aspects of the case to write about. I have often said that this vast material confuses me if not others. I have therefore decided to list all of the material, new and old, in the Bibliography.

It is wise to include the views of one of the great constitutional scholars, Professor Laurence H. Tribe of the Harvard Law School. His monumental treatise, *American Constitutional Law*, has been described by Arthur Schlesinger, Jr., as a "very remarkable feat of intellectual synthesis." California Supreme Court Justice Matthew Tobriner, himself a giant of the law, says: "We haven't had a book like Tribe's in this century. He's giving the kind of guidance sensitive judges will follow."

Tribe devotes many pages to *Gertz*. To distill what he says with such learning, clarity, and sometimes eloquence is not possible. What is omitted is as important as what is quoted. The reader should, however, bear in mind that the book was published in 1978 before the latest defamation cases were decided by the Supreme Court.

Gertz represents a shift in the Court's attention from the location of defamatory falsehoods within or without a sphere of constitutional protection to the determination of the precise degree of protection to be afforded in various contexts. This shift seems attributable to two influences. The first is the *Gertz* majority's conclusion that for many situations the *New York Times* standard was too strong, its practical effect being to defeat recovery in nearly all litigated cases in which the standard had been applied. The second is the *Gertz* majority's repudiation of the plurality opinion in *Rosenbloom v. Metromedia, Inc.* and the substantial acceptance of Justice Marshall's dissent in that case.

. . . .

. . . Where the law of defamation is closely confined to the narrow purpose of compensating private individuals for injury to their reputational interests, the law is aimed at something other than content, at least in the sense that the objective is unrelated to whether government approved or disapproves the content of the message. Defamation law in this sense is ideologically neutral, and therefore is appropriately remitted to a "balancing" test. Because the reputational interest of the individual is significant, and may indeed be of federal constitutional dimension, the crucial question is the degree to which the law of defamation actually constrains the communication of truthful information.

. . . .

In other contexts, the present majority of the Court has indicated skepticism toward the substance and reality of a "chilling" effect on the exercise of first amendment rights flowing from the mere threat of sanctions, and it must be assumed that a similar attitude in part underlies the *Gertz* decision. And for many the real problem is the power and unaccountability of the institutional press, not its weakness or timidity. But entirely different premises also serve to justify the *Gertz* formulation. The Court has been largely guessing that rules making it more difficult for defamed individuals to recover damages create "breathing space" for the exercise of first amendment rights. Yet a publisher's decision to print or broadcast a libelous story is only partly influenced by the probability of winning or losing a lawsuit. While the publication decision involves a complex calculus, the salient cost factors are likely to be the probability that the publisher will be sued, and the cost of defending if suit is brought. Rules affecting the publisher's ultimate liability are thus likely to be marginal considerations in the decision to publish. One commentator's analysis concludes that the *New York Times* privilege has failed to prevent self-censorship because it does little to reduce the costs of defending against libel claims.

In little more than two decades, the Supreme Court handed down several landmark decisions that defined the constitutional guidelines in the troublesome area of defamation. It appeared that there was little more for the Court to decide except for certain largely peripheral aspects. Then, on June 26, 1985, the Court decided *Dun & Bradstreet, Inc. v. Greenmoss Builder, Inc.* The judgment in favor of Greenmoss was affirmed, but there was no majority opinion. Justice Powell, who had written the opinion of the Court in *Gertz* eleven years earlier, announced the judgment of the Court and delivered an opinion in which only Justices Rehnquist and O'Connor fully joined. Other opinions in the case were delivered by Chief Justice Burger and Justice White, concurring only in the judgment, and Justice Brennan, with whom Justices Marshall, Blackmun, and Stevens joined, dissenting.

Was this, then, the situation of *Rosenbloom* all over again? *Rosenbloom* too was only a plurality opinion, but at first it was given the effect of a majority decision. State courts generally assumed that just as public officials and public figures had to prove actual malice in the *New York Times* sense, private persons involved in matters of public interest had to prove actual malice in order to prevail in a defamation action. Then came *Gertz*, and the courts were disabused of their interpretation of *Rosenbloom*. Even the U.S. Court of Appeals for the Seventh Circuit had shared the common error when it affirmed the dismissal of *Gertz* in the first trial on *Rosenbloom* grounds. It was only after the Supreme

Court decided otherwise and there was a retrial resulting in a *Gertz* victory that the Seventh Circuit upheld the new view with respect to private persons. There followed case after case, as we have seen, in which the highest court reaffirmed the position it had taken in *Gertz*.

To repeat, one must be very careful in reaching conclusions about the effect of plurality opinions. This is especially true in considering *Greenmoss*. It is necessary to ascertain the precise factual situation that gave rise to the judgment and the differing opinions. We start with the unanimous opinion of the Supreme Court of Vermont where the case was first reviewed. It was decided by that court on April 15, 1983, a little more than two years prior to the Supreme Court judgment. Greenmoss, a building contractor, brought a defamation action against Dun & Bradstreet, a credit-reporting agency that had issued an erroneous credit report to five of the contractor's creditors. The trial court had entered judgment in favor of Greenmoss for $50,000 in compensatory damages and $300,000 in punitive damages. At the same time, the trial court had granted the motion of Dun & Bradstreet for a new trial because the instructions to the jury were thought erroneous.

Thereupon, several questions of law were certified by the trial court to the state supreme court. In response, that court held that (1) as a matter of federal constitutional law, qualified protections afforded the media in "private" defamation actions, pursuant to the First and Fourteenth Amendments, do not extend to defamation actions involving nonmedia defendants; (2) there is no qualified common-law privilege for credit-reporting agencies such as Dun & Bradstreet in defamation actions; (3) the trial court did not abuse its descretion in denying the defendant's motion to set aside the verdict on the issue of punitive damages; and (4) any error by the trial court in instructing on the standards of liability under the U.S. Supreme Court decisions affording qualified protections to media in "private" defamation action was harmless error. Therefore, the trial court's original jury verdict for Greenmoss was affirmed and the order for a new trial set aside.

The Vermont Supreme Court stressed that Dun & Bradstreet operated a business in which factual and financial reports about business enterprises are issued exclusively to subscribers to its service. These reports are purportedly based on information elicited from the business itself, the business's banking and credit sources, trade suppliers, and public records. When Greenmoss's president met with its principal creditor, a bank, to discuss the possibility of future financing, it was informed by the bank that it had just received a credit report issued by Dun & Bradstreet that Greenmoss had recently filed a voluntary petition in bankruptcy. This was totally false; Greenmoss had never suffered a major economic reversal, and its financial condition was sound. As a result, the bank put off any consideration of credit to Greenmoss and then terminated its credit, allegedly for reasons other than the unfavorable report.

Greenmoss demanded that Dun & Bradstreet immediately correct the report and give it a list of those creditors who had received the false report so that it might reassure them. Dun & Bradstreet refused to give Greenmoss such a list.

On the basic issue whether the *Gertz* rule would apply both to media and nonmedia defendants in defamation cases, the Vermont Supreme Court had much to say, but its view that there is a basic distinction between media and nonmedia cases was not adopted by the U.S. Supreme Court, so I say nothing of it here, especially since the highest court played with the distinction before discarding it.

The losing party, defendant Dun & Bradstreet, appealed to the U.S. Supreme Court. It reduced the issue to whether the First Amendment's limitations on the award of presumed and punitive damages for libel, recognized in *Gertz*, apply to nonmedia defendants. It declared that there could be no recovery for compensatory, or "general," damages against a nonmedia defendant, absent a showing of actual malice as defined in *New York Times*. It argued that the law of libel would become too complex if there had to be a threshhold ruling on the defendant's status and that in any event it would be too difficult to apply any such a distinction.

After the original argument before the Supreme Court on March 21, 1984, the Court entered an order on July 5, 1984, that requested the parties to brief and argue the following issues:

1. Whether, in a defamation action, the constitutional rule of *New York Times* and *Gertz* with respect to presumed and punitive damages should apply where the suit is against a nonmedia defendant; and

2. Whether, in a defamation action, the constitutional rule of *New*

York Times and *Gertz* with respect to presumed and punitive damages should apply when the speech is of a commercial or economic nature.

Significant *amicus curiae* (interested-party) briefs were filed. The one by the Information Industry Association vigorously argued that the *New York Times-Gertz* rule should apply irrespective of the status of the defendant and that the fact that the speech involves commercial or economic information does not deprive the publisher of First Amendment protection against the unrestricted imposition of presumed or punitive damages. The brief pointed out that the association represented approximately three hundred information publishers and information-services organizations. Dow Jones & Company, in its *amicus* brief in support of Dun & Bradstreet, pointed out that it published the *Wall Street Journal* and was also involved in the dissemination of information through a variety of electronic news media. A somewhat surprising *amicus* brief was filed by the American Federation of Labor and Congress of Industrial Organizations (AFL-CIO) in support of the Dun & Bradstreet position. The AFL-CIO, it declared, is a federation of ninety-five national and international trade unions with a total membership of 13 million working people. It opined that if Dun & Bradstreet is not part of the media, neither is the AFL-CIO or its affiliated unions, and if the financial reports at issue are speech of a commercial or economic nature, so is much of the speech of the unions. Thus the unions would be faced with an increased threat of defamation actions.

We come now to what Justice Powell and his Supreme Court associates said about the case in voting 5–4 to affirm the judgment of the Supreme Court of Vermont. The case was decided not on the media-nonmedia issue raised in the appeal and in the request of the Supreme Court in connection with the reargument of the case but on the distinction between matters of public interest and those purely private.

Just as he had done earlier in *Gertz*, Justice Powell began his opinion in *Greenmoss* with a clear statement of the issue as he and Justices Rehnquist and O'Connor saw it:

In *Gertz v. Robert Welch, Inc.*, 418 U.S. 323 (1974), we held that the First Amendment restricted the damages that a private individual could obtain from a publisher for a libel that involved a matter of public concern. More specifically, we held that in these circumstances the First Amendment prohibited awards of presumed and punitive damages for false and defamatory statements unless the plaintiff shows "actual malice," that is, knowledge of falsity or reckless disregard for the truth. The question presented in this case is whether this rule of *Gertz* applies when the false and defamatory statements do not involve matters of public concern.

Justice Powell's opinion may be summed up in these excerpts:

We have never considered whether the *Gertz* balance obtains when the defamatory statements involve no issue of public concern. To make this determination, we must employ the approach approved in *Gertz* and balance the State's interest in compensating private individuals for injury to their reputation against the First Amendment interest in protecting this type of expression. This state interest is identical to the one weighted in *Gertz*. There we found that it was "strong and legitimate." 418 U.S. at 348. . . .

The First Amendment interest, on the other hand, is less important than the one weighed in *Gertz*. We have long recognized that not all speech is of equal First Amendment importance. It is speech on "matters of public concern" that is "at the heart of the First Amendment's protection." *First National Bank of Boston v. Bellotti*, 435 U.S. 765, 776 (1978), quoting *Thornhill v. Alabama*, 310 U.S. 88, 101 (1940). . . . In contrast, speech on matters of purely private concern is of less First Amendment concern. 461 U.S. at 146–147. . . . As a number of state courts, including the court below, have recognized, the role of the Constitution in regulating state libel law is far more limited when the concerns that activated *New York Times* and *Gertz* are absent. . . . In light of the reduced constitutional value of speech involving no matters of public concern, we hold that the state interest adequately supports awards of presumed and punitive damages—even absent a showing of "actual malice."

Chief Justice Burger's opinion was quite brief. He asserted that he had dissented in *Gertz* because regarding the ordinary private citizen, he objected to the abandonment of the traditional trend of the law up to that time. He preferred to allow this area of the law to evolve rather than to embark on a new doctrinal basis. "*Gertz*, however, is now the law of the land, and until it is overruled, it must, under the principle of *stare decisis*, be applied by this Court." "The single question before the Court today is whether

Gertz applies to this case." He agreed with the plurality opinion "that *Gertz* is limited to circumstances in which the alleged defamatory expression concerns a matter of general public importance, and that the expression in question here relates to a matter of essentially private concern." His belief remained that as suggested by Justice White, *Gertz* should be overruled. He also believed that *New York Times* should be reconsidered so that at the very least, a writing should be actionable if it could have been found untrue with the exercise of reasonable care.

As with his dissenting opinion in *Gertz*, Justice White dealt with the *Greenmoss* issues more fully. Although he had joined the judgment and opinion in *New York Times* and decisions extending it, he had come to harbor increasing doubts about the soundness of the Court's approach and some of the assumptions underlying it. He had come to believe that the Court had "struck an improvident balance in the *New York Times* case between the public's interest in being fully informed about public officials and public affairs and the competing interest of those who have been defamed in vindicating their reputation."

He went on more fully regarding the vices of *New York Times*:

> The *New York Times* rule thus contenances two evils: first, the stream of information about public officials and public affairs is polluted and often remains polluted by false information; and second, the reputation and professional life of the defeated plaintiff may be destroyed by falsehoods that might have been avoided with a reasonable effort to investigate the facts. In terms of the First Amendment and reputational interests at stake, these seem grossly perverse results.

And more specifically about the failings of *Gertz*:

> Although there was much talk in *Gertz* about liability without fault and the unfairness of presuming damages, all of this, as was the case in *New York Times*, was done in the name of the First Amendment, purportedly to shield the press and others writing about public affairs from possibly intimidating damages liability. But if protecting the press from intimidating damages liability that might lead to excessive timidity was the driving force behind *New York Times* and *Gertz*, it is evident that the Court engaged in severe overkill in both cases.
> In *New York Times*, instead of escalating the plaintiff's burden of proof to an almost impossible level, we could have achieved our stated

goal by limiting the recoverable damages to a level that would not unduly threaten the press. Punitive damages might have been scrutinized as Justice Harlan suggested in *Rosenbloom*, 403 U.S. at 77, or perhaps even entirely forbidden. Presumed damages to reputation might have been prohibited, or limited, as in *Gertz*. Had that course been taken and the common-law standard of liability been retained, the defamed public official, upon proving falsity, could at least have had a judgment to that effect. His reputation would then be vindicated; and to the extent possible, the misinformation circulated would have been countered. He might have also recovered a modest amount, enough perhaps to pay his litigation expenses. At the very least, the public official should not have been required to satisfy the actual malice standard where he sought no damages but only to clear his name. In this way, both First Amendment and reputational interests would have been far better served.

Thus, while Justice White joined in affirming the *Greenmoss* judgment, he had heavy reservations about the direction of the law of defamation. It is clear that he would have preferred that we live with the common law, at least with respect to the substantive rights of individuals.

The dissent by Justice Brennan, joined by Justices Marshall, Blackmun, and Stevens, is twice as long as the plurality opinion of Justice Powell. He declared that Justice Powell had in effect undermined *Gertz* by introducing what he regarded as the new element of matters of public or general interest. *Gertz*, he said, does not make such a distinction, and it is really not justified in the plurality opinion. Having said this and much more in opposition to that opinion, he concluded by declaring that "Greenmoss Builders should be permitted to recover for any actual damage it can show resulted from Dun and Bradstreet's negligently false credit report, but should be required to show actual malice to receive presumed or punitive damages."

Justice Brennan made one statement that was mistaken, as I read the opinions in the case. He said that at least six members of the Court agreed that "the rights of the institutional media are no greater and no less than those enjoyed by other individuals or organizations engaged in the same activities." I do not see that the Court has indicated that it expressly rejects the media-nonmedia distinction as a constitutional matter. It simply did not decide the case on that basis, possibly because it was easier to do so on another basis. It is not impossible that in a more appropriate context it will embrace the distinction in at least a limited fashion. It may yet be impressed by what the Supreme Court of Vermont and a majority of other jurisdictions say on the subject of the distinction between media and nonmedia publication.

Some are troubled because the Court seems to have created a new category of expression, thus further complicating an already complex field of the law. Until *Greenmoss*, the Court seemed to have dropped the common-law rules of defamation in which there might be recovery without proof of either fault or injury. That seemed to be the meaning of *Gertz*. Now it seems to be saying that after all, the common law will apply and not *New York Times* or *Gertz*—if the aggrieved party is a private person and the defamatory expression does not relate to a matter of public concern.

Some questions remain unanswered but may be resolved later. Who determines whether the material is of public concern—the trier of the facts or the court? We now know that the burden of proof as to falsity lies with the plaintiff, at least in public-interest cases. The fact of publication remains the responsibility of the defendant as at common law.

There remains the issue of punitive damages. Under both *New York Times* and *Gertz*, such damages may be recovered only if there is *actual malice*, as defined in *New York Times*, not malice as at common law. But if the defamation is sufficiently heinous, the jury will somehow find a way to enlarge actual damages.

In some moods, I think that there are three principal opponents of permitting aggrieved parties to recover for defamation: (1) those who would abolish the action of libel completely; require proof of actual malice in all instances, public or private; or limit recovery in every case to actual damages, excluding punitive damages completely; (2) individuals or entities such as the media with a pecuniary stake in defending such actions; and (3) rigid civil libertarians with an inflexible belief in an absolute privilege for all expression under the First Amendment or ivory-tower academics without much experience.

It seems to me that injury to the reputation can be at least as serious as bodily harm, which is compensated in personal-injury cases. A blatant enough lie or misstatement about a professional, business, or layperson can destroy or reduce a practice, a business, standing in the community, or self-esteem. Freedom of speech and the press, important as they are, should not be the sole consideration or always the most important. In a civilized society, we owe it to one another not to be careless or trifling with reputations. At the very least, ordinary care ought to be expended to ascertain the truth.

Times and *Gertz* provided litigants and lawyers with reasonable certainty of the circumstances in which their rules applied and the consequences thereof. There is not the same assurance with respect to *Greenmoss*. It may prove as evanescent as *Rosenbloom*. Virtually all the lower courts assumed that *Rosenbloom* reflected the true state of the law, even though the opinion represented only a plurality of the Court. With *Gertz*, that misconception was corrected. Then came *Greenmoss* to complicate the situation once more. One will have to await further rulings of the highest court to learn the "final" meaning of *Gertz*.

So the story of my landmark libel case ends—at least for the present. I am sure that time will bring changes in the law of defamation. But for me, nothing can diminish the fulfillment that I have been privileged to experience in the more than fourteen years of the saga.

Dr. Peter Irons, in *The Courage of Their Convictions*, tells the stories of sixteen people, including Elmer Gertz, who fought their way to the highest court of the land despite every kind of difficulty. The *Journal of the American Bar Association* says that every lawyer should read Dr. Irons's book because it teaches us about the roots of justice and why we should struggle so that it may prevail.

As one of those fortunate people, I know what the others have endured. I went through two trials, two reviews in the court of appeals, two battles in the Supreme Court, three civil rights cases for a client, and an appeal in connection with one of them. I had to contend with delays, defeats, and near disasters.

I could not permit myself to surrender, despite the accumulation of years and the disabilities that are a necessary part of aging. I had to remain confident while others despaired. Now that it is all over, I know the supreme joy of triumphing in a cause that transcends all that is personal, for I have contributed to the law in a truly meaningful fashion.

Bibliography
Index

■ Bibliography

I have deposited virtually every item listed in the following Bibliography, as well as other material relating to the *Gertz* case and defamation generally, in the special collection of the Morris Library, Southern Illinois University at Carbondale.

Articles, Notes, Commentaries

A.B.A. Journal. Special issue: thirteen articles on the Supreme Court, its justices, and oral argument in the Court. June 15, 1986.

Abrams, Floyd. "The Supreme Court Turns a New Page in Libel." *A.B.A. Journal,* August 1984.

Akron Law Review. "Symposium—First Amendment Rights to Free Speech and a Free Press. Change and Continuity." Articles by Ernest G. Giglio, Sanda Bradley, James E. Moliterno, Thomas W. Renwane, Sheryl S. Kants, and Cary Douglas Caesar. Vol. 12, No. 2, Fall 1978.

Albergo, Janine. "The Supreme Court Creates New Hurdle for Libel Defendants: *Dun & Bradstreet, Inc. v. Greenmoss Builders, Inc.*," *St. John's Law Review,* Vol. 60, No. 1, Fall 1983.

Albert, James. "The Remedies Available to Candidates Who Are Defamed by Television or Radio Commercials of Opponents." *Vermont Law Review,* Vol. 11, 1986.

Allen, Gary. "Control of the Media." *American Opinion,* May 1983.

Allport, Michael B., and Steven C. Baldwin. "Defamation and State Constitutions: The Search for a State Law Based Standard after *Gertz.*" *Williamette Law Review,* Vol. 19, No. 4, Fall 1983.

Amspecher, Catherine L., and Randel Steven Springer. "Humor, Defamation, and Intentional Infliction of Emotional Distress: The Potential Predicament for Private Figure Plaintiffs." *William and Mary Law Review,* Vol. 31, Fall 1990.

Anderson, David A. "Libel and Press Self-Censorship." *Texas Law Review,* Vol. 53, No. 3, March 1975.

———. "The Selective Impact of Libel Law." *Columbia Journalism Review,* May-June 1975.

Angle, Margaret S. "Media Freedom of Speech and Press—Defamation—*Gertz v. Robert Welch, Inc.*" *Wisconsin Law Review,* Vol. 1974, No. 4.

Arbetman, Lee, and Bob Hayman. "The Court Takes Another Look at Protection for Defendants in Defamation Cases." *Preview of United States Supreme Court Cases*, 1984–85 Term, Issue No. 1, September 18, 1984.

Armenakis, Diana L. "Privacy and Summary Judgment: New Test, New Beneficiaries." *Seton Hall Law Review*, Vol. 6, No. 3, Spring 1975.

Armstrong, Michael J. "A Barometer of Freedom of the Press: The Opinions of Mr. Justice White." *Pepperdine Law Review*, Vol. 8, No. 1, 1980.

Ashdown, Gerald G. "*Gertz* and *Firestone*. A Study in Constitutional Policy-Making." *Minnesota Law Review*, Vol. 61, No. 4, April 1977.

Austin, Bradford L. "Newspaper or Broadcaster that Publishes Defamatory Falsehoods about Individual Who Is neither Public Official nor Public Figure May Not Claim Constitutional Privilege against Liability for Injury Inflicted by Those Statements—*Gertz v. Robert Welch, Inc.*" *Drake Law Review*, Vol. 24, No. 2, Winter 1975.

Authors Guild Bulletin. "Full Text of the Authors League Symposium on Libel." October 1981. (Discusses the cases since *New York Times v. Sullivan*, including *Gertz*. Also has brief article on *Pring* case.)

———. "Libel and Invasion of Privacy—The Contract Committee Survey." June–July 1981.

———. "More Publishers to Provide Libel Protection for Authors." April–May 1982.

Avery, Phyllis Ann, and John D. Stevens. "Effects of *Gertz* Decision in One Circuit." *Journalism Quarterly*, Vol. 61, No. 4, Winter 1984.

Backer, Braden C. "Constitutional Protections of Critical Speech and the Public Figure Doctrine: Retreat by Reaffirmation." *Wisconsin Law Review*, Vol. 1980, No. 3.

Baker, C. Edwin. "Scope of the First Amendment Freedom of Speech." *UCLA Law Review*, Vol. 25, No. 5, June 1978.

Barkley, Richard. "The Evolution of a Public Issue: *New York Times* through *Greenmoss*." *University of Colorado Law Review*, Vol. 57, No. 4, Summer 1986.

Barnes, Richard L. "The Constitutional Fault Test of *Gertz v. Robert Welch, Inc.* and the Continued Viability of the Common Law Privileges on the Law of Defamation." *Arizona Law Review*, Vol. 20, No. 3.

Berritt, Gail J. "The Fact-Opinion Deduction in Libel Law: The Second Circuit Adopts a More Comprehensive Approach." *Brooklyn Law Review*, Vol. 52.

Barron, Jerome A. "The Search of Media Accountability." *Suffolk University Law Review*, Vol. 19, No. 4, Winter 1985.

Bayer, James R. "Defamation Extension of the 'Actual Malice' Standard to Private Litigants. *Colson v. Stieg*." *Chicago Kent Law Review*, Vol. 59, No. 4, 1983.

Beckerle, Carol A. "The Effect of *Gaeta v. New York News, Inc.* on New York's Private Libel Plaintiffs." *Albany Law Review*, Vol. 50, No. 11, Fall 1985.

Beroukas, Eudoxia. "The Over-Constitutionalization of Libel Law: *Philadelphia Newspapers, Inc. v. Hepps*," *DePaul Law Review*, Vol. 36, No. 3, Spring 1987.

Beschle, Donald L., Neil J. Fogarty, Peter Jude Niemiec. "Freedom of the Press: Libel." *Annual Survey of American Law*, New York University School of Law, 1974–75, Winter 1975.

BeVier, Lillian R. "The First Amendment and Political Speech: An Inquiry into the Substance and Limits of Principle." *Sanford Law Review*, Vol. 30, No. 2, January 1978.

Black, Bob. "A Constitutional Revolution in the Law of Libel: *New York Times* and *Gertz* Applied." *Texas Tech Law Review*, Vol. 11, No. 3, Spring 1980.

Bloom, Lackland H., Jr. "Proof of Fault in Media Defamation Litigation." *Vanderbilt Law Review*, Vol. 38, No. 2, March 1985.

Bloustein, Edward J. "The First Amendment and Privacy: The Supreme Court Justice and the Philosopher." *Rutgers Law Review*, Vol. 28, No. 1, Fall 1974.

Boisseau, Merribeth. "*Time, Inc. v. Firestone*: The Supreme Court's Restrictive New Libel Ruling." *San Diego Law Review*, Vol. 14, No. 2, 1977.

Borrus, Bruce J. "Defamation and the First Amendment: Protecting Speech on Public Issues." *Washington Law Review*, Vol. 56, 1980–81.

Boyken, Jeff. "*Dun & Bradstreet, Inc. v. Greenmoss Builders, Inc.* . . . The Actual Malice Standard of *Gertz v. Robert Welch, Inc.*" *Pepperdine Law Review*, Vol. 14, No. 2, 1987.

Branscomb, Melinda J. "Liability and Damages in Libel and Slander Law." *Tennessee Law Review*, Vol. 47, No. 4, Summer 1980.

Brill, Steven. "Redoing Libel Law." *American Lawyer*, September 1984.

Brody, James Patrick. "Defamation Law of Wisconsin." *Marquette Law Review*, Vol. 65, No. 4, Summer 1982.

Brooklyn Law Review. Symposium: Defamation in Fiction: articles by Joel M. Gore, Frederick Schauer, Marc A. Franklin, Paul A. LeBel, Diane Leenheer Zimmerman, David A. Anderson, Martin Garbus, Richard Kurnit. Vol. 51, No. 2, Winter 1985.

Brosnahan, James J. "From *Times v. Sullivan* to *Gertz v. Welch*: Ten Years of Balancing Libel Law and the First Amendment." *Hastings Law Journal*, Vol. 26, No. 3, January 1975.

Brown, Jeffrey Paige. "*Wolston v. Reader's Digest Association, Inc.*: The Definition of Public Figure Is Narrowed." *North Carolina Law Review*, Vol. 58, No. 5, June 1980.

Brown, Joseph Kent. "Florida Defamation Law and the First Amendment: Protecting the Reputational Interests of the Private Individual." *Florida State University Law Review*, Vol. 113, No. 1, Spring 1983.

Burnside, Janet R. "Private Plaintiff versus Member News Media—An Application of *Gertz v. Robert Welch, Inc.*" *Ohio State Law Journal*, Vol. 36, No. 4, 1975.

Burt, Dan M., and Anthony S. Murry. "The Public-Figure Defamation Case—Westmoreland Counsel Recount Their Strategy." *Trial*, Vol. 21, No. 10, October 1985.

Butler, Richard L. "Libel and the First Amendment. *Time, Inc. v. Firestone.*" *Nebraska Law Review*, Vol. 56, No. 2, 1977.

Cahn, Miriam E. "The Triumph of the Press: New Jersey Departs from Federal Trends in Libel Law." *Rutgers Law Review*, Vol. 36, Nos. 1, 2, Fall 1983–Winter 1984.

California Law Review. Symposium: New Perspectives in the Law of Defamation. Eleven experts, including Gerhard Casper, Marc A. Franklin, James Reston, Frederik Schauer; also Thomas, Jeffrey E.: "Statements of Fact, Statements of Opinion, and the First Amendment." Vol. 74, No. 3, 1986.

Campbell, Dennis. "Free Press in Sweden and America: Who's the Fairest of Them All?" *Southwestern University Law Review*, Vol. 87, No. 1, 1976.

Caputo, Phil. "Julius Echeles, Defense." *Chicago Free Press*, October 26–November 2, 1970.

Carman, Charles A. "*Hutchinson v. Proxmire* and the Neglected Fair Comment Defense: An Alternative to 'Fair Comment.'" *DePaul Law Review*, Vol. 30, No. 2, Fall 1980.

Carroll, William Richard. "Constitutional Law—First Amendment—Freedom of the Press in Constitutional Privilege for Defamation. . ." *Duquesne Law Review*, Vol. 14, No. 1, Fall 1975.

Center Magazine. Symposium: Privacy, Government, and the Media. Articles by Arthur Miller, James Sheelow, Melville Nimmer, Albert Picherell, and Jeremiah S. Gutman. Vol. 15, No. 5, September–October 1982.

Chany, Jerry. "*Gertz*, a Press Blessing in Disguise—'Opinion' Dicta Now Law of Libel?" *Media Law Notes*, Vol. 10, No. 2, February 1983.

Chicago Daily Law Bulletin. Articles on second trial of *Gertz v. Robert Welch, Inc.*: April 17, 1981; April 21, 1981; April 22, 1981; April 23, 1981.

Christie, George C. "Defamatory Opinion and the Restatement (Second) of Torts." *Michigan Law Review*, Vol. 75, No. 8, August 1977.

———. "Injury to Reputation and the Constitution: Confusion and Conflicting Approaches." *Michigan Law Review*, Vol. 75, No. 1, November 1976.

―――. "Underlying Contradictions in the Supreme Court's Classification of Defamation." *Duke Law Journal*, Vol. 1981, No. 5.
Chupack, Joel L. "Protection from Defamation: *Hutchinson v. Proxmire.*" *Decalogue Journal*, Summer 1982.
Cohen, Jeremy. "Oregon Defamation: Which Guarantee of Protection?" *Williamette Law Review*, Vol. 23, Spring 1987.
Cohen, Melissa A. "State Court Approaches in Developing a Post-*Gertz* Standard of Liability." *Annual Survey of American Law*. State Courts Issue, 1984 Volume.
Cole, Christopher. "Press to Trial: The Press Clause, The Libel Dilemma and the Media-Nonmedia Distinction." *Syracuse Law Review*, Vol. 39, November, 1989.
Collins, Erik L., and J. Douglas Drushal. "The Reaction of the State Courts to *Gertz v. Robert Welch, Inc.*" *Case Western Law Review*, Vol. 28, No. 2, Winter 1978.
Collins, Erik L., and Gretchen M. Smith. "Awards of Damages for Mental Anguish without Proof of Harm to Reputation: Is There Parasitic or Independent Life after *Gertz*?" *Mercer Law Review*, Vol. 38, No. 3, Spring 1987.
Columbia Journalism Review. "On the Libel Front" (articles by C. T. Hanson, Nancy Madlin, Pat Deddy, and Gilbert Cranberg). January–February 1983.
Comegys, Rowena Scott. "Potter Stewart: An Analysis of His Views on the Press as Fourth Estate." *Chicago Kent Law Review*, Vol. 59, No. 1, 1982.
Comm/Ent. Articles relating to *Gertz*: Robert M. Wise. "The Athlete as Public Figure in Light of *Gertz v. Robert Welch, Inc.*" Marc A. Franklin, "What Does 'Negligence' Mean in Defamation Cases?" Frank G. Houdek, "Constitutional Limitations on Libel Actions: A Bibliography of *New York Times v. Sullivan* and Its Progeny, 1964–1984." Vol. 6, No. 2, Winter 1984.
Corbelli, James. "Fame and Notoriety in Defamation Litigation." *Hastings Law Journal*, Vol. 34, March 1983.
The Cost of Libel: Economics and Policy Implications. A Conference Report. Gannett Center for Media Studies, Columbia University, 1986.
Cox, Archibald. "Freedom of Expression in the Burger Court." *Harvard Law Review*, Vol. 94, No. 1, November 1980.
Cuozzi, William F., and Lee Sporn. "Private Lives and Public Concerns: The Decade Since *Gertz v. Robert Welch, Inc.*" *Brooklyn Law Review*, Vol. 51, No. 2, Winter 1985.
Daniloff, Deborah. "Employer Defamation." *Hastings Law Journal*, Vol. 40, No. 3, March 1989.
Dato, Robert M. "The Effect of Passage of Time on Inactive Public Figures." *Federal Communications Law Journal*, Vol. 35, No. 2, Summer 1983.

Davis, Chee. "The Firestone Case: A Judicial Exercise in Press Censorship." *Emory Law Journal*, Vol. 25, 1976.
Del Russo, Alexander D. "Freedom of the Press and Defamation: Attacking the Bastion of *New York Times Co. v. Sullivan.*" *St. Louis University Law Journal*, Vol. 25, No. 3, 1981.
DeVore, P. Cameron, and Marshall J. Nelson. "Punitive Damages in Libel Cases after *Browning-Ferris.*" *Comm/Ent*, Vol. 12, 1989.
Diamond, John L. "*Philadelphia Newspapers v. Hepps*: Unanswered Defamation Questions." *Comm/Ent*, Fall 1987.
Dickinson Law Review. An entire issue devoted to defamation: Introduction by Elmer Gertz; articles by Henry R. Kaufman, Robert Gilson, Medelyn Leopold, Randall P. Bezanson, Kathryn L. Ingle, Robert D. Sack, Richard J. Tote, David J. Branson, Sharon A. Sprague, Jane E. Kirtly, Ronald H. Surkin, most in collaboration, all relevant to *Gertz*. Vol. 90, November 3, Spring 1986.
Doneberg, Barbara A. "The Reform of the Innocent Construction Rule in Illinois." *Chicago Kent Law Review*, Vol. 60, No. 2, 1984.
Donovan, Paul F. "Private Individuals Defamed in Newspaper Need Only Prove Negligence for Recovery in Massachusetts." *Suffolk University Law Review*, Vol. 10, No. 1, Fall 1975.
Dorfman, Ron. "The Police and Deadly Force." *Chicago Lawyer*, Vol, 2, No. 6, June 4, 1979.
Dorothy, Wade L. "Communication Law: Defamation—Public Figure or Private Individual?" *Washburn Law Journal*, Vol. 16, No. 1, Fall 1976.
Doyle, Thomas J. "The Nonmedia Figure and Strict Liability in California." *University of San Francisco Law Review*, Vol. 18, No. 2, Winter 1984.
Drake Law Review. "The Gertz Fault Standard." Vol. 35, No. 1, 1985–86.
Dreschel, Bob. "Has the *Gertz* Case Hurt the Press." *Twin City Journalism Review*, Vol. 3, No. 5, October–November 1975.
Dreschel, Robert E., and Deborah Moon. "Corporate Libel Plaintiffs and the News Media: An Analysis of the Public-Private Figure Distinction after *Gertz.*" *American Business Law Journal*. Vol. 21, No. 2, Summer 1983.
Eaton, Joel D. "The American Law of Defamation Through *Gertz v. Robert Welch, Inc.* and Beyond: An Analytical Primer." *Virginia Law Review*, Vol. 61, No. 7, 1975.
Editor and Publisher. Compilation of 136 Supreme Court Decisions involving the First Amendment. July 3, 1976, and July 17, 1976.
Epstein, Richard A. "Was *New York Times v. Sullivan* Wrong?" *University of Chicago Law Review*, Vol. 53, 1986.
Ester, Elizabeth K. "*Street v. National Broadcasting Co.*: Libel and Invasion of Privacy." *Northwestern University Law Review*, Vol. 77, No. 1, March 1982.

Faerber, Richard F. "Defamation, Advertising, and *Gertz*: Public Controversy and Media Access." *Arizona State Law Journal*, Vol. 1982, No. 1.

Feinstein, Terri S. "Persistence of Illogic: Further Constitutional Aspects of the Law of Defamation." *Hofstra Law Review*, Vol. 5, No. 3, Spring 1977.

Fetzer, Patricia Nassif. "The Corporate Defamation Plaintiff as First Amendment's 'Public Figure': Nailing the Jelly Fish." *Iowa Law Review*, Vol. 68, No. 1, October 1982.

Finan, Eileen. "The Fact-Opinion Determination in Defamation." *Columbia Law Review*, Vol. 88, No. 9, May 1988.

Finical, Scott M. "Defamation of a Police Officer in a Citizen Complaint: Vindicating the Rights of 'The Blue' in Arizona." *Arizona Law Review*, Vol. 24, No. 3, 1982.

Fishman, Cliff. "Constitutional Law-First Amendment—Libel—Public Figure—*Time, Inc. v. Firestone*." *New York Law School Law Review*, Vol. 22, November 4, 1978.

Fitzpatrick, Tom. (Account of Nuccio trial.) *Chicago Sun-Times*, December 1, 1970.

Fleisher, Richard E., and Edward Eckhart. "At Your Own Risk and Beyond: Developments in the Law of Defamation." *Arkansas Law Review*, Vol. 29, No. 3, Fall 1975.

Florence, Heather Grant. "Libel Law 1980: A Map of Tricky Territory." *Publishers Weekly*, Vol. 217, No. 12.

Forbes, Randall J., Lance A. Pool, and John F. Thompson. "Federalization of State Defamation Law." *Washburn Law Journal*, Vol. 15, No. 2, Spring 1976. (In same issue, see note on libel in Kansas Judicial Survey.)

Forers, Lois G. "Libel, Privacy and the First Amendment." *William Mitchell Law Review*, Vol. 15, 1989.

Fowler, Tracy H. "Modernizing Defamation Law in Utah." *Utah Law Review*, Vol. 1980, No. 3.

Frakt, Arthur N. "Defamation Since *Gertz v. Robert Welch, Inc.*: The Emerging Common Law." *Rutgers Camden Law Journal*, Vol. 10, No. 3, Spring 1979.

———. "The Evolving Law of Defamation: *New York Times v. Sullivan* to *Gertz v. Robert Welch, Inc.* and Beyond." *Rutgers Camden Law Journal*, Vol. 6, No. 3, Winter 1975.

Franklin, Marc A. "Good Names and Bad Law: A Critique of Libel Law and a Proposal." *University of San Francisco Law Review*, Vol. 18, No. 1, Fall 1983.

———. "Libel Gets Tougher." *More—The Media Magazine*. Vol. 8, No. 2, February 1978.

———. "Suing Media for Libel: A Litigation Study." *American Bar Foundation Research Journal*, Vol. 1981, No. 3.

Gallagher, Lori. "New Mexico Adopts Ordinary Negligence Standards for Defamation of a Private Figure: *Marchiando v. Brown.*" *New Mexico Law Review*, Vol. 13, No. 3, Summer 1983.

Garbus, Martin. "The Many Costs of Libel." *Publishers Weekly*, Vol. 230, No. 10, September 5, 1986.

Garment, Leonard. "Nixon and Privacy." *New Yorker*, April 17, 1989.

Gasperini, Edwin L. "New Shift in the Libel Law." *Public Relations Journal*, December 1974.

Gerdts, Charles W., III, and Kevin J. Wolf. "State Court Reaction to *Gertz v. Robert Welch, Inc.*: Inconsistent Results and Reasoning." *Vanderbilt Law Review*, Vol. 29, No. 6, November 1976.

Gertz, Elmer. "Finding of 'Actual Malice' in Defamation Is Subject to Review"; Wayne B. Giampietro, "Plaintiffs Given Wide Choice of Forum." *Constitutional Law and Liberty*, Vol. 10, No. 4, March–April 1984.

_____. "Gertz on Gertz." *Trial*, Vol. 21, No. 10, October 1985.

_____. "*Greenmoss Builders, Inc. v. Dun & Bradstreet, Inc.* Invites Controversy." *John Marshall Law Review*. Vol. 19, No. 4, Summer 1986.

_____. "I Am No longer a Mere Person—I Am a Legal Landmark." *Student Lawyer*, Vol. 4, No. 2, October 1985.

_____. "Living with a Landmark Libel Case." *Media Law Notes*, Vol. 12, No. 2, February 1985.

_____. "Privacy Law—A Personal View." *Loyola Quarterly of Public Issues and the Law*, Spring 1988.

_____. "Review of Suing the Press." *Trial*, Vol. 22, No. 23, December 1986.

_____. "The Search for Consistency in Constitutional Defamation Law." *Comm/Ent*, Vol. 10, No. 4, Summer 1988.

_____. "What You Read in the Press of Lando—It Ain't Necessarily So." *Chicago Lawyer*, Vol. 2, No. 8, May 1, 1979.

Gertz, Elmer, and Wayne B. Giampietro. "The Gertz Libel Doctrines Grow with the Years." *Constitutional Liberty*, Vol. 9, No. 1, September 1982.

Giampietro, Wayne B. "The Constitutional Rules of Defamation, or It's Libel but Is He Liable?" *Illinois Bar Journal*, Vol. 64, No. 1, December 1975.

Giampietro, Wayne B., Penny Nathan Kahan, and Teresa Nuccio. "Defamation Suits and Law Firm Break-ups." *Illinois Bar Journal*, Vol. 77, No. 10, September 1989.

Giorkaris, Virginia M. "Confusion Persists in the Distinction Between Fact and Fiction in Defamation Action." *JMKC Law Review*, Vol. 54, No. 4, 1986.

Gleason, Timothy W. "The Fact/Opinion Distinction in Libel." *Comm/Ent*, Spring 1988.

Godofsky, Stanley. "Protection of the Press from Prior Restraint and Harassment under Libel Laws." *University of Miami Law Review*, Vol. 29, No. 3, Spring 1975.
Goodwin, Alfred T. "Press-Court Relations: Can They Be Improved?" *Hastings Constitutional Law Quarterly*, Vol. 7, No. 3, Spring 1980.
Gordon, David. "Two Libel Decisions Face New Approach in Courses." *Journalism Educator*, April 1977.
Grandjean, Dalma C. "Does Freedom of the Press Allow for Protection of a Rape Victim's Identity? A Comment on *Cox Broadcasting Corp. v. Cohn*." *University of Dayton Intramural Law Review*, Vol. 1, No. 1, January 1976.
Green, Leon. "Political Freedom of the Press and the Libel Problem." *Texas Law Review*, Vol. 54, No. 3, February 1978.
Green, Michael. "*Dun & Bradstreet v. Greenmoss*: Cutting Away the Protective Mantle of *Gertz*." *Hastings Law Journal*, Vol. 37, No. 6, July 1986.
Greenfield, James J. "Defamation and the First Amendment in the 1978 Term: Diminishing Protection for the Media." *University of Cincinnati Law Review*, Vol. 48, No. 4, 1979.
Greenfield, Phillip G. "Private Reputation vs. Freedom of Speech." *Missouri Law Review*, Vol. 53, No. 1, Winter 1988.
Grossman, Ron. "Camp Conspiracy—At a John Birch Society Retreat Kids Hear a Reveille for America." *Chicago Tribune*, September 8, 1989, Sec. 5, p. 1.
Gunnison, Michael J. "General Public Figures Since *Gertz v. Robert Welch, Inc.*" *St. John's Law Review*, Vol. 58, No. 2, Winter 1984.
Hager, John W. "Civil Libel and Slander in Oklahoma—An Update." *University of Tulsa Law Journal*, Vol. 14, No. 1, 1978.
Hale, F. Dennis. "The Future of Strict Liability in Libel." *Communications and the Law*, Vol. 5, No. 2, Spring 1983.
Hamilton, Douglas C. "As Time Goes By: *Gertz v. Robert Welch, Inc.* and Its Effect on California Defamation Law." *Pacific Law Journal*, Vol. 6, No. 2, July 1975.
Hanley, Robert F. "*Gertz v. Welch*: Radical Changes in the Law of Libel." *Chicago Bar Record*, Vol. 57, No. 1, July–August 1975.
Hannigan, Thomas H., Jr. "First Amendment Theory Applied to the Right of Publicity." *Boston College Law Review*, Vol. 19, No. 2, January 1978.
Harvard Civil Rights/Civil Liberties Law Review. First Amendment symposium: articles by Edward M. Kennedy, Robert Meister, John H. F. Shattuck, Fritz Byers, Charles R. Nesson, Andrew D. Koblanz, G. Michael Fenner, James L. Koley, Craig M. Bradley, Don Lively, James R. Ferguson, Priha Lahar. Vol. 16, No. 2, Fall 1981.
Hastings Law Journal. "First Amendment and the Media": articles by Justices Potter Stewart and William O. Douglas, Melville B. Nimmer,

Roscoe L. Barrow, James C. Goodale, P. Cameron DeVere, Marshall J. Nelson, and James J. Brosnahan, all relevant to *Gertz*. Vol. 26, No. 3, January 1975.

Heidig, Edward G. "Ollman v. Evans: Skinning the Membrane of Fact versus Opinion." *Tort & Insurance Law Journal*, Vol. 23, No. 1, Fall 1987.

Helfgot, Ira N. "*Wolston v. Reader's Digest Association, Inc.*—A Chilling Effect on the Media's Privilege." *Decalogue Journal*, Vol. 26, No. 2, Summer 1980.

Helle, Steven. "Judging Public Interest in Libel: The Gertz Decision's Contribution." *Journalism Quarterly*, Spring 1984.

Hentoff, Nat. "Free Speech: The Price Is Going Up." *The Progressive*, May 1983.

Hermann, Donald H. J. "Patterns of Life in Law: A Consideration of Contemporary American Legal Biography." *DePaul Law Review*, Vol. 24, No. 41, Summer 1975.

Herron, Matthew. "The Law of Libel—Constitutional Privilege and the Private Individual: Round Two—*Gertz v. Robert Welch, Inc.*" *San Diego Law Review*, Vol. 12, No. 2, 1975.

Hickman, Paula H. "A New Standard of Fault for the Reportorial Privilege." *Louisiana Law Review*, Vol. 37, No. 1, Fall 1976.

Higdon, Philip R. "The Burger Court and the Media: A Ten-Year Perspective." *Western New England Law Review*, Vol. 2, Issue 4, Spring 1980.

Hilbert, John. "A Criticism of the *Gertz* Public Figure/Private Figure Test in the Context of the Corporate Defamation Plaintiff." *San Diego Law Review*, Vol. 18, Nos. 4 and 5, 1981.

Hill, Alfred. "Defamation and Privacy Under the First Amendment." *Columbia Law Review*, Vol. 76, No. 8, December 1976.

Hill, J. Graham. "*Gertz v. Robert Welch, Inc.*: Defamation and Freedom of the Press—The Struggle Continues." *Southwestern Law Journal*," Vol. 28, No. 5, Winter 1974.

Hofstra Law Review. Symposium on the press clause, dedicated to Justice Potter Stewart: See especially James L. Oakes, "Proof of Actual Malice in Defamation Actions: An Unsolved Dilemma." Vol. 7, No. 3, Spring 1979.

Holdridge, John. "Libel Law: The Burden of Proof, Summary Judgment, and the Choice Between Truth and Privacy." *Annual Survey of American Law*, Issue 2, 1987.

Holisky, Jerald B. "*Costello v. Capital Cities Communications, Inc.*: Illinois Innocent Construction Rule Prevails over the Constitutional Privilege for Expression of Opinion." *John Marshall Law Review*, Vol. 21, No. 2, Winter 1988.

Huckaby, James, Jr. "Freedom of the Press—Denial of a Right of Public Access to the Press. *Miami Herald Publishing Company v. Tornillo*." *Emory Law Journal*, Vol. 24, No. 1, Winter 1975.

Hulme, James H. "Vindicating Reputation: An Alternative to Damages as a Remedy for Defamation." *American University Law Review*, Vol. 30, 1987.

Hunter, Howard D. "A Reprise on *Herbert V. Lando* and the Law of Defamation." *Kentucky Law Journal*, Vol. 76, 1982–83.

Ingber, Stanley. "Defamation: A Conflict Between Reason and Decency." *Virginia Law Review*, Vol. 65, No. 5, June 1979.

Iowa Law Review. "Symposium: Toward a Resolution of the Expanding Conflict between the Press and Privacy Interests": articles by Randall B. Bezanson, Dorsey D. Ellis, Jr., Don R. Pember, Geoffrey Palmer, and William E. Lee. Vol. 64, No. 5, July 1979.

Jacobs, Eric M. "Protecting the First Amendment Right to Petition Immunity for Defendants in Defamation Actions Through Application of the *Noerr-Pennington Doctrine*." *American University Law Review*, Vol. 31, No. 1, Fall 1981.

James, John P. "Corporate Plaintiffs in Libel Actions. *Rosenbloom Resurrected?*" *Western New England Law Review*, Vol. 1, Issue 4, Spring 1979.

Jeffries, John Calvin, Jr. "A Comment on the Constitutionality of Punitive Damages." *Virginia Law Review*, Vol. 72, 139, 1986.

Jenkins, Bruce S. "The Integrity of Words." *Utah Law Review*, No. 2, 1988.

Jess, Paul. "Gertz Decision: Chance to Improve Unit on Libel Law." *Journalism Educator*, January 1976.

John Marshall Law Review. "Fifth Annual Benton National Moot Court Competition." (Deals to a large extent with *Gertz v. Robert Welch, Inc.*) Vol. 20, No. 4, Summer 1987.

———. "Fourth Annual Benton National Moot Court Competition. (Deals largely with the *Gertz* case.) Vol. 19, No. 4, Summer 1986.

Jollymore, Nicholas J. "The Constitutionality of Punitive Damages in Libel Actions." *Fordham Law Review*, Vol. 45, No. 6, May 1977.

Jones, Lawrence A. "*Time, Inc. v. Firestone*: Is Rosenbloom Really Dead?" *University of Miami Law Review*, Vol. 31, No. 1, Fall 1976.

Kalm, Lind. "The Burden of Proving Truth or Falsity in Defamation: Setting a Standard for Cases Involving Nonmedia Defendants." *New York University Law Review*, October 1987.

Kaminsky, Alan. "Defamation Law: Once a Public Figure Always a Public Figure?" *Hofstra Law Review*, Vol. 10, No. 3, Spring 1982.

Kaplan, Seth A. "Fact and Opinion After *Gertz V. Robert Welch, Inc.* The Evolution of a Privilege." *Rutgers Law Review*, Vol. 34, No. 1, Fall 1981.

Karinja, Mark T. "Defamation Conflict in the Definition of 'Public Figure.'" *Seton Hall Law Review*, Vol. 10, No. 4, 1980.

Karp, Diane. "The Demise of the Public Figure in Defamation Cases and the Assent of a Responsible Press—*Time, Inc. v. Firestone*." *DePaul Law Review*, Vol. 26, No. 4, Summer 1977.

Kaufman, Irving R. "Press, Privacy and Malice: Reflections on *New York v. Sullivan.*" *New York State Bar Journal*, July 1984.

Keeton, W. Page. "Defamation and Freedom of the Press." *Texas Law Review*, Vol. 54, No. 6, August 1976.

Kendall, Patricia Jo. "Defamation—*Colson v. Stieg.*" *Illinois Bar Journal*, Vol. 71, No. 7, March 1983.

Kentucky Law Journal. "The First Amendment: A Symposium": articles by Howard O. Hunter, Jerome A. Barron, William H. Erickson, Dwight I. Teeter and S. Griffin Sinze, Doug Rendlemar, Raymond L. Yasser, Francis H. Heller, Gerald J. Thain. Vol. 67, No. 4, 1978–79

Kohler, David C. "Toward a Modern Defamation Law in Virginia: Questions Answered, Questions Raised." *University of Richmond Law Review*, Vol. 21, No. 1, Fall 1986.

Kohn, Shalom L. "Chapski and the Loss of Innocence." *Chicago Bar Record*, Vol. 21, No. 1, Fall 1986.

Kohn, William I. "State Tort Action for Libel after *Gertz v. Robert Welch, Inc.*: Is the Balance of Interest Leaning in Favor of the News Media?" *Ohio State Law Journal*, Vol. 36, No. 3, 1975.

Kovner, Victor A. "Disturbing Trends in the Law of Defamation: A Publishing Attorney's Opinion." *Hastings Constitutional Law Quarterly*, Vol. 3, No. 2, Spring 1976.

Kreuzer, Adam. "More Speech, Less Litigated: Extending the Noerr v. Pennington Doctrine to the Law of Defamation." *John Marshall Law Review*, Vol. 18, No. 3, Spring 1985.

Landis, Debra T. "Criticism or disparagement of attorney's character, competence, or conduct as defamation." 46 ALR 4th 326.

Lange, David. "The Speech and Press Clauses." *UCLA Law Review*, Vol. 23, No. 1, October 1975. (See also Melville B. Nimmer, "Speech and Press: A Brief Reply.")

Langvardt, Arlene W. "Media Defendants, Public Concerns, and Public Plaintiffs: Toward Fashioning Order from Confusion in Defamation Law." *University of Pittsburgh Law Review*, Vol. 49, No. 1, Fall 1987.

Large, Douglas B., and Kristopher Kellman. "Losing the Struggle to Define the Proper Balance Between the Law of Defamation and the First Amendment—*Gertz v. Robert Welch, Inc.*—One Step Forward, Two Steps Back." *Pepperdine Law Review*, Vol. 2, No. 2, 1975.

LaRue, Lewis H. "Living with *Gertz*: A Practical Look at Constitutional Libel Standards." *Virginia Law Review*, Vol. 67, No. 2, March 1981.

Laughlin, Michael J. "New Standards in Media Defamation Cases. *Gertz v. Robert Welch, Inc.*" *California Western Law Review*, Vol. 12, No. 1, Fall 1975.

Le Bel, Paul A. "Refining the Tort of Defamation: An Accommodation of the Competing Interests Within the Current Constitutional Framework." *Nebraska Law Review*, Vol. 66, No. 2, 1987.

Bibliography ■ 263

Lee, Douglas E. "Public Interest, Public Figures, and the Corporate Defamation Plaintiff." (*Jadwin v. Minneapolis Star & Tribune.*) *Northwestern University Law Review*, Vol. 81, No. 2, Winter 1987.

Lee, Gary L. "Strict Liability Versus Negligence: An Economic Analysis of the Law of Libel." *Brigham Young University Law Review*, 1981.

Lee, William E. "The Supreme Court on Privacy and the Press." *Georgia Law Review*, Vol. 12, No. 2, Winter 1978.

Lehmann, Michael P. "Triangulating the Limits on the Tort of Invasion of Privacy: The Development of the Remedy in Light of the Expansion of Constitutional Privilege." *Hastings Constitutional Law Quarterly*. Vol. 3, No. 2, Spring 1976.

Leitner, Jerome M. "Defamation." (In 1979 survey of New York law.) *Syracuse Law Review*, Vol. 31, No. 1, Winter 1980.

Levin, Leslie C. "Constitutional Privilege to Republish Defamation." *Columbia Law Review*, Vol. 77, No. 8, December 1977.

Levin, Steven Michael. "Libel and Slander—A State Is Precluded from Imposing Liablity Without Fault Presumed or Punitive Damages in the Absence of *New York Times* Malice in *Gertz v. Robert Welch, Inc.*" *Loyola University of Chicago Law Journal*, Vol. 6, No. 1, Winter 1975.

Lewis, Anthony. "Annals of the Law in Libel." (The *New York Times* and subsequent cases, including *Gertz.*) *New Yorker*, November 5, 1984.

———. "*New York Times v. Sullivan* Reconsidered: Time to Return to 'The Central Meaning of the First Amendment.'" *Columbia Law Review*, Vol. 83, No. 3, April 1983.

Lewis, John B., and Bruce L. Ottley. "*New York Times v. Sullivan*—Its Continuing Impact on Libel Law." *Trial*, Vol. 21, No. 10, October 1985.

Light, Jonathan D. "*Gertz v. Robert Welch, Inc.* Redefined Defamation for a Private Citizen." *New England Law Review*, Vol. 10, No. 2, Spring 1985.

Lusky, Louis. "Public Trial and Public Right: The Missing Bottom Line." *Hofstra Law Review*, Vol. 8, No. 2, Winter 1980.

McAvoy, Terence P. "A Way Out of Defamation's Maze of Confusion." *John Marshall Law Review*, Vol. 20, No. 1, Fall 1986.

McCardy, William Osler. "How State Courts Have Responded to *Gertz* in Setting Standards of Fault." *Journalism Quarterly*, Autumn 1979.

McChrystal, Michael K. "Reconciling Defamation Law and the Free Enterprise System When the Media Provides Consumer or Investor Information." *Texas Tech Law Review*, Vol. 17, 1986.

McCloskey, Margaret E. "Suing the Artist for Libel—The Pendulum Swings Back." *Illinois Bar Journal*, Vol. 71, No. 2, October 1982.

McKeever, Joyce. "Constitutional Law—Freedom of the Press—Right of Privacy—Publication of True Information on the Public Record." *Duquesne Law Review*, Vol. 14, No. 3, Spring 1976.

McKennon, Donald J. "*Time, Inc. v. Firestone*: More Than a New Public Standard?" *St. Louis University Law Journal*, Vol. 20, No. 4, 1976.

McKey, Arthur Duncan. "Defamation Law After *Time, Inc. v. Firestone.*" *Idaho Law Review*, Vol. 13, No. 1, Winter 1976.

Magaziner, Fred T. "Corporate Defamation and Product Disparagement: Narrowing the Analogy to Personal Defamation." *Columbia Law Review*, Vol. 75, No. 5, June 1975.

Malone, Linda, and Rodney A. Smolla. "The Future of Defamation in Illinois after *Colson v. Stieg* and *Chopski v. Copley Press, Inc.*" *DePaul Law Review*, Vol. 32, No. 2, Winter 1983.

Marando, Michael P. "*Time, Inc. v. Firestone*: Free Press Versus the Right to Reputation—A Continuing Struggle to Define the Obscure." *Ohio Northern University Law Review*, Vol. 12, No. 1, 1977.

Marshall, Charles T., and F. Scott McCown. "Examining the Institutional Interpretation of the PRESS Clause." *Texas Law Review*, Vol. 58, No. 1, December 1979.

Martin, Jeffrey C. "First Amendment Limitations on Public Disclosure Actions." *University of Chicago Law Review*, Vol. 45, No. 1, Fall 1977.

Mather, T. Michael. "Experience with *Gertz* 'Actual Injury' in Defamation Cases." *Baylor Law Review*, Vol. 38, No. 4, Fall 1986.

Matheson, Scott M., Jr. "Procedure in Public Person Defamation Cases: The Impact of the First Amendment." *Texas Law Review*, Vol. 66, No. 2, December 1987.

Meikeljohn, Donald. "Public Speech in the Burger Court: The Influence of Justice Black." *University of Toledo Law Review*, Vol. 8, No. 2, Winter 1977.

_____. "Public Speech in the Supreme Court Since *New York Times v. Sullivan.*" *Syracuse Law Review*, Vol. 26, No. 3, Summer 1975.

Meltzer, Donald. "Toward a New Standard of Liability for Defamation in Fiction." *New York University Law Review*, Vol. 58, No. 5, November 1983.

Mercer Law Review. Symposium: libel (entire issue). Vol. 38, No. 3, Spring 1987.

Mertz, Neil. "Constitutional Limitations on Libel Actions." *Baylor Law Review*, Vol. 28, No. 1, Winter 1976.

Mobley, Jeffrey. "Libel and 'False Light' Invasion of Privacy in Kentucky." *Kentucky Law Journal*, Vol. 70, No. 2, 1981–82.

Molchen, William E., II. "New York Times Standard Is Inapplicable to a Defamed Individual Who Is neither a Public Official nor a Public Figure; and Only Actual Injury Is Compensable Absent Showing of Actual Malice." *Villanova Law Review*, Vol. 20, No. 4, 1974–75.

Moll, Nessa E. "In Search of the Corporate Private Figure: Defamation of the Corporation." *Hofstra Law Review*, Vol. 6, No. 2, Winter 1978.

Moore, Kevin M. "Fair Comment and Music Criticism: New York Law Under the Constitutional Defenses to Libel." *Syracuse Law Review*, Vol. 37, 1986.

Moses, Becky. "Performer's Right of Publicity: A Limitation on News Privilege." *Cleveland State Law Review*, Vol. 26, No. 4, 1977.

Moses, Susan M. "Award of Punitive Damages Permissible under the Doctrine of Respondent Superior in First Amendment Cases, *Embry v. Holly*." *University of Baltimore Law Review*, Vol. 12, No. 1, Fall 1982.

Mullen, John C. "*Troman v. Wood*: A Landmark Libel Decision in Illinois." *Chicago Bar Record*, Vol. 58, No. 2, September–October 1976.

Murnaghan, Francis D., Jr. "*Ave* Defamation, *Atque Vale* Libel and Slander." *University of Baltimore Law Review*, Vol. 6, No. 1, Fall 1976.

The National Voter. "Individual Rights." Vol. 25, No. 3, Fall 1975.

Naumann, Steven T. "The Return of a Content Based Standard for Private Plaintiff Defamation in *Dun & Bradstreet, Inc. v. Greenmoss Builders, Inc.*" *Chicago-Kent Law Review*, Vol. 62, No. 2, 1985.

Neier, Aryeh. "The Libel Dilemma. The Case for a Right to Reply"; Martin Garbus, "Abolish Libel—The Only Answer." *The Nation*, October 8, 1983.

Nelson, Robert D. "Media Defamation in Oklahoma: A Modest Proposal and New Perspectives—Part I." *Oklahoma Law Review*, Vol. 34, 1981.

———. "Media Defamation in Oklahoma: A Modest Proposal and New Perspectives—Part II." *Oklahoma Law Review*, Vol. 34, 1981.

News Media and the Law. Published by the Reporters Committee for Freedom of the Press. Each issue contains news and comment on libel, privacy, and related subjects.

New York Law Forum. "Confrontation: A Free Press in a Free Society—A Symposium Dedicated to Morris L. Ernst." Vol. 20, No. 3, Winter 1975. (See especially the article by Francis X. Beytagh, "Privacy and a Free Press. A Contemporary Conflict in Values.")

Nichols, Dale K. "The Involuntary Public Figure Class of *Gertz v. Robert Welch*: Dead or Merely Dormant?" *Journal of Law Reform*, Vol. 14, No. 1, Fall 1980.

Nimmer, Melville B. "Speech and Press: A Brief Reply." *UCLA Law Review*, Vol. 23, No. 1, October 1975. (See also David Lange, "The Speech and Press Clauses.")

Nizer, Louis. "Don't Give the First Amendment a Bad Name"; Victor A. Kovner, "Response to Remarks of Louis Nizer." *Communications and the Law*, August 1984.

Nocera, Joseph. "McDonald's War—John Birch Is No Longer Society's Only Martyr." *The New Republic*, October 3, 1983.

Northern Kentucky Law Review. First Amendment symposium: articles on various phases of defamation law, with references to *Gertz v. Robert Welch, Inc.* Vol. 15, No. 1, 1988.

O'Brien, David M. "The First Amendment and the Public's Right to Know." *Hastings Constitutional Law Quarterly*, Vol. 7, No. 3, Spring 1980.

O'Halloran, Hugh J. "Journalistic Malpractice: The Need for a Professional Standard of Care in Defamation Cases." *Marquette Law Review*, Vol. 72, No. 1, Fall 1988.

O'Hern, Steven K. "Expungement: Lies That Can Hurt You in and out of Court." *Washburn Law Journal*, Vol. 27, No. 3, Spring 1988.

Okerson, Eric C. "Restaurant Owner Must Prove Actual Malice to Recover Damages for a Defamatory Statement of Opinion Concerning the Quality of His Restaurant." *Tulane Law Review*, Vol. 52, No. 3, April 1978.

Ottley, Bruce L., John Bruce Lewis, and Young Lee Jim Ottley. "*New York Times v. Sullivan*: A Retrospective Examination." *DePaul Law Review*, Vol. 33, No. 4, Summer 1984.

Overend, William. "John Birch Society Still Fighting Communists." *St. Paul Sunday Pioneer Press*. October 10, 1982. This article originated with the *Los Angeles Times*.

Park, Susan Kee-Young. "Defamation: A Study in Hawaii Law." *University of Hawaii Law Review*. Vol. 1, No. 1, 1979.

Parker, John C. "Libel: The Application of *Gertz v. Robert Welch, Inc.*" *Washington and Lee Law Review*, Vol. 34, No. 2, Spring 1977.

Pell, Eve. "Libel as a Political Weapon." *The Nation*, Vol. 232, No. 22, June 6, 1981. (See also editorial, "Libel Overkill.")

Pember, Don R., and Dwight L. Teeter, Jr. "Privacy and the Press since *Time, Inc. v. Hill*." *Washington Law Review*, Vol. 50, 1974.

Petrus, Barbara A. "Defamation and the First Amendment in the Corporate Context." *Albany Law Review*, Vol. 46, No. 2, Winter 1982. Reprinted in *Publishing, Entertainment, Advertising, and Allied Fields Law Quarterly*, Vol. 21, No. 2, Fall 1982.

Phillips, Herbert C. "Washington and New York Respond to *Gertz*." *Denver Law Journal*, Vol. 55, No. 1, 1978.

Phillips, Jerry J. "Defamation, Invasion of Privacy and the Constitutional Standard of Care." *Santa Clara Law Review*, Vol. 16, No. 1, 1975.

Pick, Grant. "He's Earned a Moral Fortune." *Student Lawyer*, Vol. 9, No. 1, September 1980.

Pilpel, Harriet F. "Cases of Libel and the Right to Privacy Raise Serious and Inhibiting Questions." *Publishers Weekly*, Vol. 213, No. 13, March 27, 1978.

Pilpel, Harriet F., and Laurie R. Rockett. "Libel, Advertising and Freedom of the Press." *Publishers Weekly*, Vol. 209, No. 9, March 1, 1976.

Pilpel, Harriet F., and Alan V. Schwarz. "When Is a Libel Not a Libel?" *Publishers Weekly*, December 16, 1974.

Plunkett, Jeffrey A. "The Constitutional Law of Defamation: Are All Speakers Protected Equally?" *Ohio State Law Journal*, Vol. 49, No. 1, 1983.

Polelle, Michael J. "The Unconstitutionality of the Qualified Truth Defense to Libel Actions." *John Marshall Journal of Practice and Procedure*, Vol. 11, No. 2, Winter 1977–78.

Porter, Gregory Douglas. "Self-Censorship after *Herbert v. Lando*: The Need for Special Pre-Trial Procedure in Defamation Action." *North Carolina Law Review*, Vol. 58, No. 5, June 1980.

Powell, Lewis F., Jr., Justice. "What Really Goes on at the Supreme Court." *American Bar Association Journal*, June 1980.

Prager, Eileen Carroll. "Public Figures, Private Figures and Public Interest." *Stanford Law Review*, Vol. 30, No. 1, November 1977.

Press Censorship Newsletter. Published by the Reporters Committee for Freedom of the Press; each issue contains material on libel and related matters. The publication subsequently became *News Media and the Law.*

Rahdert, George K., and David M. Snyder. "Rediscovering Florida's Common Law Defenses to Libel and Slander." *Stetson Law Review*, Vol. 11, No. 1, Fall 1981.

Rees, William J. "The First Amendment Does Not Protect the Publicizing of Unnewsworthy Private Facts." *Vanderbilt Law Review*, Vol. 29, No. 3, April 1976.

Reuben, Don. "Libel-Law Reform That Would Chill the Working Press." *Chicago Tribune*, December 12, 1988, Sec. 1, p. 19.

Rinzler, Carol E. "Any Resemblances to Actual Logic Is Purely Coincidental. The Perplexing Problem of Libel in Fiction." *Publishers Weekly*, Vol. 227, No. 26, June 28, 1985.

Roberts, S. A. "Damages—Recovery of Punitive Damages Held Unconstitutional in Defamation Action Where Plaintiff Is a Public Figure and Liability Is Based on Actual Malice. *Maheu v. Hughes Tool Co."* *Cumberland Law Review*, Vol. 6, No. 1, Spring 1975.

Robertson, David W. "Defamation and the First Amendment: In Praise of *Gertz v. Robert Welch, Inc*"; see also David A. Anderson, "A Response to Professor Robertson: The Issue Is Control of Press Power." *Texas Law Review*, Vol. 54, No. 2, January 1976.

Roby, Katherine S., and Pamela S. Yeary. "Defamation: The Kansas Requirement that Private Plaintiffs Prove Injury to Reputation before Recovering for Emotional Harm." *Washburn Law Journal*, Vol. 23, No. 2.

Roe, Richard L. "Summary Judgments in Public Figure Libel Suits: How High a Burden of Proof"; see also Peter de Lacy, "Who Must Prove What in Libel Actions?" *Preview of United States Supreme Court Cases*, 1985–86 Term, Issue No. 6, December 20, 1985.

Rose, Laurence M. "Interstate Libel and Choice of Law: Proposals for the Future." *Hastings Law Journal*, Vol. 30, No. 5, May 1979.

Rosen, Mark L. "Media Lament—The Rise and Fall of Involuntary Public Figures." *St. John's Law Review*, Vol. 54, No. 31, Spring 1980.

Rosenblatt, Stephen W. "Adjusting the Defamation Standard." *Mississippi Law Review*, Vol. 46, No. 2, Spring, 1975.

Saadek, Laura L. "*Dun & Brandstreet, Inc. v. Greenmoss Builders, Inc.*: The Supreme Court Further Muddies the Defamation Waters." *Loyola of Los Angeles Law Review*, Vol. 20, No. 1, November 1986.

Sackett, Harvey P. "The *Gertz* Case: Unbalancing Media Rights and Reputational Interests." *Western State University Law Review*, Vol. 2, No. 2,

Spring 1975. (In the same issue there is a note on *Maheu v. Hughes Tool Co.* by Theodore A. Anderson that also discusses *Gertz*.)

Sales, James B., and Kenneth B. Cole, Jr. "Punitive Damages: A Relic That Has Outlived Its Origins." *Vanderbilt Law Review*, Vol. 37, 1989.

Schaefer, Walter V. "Defamation and the First Amendment: The Coen Lecture." *University of Colorado Law Review*, Vol. 52, Fall 1980.

Schaplowsky, Richard L. "The First Amendment Does Not Insulate the Press from Liability in a Defamation Action Brought by a Private Person Even Though She Is a Party in a Widely Publicized Divorce Proceeding. *Time, Inc. v. Firestone* . . . " *Seton Hall Law Review*, Vol. 7, No. 4, Summer 1976.

Schauer, Frederick T. "Language, Truth, and the First Amendment. An Essay in Memory of Harry Canter." *Virginia Law Review*, Vol. 64, No. 2, March 1978.

_____. "The Second Best First Amendment." *William and Mary Law Review*, Vol. 31, No. 1, Fall, 1989.

Schwartz, Charles W. "Story Defaming Lower Level Official Must Reveal That It Refers to His Official Conduct before *New York Times* Privilege Applies . . . " *Texas Law Review*, Vol. 55, No. 3, February 1977.

Shaman, Jeffrey M. "Revitalizing the Clear-and-Present-Danger Test. Toward a Principled Interpretation of the First Amendment." *Villanova Law Review*, Vol. 22, No. 1, 1976–77.

Shepard, Paul C. "Freedom to Defame." *Wake Forest Law Review*, Vol. 11, No. 1, March 1975.

Shiffrin, Steven. "Defamatory Non-Media Speech and First Amendment Methodology." *UCLA Law Review*, Vol. 25, No. 5, June 1975.

Shore, Laurence. "Defamation and Employment Relationships." *Emory Law Review*, Vol. 38, 1989.

Shneider, Gordon. "A Model for Relating Defamatory 'Opinions' to First Amendment Protected 'Ideas.'" *Arkansas Law Review*, Vol. 43, No. 1.

Shorey, Susan Gail. "The Constitutional Law of Defamation—Recent Developments and Suggested State Court Responses." *Maine Law Review*, Vol. 33, No. 2, 1981.

Silver, Isidore. "Libel, the Higher Truths of Art, and the First Amendment." *University of Pennsylvania Law Review*, Vol. 12, No. 5, May 1978.

_____. "Libel, a Weapon for the Right." *The Nation*, Vol. 226, No. 14, May 20, 1978.

Slough, M. C. "Swift Currents of Change in the Law of Defamation." *Journal of the Kansas Bar Association*, Spring 1976.

Smith, Barry F. "The Rising of Libel Litigation: Implications of the *Gertz* Negligence Rule." *Montana Law Review*, Vol. 44, No. 1, Winter 1983.

Smolla, Rodney A. "*Dun & Brandstreet, Hepps and Liberty Lobby*. A New Analysis Primer on the Future Course of Defamation." *Georgetown Law Journal*, Vol. 75, No. 5, June 1987.

_____. "Intertwining the Constitution and the Common Law: Evolving Doctrines of Defamation in Arkansas." *Arkansas Law Notes*, 1983.

———. "Let the Author Beware: The Rejuvenation of the American Law of Libel." *University of Pennsylvania Law Review*, Vol. 132, No. 1, December 1983.

Smolla, Rodney A., and Michael J. Gaertner. "The Annenberg Libel Reform Proposal: The Case for Enactment." *William and Mary Law Review*, Vol. 31, No. 1, Fall 1989.

Sniscak, Thomas J. "Libel Becomes Viable: The Narrow Application of Limited Public Figure Status in Current Defamation Law." *Ohio Northern University Law Review*, Vol. 7, No. 1, 1980.

Soupper, Samuel. "The First Amendment Privilege and Public Disclosure of Private Facts." *Catholic University Law Review*, Vol. 25, No. 2, Winter 1976.

Sowle, Kathryn Dix. "Defamation and the First Amendment: The Case for a Constitutional Privilege of Fair Report." *New York University Law Review*. Vol. 54, No. 3, June 1979.

Spahn, Thomas E. "Libel and Slander in Virginia." *University of Richmond Law Review*, Vol. 17, No. 4, Summer 1983.

Spak, Michael. "Recent Developments Involving Defamation—*Gertz v. Robert Welch, Inc.*" *Chicago-Kent Law Review*, Vol. 50, No. 2, Fall–Winter 1973.

Spar, Rebecca. "Model Jury Instructions for the 'Actual Malice' Standard." *Rutgers Law Review*, Vol. 39.

Spencer, Dale R. "Establishment of Fault in Post-*Gertz* Libel Cases." *Saint Louis University Law Journal*, Vol. 21, No. 2, 1977.

Speranza, William J. "Reply and Retraction in Actions Against the Press for Defamation: The Effect of *Tornillo* and *Gertz*." *Fordham Law Review*. Vol. 43, No. 2, November 1974.

Sprayer, Abigail. "Free Speech and Defamation Law—*Gertz v. Robert Welch, Inc.*" *Chicago-Kent Law Review*, Vol. 51, No. 2, 1974.

Squire, Madelyn C. "Making Sense of Employment Defendant Litigation." *Gonzaga Law Review*, Vol. 24, No. 1, 1988–89.

Stang, Alan. "Frame-Up. Richard Nuccio and the War on Police." *American Opinion*, Vol. 12, No. 4, April 1969. (This and the pamphlet reprint are the publications out of which *Gertz* originated.)

Stevens, George E. "Performing Artists as 'Public Figures': The Implication of *Gertz v. Robert Welch*." *Performing Arts Review*, Vol. 6, No. 1, 1975.

Stocker, Barbara Larkin. "An Analysis of the Distinction Between Public Figures and Private Defamation Plaintiffs Applied to Relatives of Public Persons." *Southern California Law Review*, Vol. 49, No. 5, July 1976.

Stonecipher, Harry W., and Robert Trager. "The Impact of *Gertz* on the Law of Libel." *Journalism Quarterly*, Winter 1976.

Suddath, Thomas H., Jr. "*Waldbaum v. Fairchild Publications, Inc.* Giving Objectivity to the Definition of Public Figures." *Catholic University Law Review*, Vol. 30, No. 2, Winter 1981.

Swatsler, Todd. "The Evolution of the Public Figure Doctrine in Defama-

tion Actions." *Ohio State Law Journal*, Vol. 41, No. 4, 1980.
Sweet, David M. *"Hutchinson v. Proxmire.* The Vanishing Immunity under the Speech or Debate Clause." *Marshall Law Review*, Vol. 14, No. 1, Fall 1980.
Swing, Bradford. "Libel: A Two-Tiered Constitutional Standard." *University of Miami Law Review*, Vol. 29, No. 2, Winter 1975.
Taubenhaus, Marsha. *"Time, Inc. v. Firestone:* Sowing the Seeds of *Gertz."* *Brooklyn Law Review*, Vol. 43, No. 1, Summer 1976.
Thompson, David M. "Punitive Damages in Defamation Action Brought by Public Figures Chill First Amendment Rights and Are Unconstitutional Unless Narrowly and Necessarily Promoting Compelling State Interest." *Vanderbilt Law Review*, Vol. 28, No. 4, May 1975.
Thompson, John F. "Constitutional Law: Defamation of Private Individuals." *Washburn Law Journal*, Vol. 14, No. 3, Fall 1975.
Tiersma, Peter Meijes. "The Language of Defamation." *Texas Law Review*, Vol. 66, No. 2, December 1987.
Tone, Jeffrey R. *"Troman v. Wood*—A Negligence Standard for Private Individuals in Defamation Actions." *University of Illinois Law Forum*, Vol. 1977, No. 1.
Tracy, Donald J. "Constitutional Law First Amendment—Libel—United States Supreme Court Reaffirms Its Decision in *Gertz v. Robert Welch, Inc.* to Emphasize the Individual Injured in a Libel Action Rather than the Event Recorded in *Time, Inc. v. Firestone . . .* " *Creighton Law Review*, Vol. 10, No. 2, December 1976.
Treiger, Leslie Kim. "Protecting Satire Against Libel Claims: A Reading of the First Amendment's Opinion Privilege." *Yale Law Journal*, Vol. 98, No. 6, April 1989.
Tuchy, James. "Robert A. Sprecher: May 30, 1917–May 15, 1982." *Chicago Lawyer*, Vol. 5, No. 6, June 1982. (See also Rob Warden, "Joel Flaum Is Percy's Choice for Seventh Circuit.")
Turkington, Richard C. "Foresee Ability and Duty Issues in Illinois Torts; Constitutional Limitations to Defamation Suits Under *Gertz."* *DePaul Law Review*, Vol. 24, No. 2, Winter 1975.
Tybor, Joseph R. "On Trial—*Gertz v. Welch*, Again—A Libel 'Time Warp.'" *National Law Journal*, February 22, 1982.
Van Alstyne, William V. "The Hazards to the Press of Claiming a Preferred Position." *Hastings Law Journal*, Vol. 28, No. 3, January 1977.
Vater, Joseph A., Jr. "The Death of Retraction Statutes." *University of Pittsburgh Law Review*, Vol. 36, No. 3, Spring 1975.
Von Baur, Trowbridge. "The License to Defame Government Officials: *New York Times v. Sullivan."* *Federal Bar Journal*, December 1983.
Wade, John W. "The Communication Torts and the First Amendment." *Mississippi Law Journal*, Vol. 48, No. 4, September 1977.
Walden, Ruth, and Emile Netzhammer. "False Light Invasion of Privacy: Untangling the Web of Uncertainty." *Comm/Ent*, Vol. 9, No. 3, Spring 1987.

Wall, Tom. "Accommodation of Reputational Interests and Free Press. A Call for a Strict Interpretation of *Gertz*." *Fordham Urban Law Journal*. Vol. 11, No. 2, 1982–83.
Wanat, Daniel E. "Falsehoods, the Right of Privacy and the Constitutional Privilege: *Time, Inc. v. Hill*, Revisited." *Memphis State University Law Review*, Vol. 8, No. 1, Fall 1977.
Warden, Rob. "Gertz Case: Bad Tidings for Birchers." *Chicago Journalism Review, Chicago Lawyer*, Sec. 2, March 1983.
———. "Gertz Verdict: Leninist Label Was a Malicious Libel." *Chicago Lawyer*, Vol. 4, No. 5, May 1981.
Warner-Fredman, Berna. "Defamation in Fiction: With Malice Toward None and Punitive Damages for All." *Loyola of Los Angeles Law Review*, Vol. 16, No. 1, 1983.
Warshawsky, Meyer. "Libel, the Media, and Public Figures and Officials." *Case and Comment*, Vol. 86, No. 1, January–February 1981.
Washington and Lee Law Review. Offensive and libelous speech symposium: various writers. Vol. 47, No. 1, Winter 1990.
Watkins, John J., and Charles W. Schwartz. "Gertz and the Common Law of Defamation: Of Fault, Non-media Defendants and Conditional Privileges." *Texas Tech Law Review*, Vol. 15, No. 4, 1984.
Weiler, Daniel A. "*Gertz v. Robert Welch, Inc.*: Constitutional Privilege and the Defamed Private Individual." *John Marshall Journal of Practice and Procedure*, Vol. 8, No. 3, Spring 1975.
Weinberg, Steve. "Libel: The Press Fights Back." *Columbia Journalism Review*, November-December 1983.
Weiss, Ron. "'Guilty'—Jury Foreman Tells How Nuccio Was Convicted." *Chicago Free Press*, October 26–November 2, 1970.
Weyandt, Gregory M. "Privacy v. The Press: Inevitable Conflict?" *Marquette Law Review*, Vol. 59, No. 3, 1976.
Wheeler, Thomas E., Jr. "Media Liability for Libeling of Newsworthy Persons: Before and after *Time, Inc. v. Firestone*." *Florida State University Law Review*, Vol. 5, No. 3, Summer 1977.
Whitney, D. Charles. "Libel—New Ground Rules for an Old Ball Game." *Quill*, Vol. 62, No. 8, August 1974.
William and Mary Law Review. Special issue: "Defamation and the First Amendment: New Perspectives." Articles by William W. Van Alstyne, Marc A. Franklin, Daniel J. Bussel, Cass R. Sunstein, Frederick Schauer, Gerald G. Ashdown, Diana M. Daniels. These articles have much material on *Gertz*. Vol. 25, No. 5.
Wilson, Kinsey. "7th Circuit Upholds $400,000 Gertz Libel Award." *Chicago Daily Law Bulletin*, Vol. 128, No. 118, June 17, 1982.
Windesmith, Philip H. *1986 Annual Survey of American Law*, First Amendment I: defamation law.
Woito, Linda N., and Patrick McNulty. "The Privacy Disclosure Tort and the First Amendment: Should the Community Decide Newsworthi-

ness." *Iowa Law Review*, Vol. 64, No. 2, January 1979.
Wolf, Daniel A. "In Action for Defamation in Which Plaintiff Is Private Individual and Negligence Is the Standard of Liability. *Troman v. Wood.*" *Illinois Bar Journal*, Vol. 64, No. 8, April 1976.
Yamhure, Patricia Shahen. "*Gertz v. Robert Welch, Inc.*" *Revista Juridica de la Universidad de Puerto Rico*, Vol. 44, Nos. 1 and 2, 1975.
Zimmering, Paul L. "Liability for Defamation of Private Persons—New Standards (*Gertz v. Robert Welch, Inc.*)." *Tulane Law Review*, Vol. 49, No. 3, March 1975.
Zimmerman, Diane L. "Requiem for a Heavyweight. A Farewell to Warren and Brandeis's Privacy Tort." *Cornell Law Review*, Vol. 68, No. 3, March 1983.
Zubras, Joan A. "*Gertz v. Welch*: Reviving the Libel Action." *Temple Law Quarterly*, Vol. 48, No. 2, Winter 1975.

Anonymous Articles

"Challenging the Exclusion of Libel and Slander from Survival Statutes." *University of Illinois Law Review*, Vol. 1984, No. 2.
"Constitutional Law Damages for Libel—A New Standard for Recovery of Damages by Private Individuals Libeled in a Report of Public Interest—*Gertz v. Robert Welch*." *Brigham Young University Law Review*, Vol. 1975, No. 1.
"Constitutional Law—Reformulation of the Constitutional Privilege to Defame." *The University of Kansas Law Review*, Vol. 24, No. 2, Winter 1976.
"Constitutional Privilege Does Not Extend to Defamation Concerning a Private Individual on a Public Issue—*Gertz v. Robert Welch, Inc.* . . . " *University of Richmond Law Review*, Vol. 9, No. 27, Winter 1975.
"The De-Constitutionalization of Defamation Law—Is It Really That Far Off?" *Hamline Law Review*, Vol. 9.
"Defamation Law in the Wake of *Gertz v. Robert Welch, Inc.* The Impact on State Law and the First Amendment." *Northwestern University Law Review*, Vol. 69, No. 6, January–February, 1975.
"Defining a Public Controversy in the Constitutional Law of Defamation." *Virginia Law Review*, Vol. 69, No. 5, June 1983.
"The Editorial Function and the *Gertz* Public Figure Standard." *Yale Law Journal*, Vol. 87, No. 8, July 1978.
"Iowa Libel Law and the First Amendment: Defamation Displaced." *Iowa Law Review*, Vol. 62, No. 4, April 1977.
"Libel Actions by Private Persons—. . . *Gertz v. Robert Welch, Inc.* . . . " *ATLA Law Journal*, Vol. 36.
"Libel Actions by Private Individuals." *Harvard Law Review*, Vol. 88, No. 1, November 1974.

"Libel and the Reporting of Rumor." *Yale Law Journal*, Vol. 92, No. 1, November 1982.

"Libel—Matters of Public Interest—A Private Person May Recover Actual Damages for a Defamatory Falsehood Concerning a Matter of Public Interest Without a Showing of Actual Malice . . ." *Gonzaga Law Review*, Vol. 12, No. 1, Fall 1976.

"The Maryland Court of Appeals: State Defamation Law in the Wake of *Gertz v. Robert Welch, Inc.*" *Maryland Law Review*, Vol. 36, No. 3, 1977.

"Mediaocracy and Mistrust: Extending *New York Times* Defamation Protection to Nonmedia Defendant." *Harvard Law Review*, Vol. 95, No. 8, June 1982.

"Prejudicial Publicity in Trials of Public Officials." *Yale Law Journal*, Vol. 85, No. 1, November 1975.

"The Taxation of Defamation Recoveries." *Vanderbilt Law Review*, Vol. 37, 1984.

"Torts—Libel: A Media Publisher of an Apparent Libel Is Subject to All but Strict Liability for Actual Injury Caused a Private Individual, Who, in the Absence of Actual Malice, May Recover neither Presumed nor Punitive Damages." *Brooklyn Law Review*, Vol. 41, No. 2, Fall 1974.

Death of Robert Welch Articles

Chicago Sun-Times, January 8, 1985, p. 11.
Chicago Tribune, January 8, 1985, Sec. 2, p. 6.
Robert D. McFadden. *New York Times*, January 8, 1985, p. 6.
Newsweek. "The Birchers After Welch." January 21, 1985.

Books and Pamphlets

Abernethy, Charles F. *Civil Rights Cases and Material*. St. Paul: West, 1980.

Aharoni, Dov. *General Sharon's War Against Time Magazine*. New York: Steinmatsky, 1985.

American Bar Association. 1976 Annual Meeting. Address: "The Press and the Law," Professor Edward L. Barrett, Jr.

American Bar Association, Section of Litigation, Business Torts Litigation Committee. Midwinter meeting of November 5, 1982, Chicago. "Proving Actual Malice in a Libel Case."

Anderson, Douglas A. *A "Washington Merry-go-Round" of Libel Actions*. Chicago. Nelson-Hall, 1980.

The Associated Press Stylebook and Libel Manual. Edited by Howard Angione. New York: Associated Press, 1977.

Barrett, Edward L., Jr., and William Cohen. *Constitutional Law—Cases and Material*. 5th and 6th eds. Mineola, N.Y.: Foundation Press, 1977, 1981. (See also 1975 and 1979 supplements.)

Barron, Jerome A., and C. Thomas Dienes. *Constitutional Law: Principles and Policy—Cases and Materials*. Indianapolis: Bobbs-Merrill, 1975.

———. *Handbook of Free Speech and Free Press*. Boston and Toronto: Little, Brown, 1979.

Benoit, Gary. *Keep Us Independent*. Reprint from a November 1989 issue of *John Birch Society Bulletin*.

The Burger Court—The Counter Revolution That Wasn't. Edited by Vincent Blasi; foreword by Anthony Lewis. New Haven: Yale University Press. 1983.

Bollinger, Lee C. *The Tolerant Society—Freedom of Speech and Extremist Speech in America*. New York: Oxford University Press. Clarendon Press, 1986.

Brenner, Daniel L., and William L. Rivers. *Free but Regulated—Conflicting Traditons in Media Law*. (Collected Essays with Commentary. Many distinguished contributors.) Ames, Iowa: Iowa State University Press, 1982.

Carter, T. Barton, Marc A. Franklin, and Jay B. Wright. *The First Amendment and the Fifth Estate—Regulation of Electronic Mass Media*. Mineola, N.Y.: Foundation Press, 1986.

Communications Law, Volumes for 1975 to 1991, both inclusive. New York City. Practicing Law Institute.

Cohn, Roy M. *How to Stand Up for Your Rights and Win!* New York: Simon and Schuster, 1981.

Cohn, William, and John Kaplan. *Constitutional Law and Individual Rights*. 2d ed. Mineola, N.Y.: Foundation Press, 1982.

Congressional Quarterly's Guide to the U.S. Supreme Court. Washington, D.C.: Congressional Quarterly, 1979.

Cox, Archibald. *Freedom of Expression*. Cambridge, Mass.: Harvard University Press, 1981.

Dooley, James A. *Modern Tort Law—Liability and Litigation*, Vol. 3. Chicago: Callahan, 1977.

Dorsen, Norman, Paul Bender, and Burt Neuborne. *Political and Civil Rights in the United States*. 4th ed. Vol. 1. Boston: Little, Brown, 1976.

The Douglas Opinions. Edited by Vern Countryman. New York: Random House, 1977.

Eldredge, Laurence H. *The Law of Defamation*. Indianapolis: Bobbs-Merill, 1978.

Epstein, Benjamin R., and Arnold Forster. *The Radical Right—Report on the John Birch Society and Its Allies*. New York: Vintage Books, 1966, 1967.

Fein, Bruce E. *"New York Times v. Sullivan": An Obstacle to Enlightened Public Discourse and Government Responsibilities to the People.* Preface by Michael P. McDonald; introduction by Herbert Schnerty. Washington, D.C.: American Legal Foundation.

———. *Significant Decisions of the Supreme Court 1973–74 Term.* Washington, D.C.: American Enterprise Institute for Public Policy Research, 1975.

———. *Significant Decisions of the Supreme Court, 1975–76 Term.* Washington, D.C. American Enterprise Institute for Public Policy Research, 1977.

The First Freedom Today. Critical Issues Relating to Censorship and Intellectual Freedom. Edited by Robert B. Downs and Ralph E. McCoy. Chicago: American Library Association, 1984. (Essays by many well-known experts on constitutional matters.)

Francois, William E. *Mass Media Law and Regulation.* 2d ed. Columbus: Grid, 1978.

Franklin, Marc A. *Cases and Materials on Mass Media Law.* Mineola, N.Y.: Foundation Press, 1977. (See also 1979 supplement; see also 3d ed. 1987.)

———. *Cases and Materials on Tort Law and Alternatives.* 2d ed. Mineola, N.Y.: Foundation Press, 1979.

———. *The First Amendment and the Fourth Estate—Communications Law for Undergraduates.* 2d ed. Mineola, N.Y.: Foundation Press, 1981.

Freund, Paul, et al. *Constitutional Law-Cases and Other Problems.* 4th ed. Boston: Little, Brown, 1977. (See also 1975 supplement.)

Gertz, Elmer. *For the First Hours of Tomorrow: The New Illinois Bill of Rights.* Urbana: Institute of Government and Public Affairs, University of Illinois Press, 1972.

Gertz, Elmer. *To Life.* New York: McGraw-Hill, 1974; enl. ed., Carbondale: Southern Illinois University Press, 1990.

Gillmor, Donald M., and Jerome A. Barron. *Mass Communications Law-Cases and Comment.* 2d and 4th eds. St. Paul: West, 1974, 1984.

Ginger, Ann Fagan, and Louis H. Bell. *Police Misconduct Litigation—Plaintiff's Remedies: Vol. 15, Model Trials, American Jurisprudence.* San Francisco. Bancroft-Whitney, 1968.

Gora, Joel M. *The Rights of Reporters. The Basic ACLU Guide to a Reporter's Rights.* New York: Discuss Books, Avon, 1974.

Green, Leon, et al. *Cases on the Law of Torts.* 2d ed. St. Paul: West, 1977.

Grossman, Joel B., and Richard S. Wells. *Constitutional Law and Judicial Policy Making.* 2d ed.. New York: Wiley and Sons, 1980.

Guide to Subversive Organizations and Publications. Washington, D.C.: Committee on Un-American Activities, U.S. House of Representatives, 1951.

Gunther, Gerald. *Constitutional Law-Cases and Material*. 9th, 10th eds. Mineola, N.Y.: Foundation Press, 1975, 1980. See also 1974 and 1977 supplements.

———. *Constitutional Law*. 11th ed. Mineola, N.Y.: Foundation Press, 1985.

———. *Individual Rights in Constitutional Law*. 4th ed. Mineola, N.Y.: Foundation Press, 1986.

Haiman, Franklyn S. *Freedom of Speech*. New York. National Textbook Company, American Civil Liberties Union, 1976.

Haiman, Franklyn S. *Speech and Law in a Free Society*. Chicago: University of Chicago Press, 1981.

Heldrich, Gerard C., Jr. *The Painting of Elmer*. Authors Unlimited, 1989.

Hentoff, Nat. *The First Freedom—The Tumultuous History of Free Speech in America*. New York: Delacorte Press, 1980.

Holsinger, Ralph L. *Media Law*. New York: Random House, 1987.

Irons, Peter. *The Courage of Their Convictions*. New York: Free Press, 1988.

Kalven, Harry, Jr. *A Worthy Tradition—Freedom of Speech in America*. Edited by Jamie Kalven. Harper and Row, New York, 1988.

Kane Peter. *Errors, Lies, and Libel*. Foreword by Elmer Gertz. Carbondale: Southern Illinois University Press, 1991.

Keeton, Page, and Robert E. Keeton. *Torts—Cases and Materials*. 2d ed. St. Paul: West, 1977.

Labunski, Richard. *Libel and the First Amendment*. Transaction, 1987.

Ladenson, Robert F. *A Philosophy of Free Expression and Its Constitutional Applications*. Totowa, N.J.: Rowman and Littlefield, 1983.

Lamkin, Patricia Jean. *American Law Reports Annotated*, 3d ser. (75 ALR 3d. 616). ("Libel and Slander: Involvement—Public Controversy, other than Public Officer, Employee or Candidate, as Creating 'Public Figure' Status." "Who Is a 'Public Figure' in the Light of Gertz v. Robert Welch, Inc. . . . ") Rochester, N.Y.: Lawyers Co-operative, 1977.

Lawhorne, Clifton O. *Defamation and Public Officials—The Evolving Law of Libel*. Foreword by Howard Rusk Long. Carbondale: Southern Illinois University Press, 1971.

———. *The Supreme Court and Libel*. Foreword by Howard Rusk Long. Carbondale: Southern Illinois University Press, 1981.

Lewis, Anthony. *Make No Law: The Sullivan Case and the First Amendment*. New York: Random House, 1991.

Libel Defense Resource Center (LDRC) Bulletins on Libel and Privacy. New York: Libel Defense Resource Center, 1981–86.

Libel Defense Resource Center (LDRC) 50-State Survey 1982: Current Developments in Media Libel and Invasion of Privacy. (Prepared by leading media attorneys and law firms in all fifty states and the U.S. territories.) Edited by Henry R. Kaufman, introduction by Robert D.

Sack. New York: Libel Defense Resource Center, 1982. (Similar volumes for 1983, 1984, 1985–86, 1987, 1988, 1989, 1990.)
Libel Law under the Constitution—Marking the Twentieth Anniversary of New York Times Co. v. Sullivan. (A day devoted to aspects of libel law, in which a number of experts participated.) Washington, D.C.: American Bar Association, Forum Committee on Communications Law, American Newspaper Publishers Association, American Society of Newspaper Editors, April 13, 1984.
Libel Litigation 1988. New York: Practicing Law Institute. 1989. (Numerous references to *Gertz v. Robert Welch, Inc.*)
Littlewood, Thomas B. *Coals of Fire—The Alton Telegraph Libel Case.* Foreword by Rodney A. Smolla. Carbondale: Southern Illinois University Press, 1988.
Lockhart, William B., Yale Kamisar, and Jesse A. Choper. *Cases and Materials on Constitutional Rights and Liberties.* 4th ed. St. Paul: West, 1975; *Constitutional Law-Cases-Comments-Questions*, 5th ed. 1980. (See also 1974, 1977, and 1985 supplements.)
Lusky, Louis. *By What Right?* Charlottesville, Va.: Michie, 1975.
McCoy, Ralph E. *Freedom of the Press.* (A Bibliocyclopedia. Ten-year supplement, 1976–77.) Foreword by Robert Downs. Carbondale: Southern Illinois University Press, 1977.
Mass Media and the Supreme Court. 3d ed. Edited by Kenneth S. Devoe. New York: Hastings House, 1982.
Mayer, Michael F. *The Libel Revolution: A New Look at Defamation and Privacy.* New York: Law Arts Publishers, 1987.
Media Law Reporter Decisions. Vols. 1–13. Washington, D.C.: Bureau of National Affairs.
Mellinkoff, David. *Lawyers and the System of Justice—Cases and Notes on the Profession of Law.* St. Paul: West, 1976.
Metcalf, Slade R. *Rights and Liabilities of Publishers, Broadcasters, and Reporters.* Colorado Springs. Shepards/McGraw-Hill. 1984 (and supplements).
Minutes of the National Board of Directors of the American Civil Liberties Union on January 29, 30, 1982, and October 9, 10, 1982, with respect to establishing policy on defamation.
Mirza, Jerome. *Illinois Tort Law and Practice.* 1975 supplement. Rochester: Lawyers Co-operative, 1975.
Morris, Clarence. *Modern Defamation Law.* Philadelphia. American Law Institute, American Bar Association Committee on Continuing Professional Education, 1978.
Nelson, Harold L., and Dwight L. Teeter, Jr. *Law of Mass Communications—Freedom and Control of Print and Broadcast Media.* 4th ed. Mineola, N.Y.: Foundation Press, 1982.

Nizer, Louis. *Reflections Without Mirrors*. Garden City, N.Y.: Doubleday, 1978.
Norwick, Kenneth P., and Jerry Simon Chasen, with Henry R. Kaufman. *The Rights of Authors and Artists*. New York: Bantam Books, 1983.
Nowak, John E., Ronald D. Rotunda, and J. Nelson Young. *Handbook on Constitutional Law*. 1st and 2d eds. St. Paul: West, 1978, 1983.
Pember, Don R. *Mass Media Law*. 3d ed. Dubuque, Iowa: William C. Brown, 1984.
Polelle, Michael J., and Bruce L. Ottley. *Illinois Tort Law*. St. Paul: Butterworth, 1985.
Prosser, William L., John W. Wade, and Victor E. Schwartz. *Cases and Material on Torts*. Mineola, N.Y.: Foundation Press, 1976.
Prosser, William A., John W. Wade, and Victor E. Schwartz. *Torts—Cases and Materials*. Mineola, N.Y.: Foundation Press, 1987.
Redlich, Norman, and Bernard Schwartz. *Constitutional Law*. New York. Matthew Bender, 1983.
Restatement of Torts. (Div. 5, Defamation, Chaps. 24–27, Secs. 558–623.) Philadelphia: American Law Institute, 1977, 1978.
Rotunda, Ronald D. *Modern Constitutional Law—Cases and Notes*. 1st and 2d eds. St. Paul: West, 1981, 1985.
Sack, Robert D. *Libel, Slander, and Related Problems*. New York: Practicing Law Institute, 1980.
Sanford, Bruce W. *Libel and Privacy—The Prevention and Defense of Litigation*. 2d ed. Washington, D.C.: Law and Business, Prentice-Hall, 1991.
———. *Synopsis of the Law of Libel and the Right of Privacy*. New York. Newspaper Enterprise Association, 1977.
Schmidt, Benno, Jr. *Freedom of the Press and Public Access*. New York: Praeger, 1976.
Schomp, Gerald. *Birchison Was My Business*. New York: Macmillan, 1970.
Schwartz, Bernard. *The Ascent of Pragmatism—The Burger Court in Action*. Reading, Mass.: Addison-Wesley, 1990.
———. *Constitutional Law—A Textbook*. 2d ed. New York: Macmillan, 1979.
Smolla, Rodney A. *Law of Defamation*. New York: Clarke Boardman, 1986.
———. *Suing the Press*. New York. Oxford University Press, 1986.
Stonecipher, Harry W., and Robert Trager. *The Mass Media and the Law in Illinois*. Foreword by Howard Rusk Long. Carbondale: Southern Illinois University Press, 1976.
The Supreme Court and Individual Rights. Washington, D.C.: Congressional Quarterly, 1980.
The Supreme Court Review, 1982. Edited by Philip B. Kurland, Gerhard

Casper, and Dennis Hutchinson. (Essays on aspects of the First Amendment by Norman Dorsen, Joel Gora, L. A. Powe, Jr., and Frederick Schauer.) Chicago: University of Chicago Pres, 1983.

Tavoulareas, William P. *Fighting Back*. New York: Simon and Schuster, 1985.

Tedford, Thomas L. *Freedom of Speech in the United States*. New York: Random House, 1985.

Tribe, Laurence H. *American Constitutional Law*. Mineola, N.Y.: Foundation Press, 1978.

Turkington, Richard C., and Jeffrey M. Sherman. *Cases and Materials on the Constitutional Process*. 2d and 3d eds. Chicago, 1975, 1976.

Turkington, Richard C. *Cases and Materials on Privacy*. (Prepared solely for the use of students at Villanova University School of Law, 1977.)

United States Supreme Court Reports, Lawyers' Edition, Second Series (61 L. Ed. 2d 978). (Annotation on progeny of *New York Times v. Sullivan* in Supreme Court.)

Welch, Robert. *What Is the John Birch Society?* Reprinted from *American Opinion*, 1981.

Winfield, Richard N. Winfield, Chairman. *New York Times v. Sullivan—The Next Twenty Years*. New York: Practicing Law Institute, 1984.

Wittenberg, Philip. *The Protection of Literary Property*. Rev. Boston: Writer, 1978.

Zuckman, Harvey L., and Martin J. Gayner. *Mass Communications Law in a Nutshell*. 1st and 2d eds. St. Paul: West, 1977, 1983.

Gertz v. Robert Welch, Inc., Synopsis

1. Elmer Gertz, Plaintiff, v. Robert Welch, Inc., Defendant. Complaint filed on June 17, 1969, in the U.S. District Court for the Northern District of Illinois, Eastern Division, as Case No.69C 1288, assigned to Judge Bernard Decker. Complaint, amended complaint (filed after U.S. Supreme Court mandate), motions, briefs, memorandums of decisions, orders, transcripts of two trials, and much additional material. The amended complaint included allegations of "actual malice" and substantially increased the damages sought. The case was reassigned to Judge Joel Flaum.
2. *Gertz v. Robert Welch, Inc.*, 306 F. Supp. 310 (ND Ill. 1969):
Issue 1: Calling an attorney a Marxist and Communist-fronter is libel per se.
Issue 2: Punitive damages are recoverable where libel per se is alleged without pleading special damages. Judge Bernard Decker.
3. *Gertz v. Robert Welch, Inc.*, 322 F. Supp. 997: Grant of judgment n.o.v. dismissing case. Judge Bernard Decker.
4. *Gertz v. Robert Welch, Inc.*, 471 F.2d 801 (7th Cir 1972):

Issue 1: A false statement of fact supporting a false thesis is protected by the First Amendment.

Issue 2: Where subject of libel suit involves a matter of public interest, plaintiff must prove actual malice. Judges Knoch, Kiley, and Stevens; *reversed* 418 U.S. 323, 94, S. Ct. 2997.

5. *Gertz v. Robert Welch, Inc.*, 410 U.S. 925, 93 S. Ct. 1355, 35 L. Ed. 2d 585: Supreme Court grants certiorari.
6. *Gertz v. Robert Welch, Inc.*, 418 U.S. 323, 94 S. Ct. 2997, 41 L. Ed. 2d 789 (1974):

    Issue 1: Actual-malice standard does not apply to actual damages of private persons in libel suits.

    Issue 2: Actual malice is required to obtain punitive damages against publisher by private person.

    Issue 3: States may define standard for liability of publisher in libel as long as some fault is required. Opinion by Justice Powell.
7. *Gertz v. Robert Welch, Inc.*, 680 F.2d 527(7th Cir 1982):

    Issue 1: Law of the case applies only where the issue was actually decided in a prior decision.

    Issue 2: Public proceedings privilege does not apply where statement in proceeding is not quoted verbatim.

    Issue 3: Recklessness means entertainment of serious doubts of truth or subjective awareness of falsity.

    Judges Sprecher, Posner, and Bonsal; differentiates between federal and state libel privileges.
8. *Robert Welch, Inc. v. Gertz*, 459 U.S. 1226, 103 S. Ct. 1233, 75 L. Ed. 2d 467: Supreme Court denies certiorari, Justice Stevens abstaining (February 22, 1983).

Other Cases

Altman v. Amoco Oil Co., 85 Ill. App. 3d 104, 406 N.E.2d 142. (1st Dist. 1980).

Berkos v. National Broadcasting Company, Inc., and Peter Karl, 85-2552 (Appellate Court of Illinois Fourth Division, July 30, 1987, opinion of Presiding Justice McMorrow; Justice Jiganti dissents in part and concurs in part.)

Beauharnais v. Illinois, 343 U.S. 250 (1952).

Brown and Williamson Tobacco Corp. v. Jacobson, 713 F.2d 262 (7th Cir. 1983).

Carson v. Allied News Co., 529 F.2d 206 (7th Cir. 1976).

Catalano v. Pechous, 83 Ill. 2d. 146, 419 N.E.2d 350 (1980).

Chapski v. Copley Press et al., (Docket No. 55884, Agenda 63, May 1982); *reversed, remanded*, 92 Ill.2d 344, 442 N.E.2d 195 (1982).

Bibliography ■ 281

Coleman v. MacLennan, 78 Kan. 711, 98 P. 281 (1908).
Coursey v. Greater Niles Twp. Publishing Corp., 40 Ill. 2d 257, 237 N.E. 2d 637 (1968).
Cox Broadcasting Corp. v. Cohn, 95 S. Ct. 1029 (1974).
Curtis Publishing Co. v. Butts, 388 U.S. 130 (1967). (Decided with *Associated Press v. Walker.*)
Dun & Brandstreet, Inc. v. Greenmoss Builders, Inc., 105 S. Ct. 2939 (1985).
Farnsworth v. Tribune Co., 43 Ill.2d 286, 253 N.E.2d 408 (1969).
Garrison v. Louisiana, 379 U.S. 64 (1964).
Herbert v. Lando, 441 U.S. 153 (1979).
Hustler Magazine, Inc. v. Falwell, 485 U.S. 46, 108 S. Ct. 876, 99 L. Ed. 2d 41 (1988).
Hutchinson v. Proxmire, 443 U.S. 111, 99 S. Ct. 2675 (1979).
Janklow v. Newsweek, U.S. District Court, District of South Dakota, No. 83-4023, March 29, 1984, 378 N. W. 2d 875 (1985).
Colson v. Stieg (No. 53954, affirmed and remanded). Opinion filed February 19, 1982; rehearing denied March 25, 1982, 89 Ill.2d 205.
John v. Tribune Co., 24 Ill. 2d 437, 181 N.E.2d 105 (1962), *cert. denied*, 371 U.S. 877 (1962).
Keeton v. Hustler Magazine, Inc., 104 S. Ct. 1473 (1984).
Levinson v. Time, Inc., 89 Ill. App. 3d 338, 411 N.E.2d 1118 (1st Dist. 1980).
Lulay v. Peoria Journal-Star, Inc., 34 Ill. 2d 112, 214 N.E.2d 746.
Miami Herald Publishing Co. V. Tornillo, 418 U.S. 241 (1979).
Milkovich v. Lorain Journal Co. et al. (Supreme Court, 1990).
Monell v. Department of Social Services, 436 U.S. 658 (1978).
Monitor Patriot Co. v. Roy, 401 U.S. 265 (1971).
Near v. Minnesota, 283 U.S. 697 (1931).
Newell v. Field Enterprises, 91 Ill. 3d 735.
New York Times Co. v. Sullivan, 376 U.S. 254, 84 S. Ct. 710, (1964).
Oberman v. Dun & Bradstreet, Inc. 586 F.2d 1173 (7th Cir. 1978).
Old Dominion Branch No. 796, Nat'l. Ass'n. of Letter Carriers v. Austin, 418 U.S. 269 (1974).
Ollman v. Evans, 750 F.2d 970 (D.C. 1989), *cert. denied*, 471 U.S. 1127 (1985).
Pape v. Time, Inc., 354 F.2d 558 (7th Cir. 1965), *cert. denied*, 384 U.S. 909 (1966). See also, *Time, Inc. v. Pape*, 401 U.S. 279 (1971).
Parmelee v. Hearst Publishing Co., 341 Ill. App. 339, 93 N.E.2d 512 (1st Dist. 1950).
The People of the State of Illinois v. Heinrich, (No. 59239, Supreme Court of Illinios, September 20, 1984): *rehearing denied* November 30, 1984, 470 N.E.2d 966, reversed and remanded.

The People of the State of Illinois v. Nuccio, (No. 43820), *affirmed* 54 Ill. 2d 39 (March 1973; opinion filed March 20, 1973, 294 N.E.2d 276.

The People of the State of Illinois v. Nuccio (No. 41975) *reversed and remanded*, 43 Ill. 2d 375 (November 1969: opinion filed November 26, 1969), 253 N.E.2d 353.

Philadelphia Newspapers, Inc. v. Hepps. 106 S. Ct. 1558 (1986).

Priscilla Nelson v. Richard Nuccio et al. 131 Ill. App. 2d 2611, (1st Dist. 1971).

Rasky v. Columbia Broadcasting System, 103 Ill App. 3d 577, 431 N.E.2d 1053 (1st Dist. 1981).

Rosenblatt v. Baer, 383 U.S. 75 (1966).

Rosenbloom v. Metromedia, Inc. 403 U.S. 29, 91 S. Ct. 1811 (1971).

Spanel v. Pegler, 160 F.2d 619 (7th Cir. 1947).

St. Amant v. Thompson, 390 U.S. 727 (1968).

Time, Inc. v. Firestone (1970), 424 U.S. 448, 47 L. Ed. 2d 154, 96 S. Ct. 958.

Time, Inc. v. Hill, 385 U.S. 374, 87 S. Ct. 534 (1967).

Troman v. Wood, 62 Ill. 2d, 184, 340 N.E.2d 292 (1976).

Wolston v. Reader's Digest, 443 U.S. 157. 99 S. Ct. 2701 (1979).

Zeinfeld v. Hayes Freight Lines, 41 Ill.2d 345, 243 N.E.2d 217 (1968).

Constitutional Provisions

Illinois Constitution of 1970. Article I, Bill of Rights; Section 4, Freedom of Speech; Section 12, Right to Remedy and Justice.

Constitution of United States. First and Fourteenth amendments.

Index

Abraham Lincoln School, 152–53, 165
ACLU. *See* American Civil Liberties Union
Actor, The (Stang), 143, 162
Actual injury. *See* Damages
Actual malice. *See* Malice
Adler, Alfred, 152
Affirmative defenses. *See* Privilege
AFL-CIO. *See* American Federation of Labor and Congress of Industrial Organizations
Ahrens, John, 169
ALI. *See* American Law Institute
American Civil Liberties Union (ACLU), 3, 4, 94, 128, 148, 155; purpose of, 137; and Roger Baldwin Foundation, 136
American Constitutional Law (Tribe), 238–40
American Federation of Labor and Congress of Industrial Organizations (AFL-CIO), 242
American Jewish Congress, 149
American Law Institute (ALI), 235–37
American Newspaper Publishers Association, 191
American Opinion (*see also* "Frame-Up, Richard Nuccio and the War on Police"), 25, 34, 40–41, 142, 161; cessation of, 211; contributors to, 157; editorial policy of, 48, 146; Gertz' letter to, 6, 153, 158, 159, 160–61; ignorance of Gertz by, 52–53, 66, 139, 147; lack of retraction by, 122, 153; plaintiff's allegations of malice by, 112; Powell's findings regarding, 103–4; printing schedule of, 52, 53, 133, 157; second jury's attitude toward, 184; Stang's association with, 53–54, 112, 144, 156, 158, 162; Stanley's duties for, 51–52
American Opinion Bookstores, 53
American Society of Newspaper Editors, 191
American Youth for Democracy, 153
Antiwar movement, 3–4, 9, 104, 120
Appeals. *See* United States Court of Appeals; United States Supreme Court
Ascent of Pragmatism, The—The Burger Court in Action, (Schwartz), 101
Associated Press v. Walker, 28
Association of American Publishers, 191
Association of American University Presses, 191
Atlantic Monthly, 221
Attorneys: injury to reputation of, 89, 112, 131, 132, 136, 137–38; as public figures, 33, 75, 85–86, 88, 94, 99, 102, 108
Austill, Steve, 169
Authors League of America, 191

Baldwin, Roger (*see also* Roger Baldwin Foundation), 136, 155
Belli, Melvin, 127
Bellows, Carol, 132
Belmont Publishing Company, 34
Birchism Was My Business (Schomp), 9
Bish, George, 169
Black, Hugo L., 90, 101, 233

■ 283

284 ■ Index

Blackmun, Harry A., 102, 103, 108, 237, 239, 245
Bloom, Lois, 127
Blue Line, 16
Bon Air Hotel, Inc. v. Time, Inc., 73
Bonsal, Dudley B., 201
Boyle, James A., Jr., 42, 46, 49, 57, 84; accomplishments of, 43, 114; on appeal, 76, 77; closing argument by, 68, 156; cross-examination by, 51, 55, 60–62; and jury instructions, 64–65
Brennan, William J., 99, 101, 103, 109, 216, 233; in *Greenmoss*, 239, 245; in *Rosenbloom*, 96, 108
Brown, Barry, 127, 183, 184
Buoscio, Felix M., 14
Burger, Warren, 93, 94, 102, 103, 108; in *Greenmoss*, 239, 143; in *Houchins v. KQED*, 222; in *Hutchinson v. Proxmire*, 219–20; in *Tornillo*, 213
Burnett, Carol, 121–22, 191, 192, 193–94
Burt, John, 127

Certiorari, 83, 84–89, 209–10
Chaplinski v. New Hampshire, 105
Chicago, city of, as defendant, 3, 18, 22–23
Chicago Bar Record, 230–31
Chicago Free Press, 16
Chicago-Kent Law Review, 81
Chicago Law Enforcement Study Group, 23
Chicago Lawyer, 184–86
Chicago Peace Council, 3, 4, 5, 39, 148; Stang's testimony regarding, 170, 172
Chicago police (*see also* Police), 3–5, 9, 23–24, 25, 58, 158; and alleged intelligence file on Gertz, 1, 3, 98, 153, 164–65, 176–77
Chicago Seed, 115

Chicago Sun-Times, 14, 30, 128–29, 212, 216, 223
Chicago Tribune, 28–29, 31, 115, 159, 184, 211
Chizever, Ron, 122
Christian Science Monitor, 151
Christie, George C., 236–37
Citron, Benjamin, 2, 11–12, 15, 164
Civil Rights Act, 3, 18, 20, 23
Civil rights movement, 8–9, 27, 34, 143
Civil suits (*see also* Coroner's inquest), 3, 18–23, 39, 78, 161, 178; Gertz' testimony regarding, 59, 60; Supreme Court questioning regarding, 94, 95, 96
Clabay, Trina, 169
Clark, Corrine, 127
Closing arguments: in first trial, 68; in retrial, 174–80
Colmar v. Greater Niles Township Publishing Corp., 47
Communist affiliation and belief, 3–6, 48, 86, 94, 155, 181; accusation of, as libel per se, 29, 47, 67, 76, 174; accusation of, as opinion, 200, 210; and alleged war against police, 5, 40–41, 49, 72, 75, 79, 84–85, 159–60; and appeals court opinion, 79, 80; assertions of defendant's posttrial motions on, 188–89; character witnesses' testimony regarding, 54, 55, 56, 131, 135, 166; defendant's admissions regarding, 68, 75, 120; defendant's attempt to prove, 187; Gertz' denial of, 38–39, 58, 59, 60, 62, 148–49, 152; Gertz' reaction to accusation of, 150, 151; and injury to reputation of attorney, 112, 131, 132, 136, 137–38; and Stang's prior writing, 45, 142, 143–44, 180, 200, 201; Stang's testimony regarding, 169–71, 172; Stanley's

Index

testimony regarding, 140–42, 145; and summary judgment motions, 119, 120
Comparative negligence, 188
Conditional privilege. *See* Privilege
Conscientious error, 26
"Constitutional Rules of Defamation, The" (Giampietro), 227
Contributory negligence, 121, 187–88, 230
Cook County Circuit Court (*see also* Civil suits), 18
Coroner's inquest, 69, 78, 94, 99–100, 153, 171; Nuccio's failure to testify at, 6, 17, 88–89
Courage of Their Convictions, The (Irons), 247
Court costs, 87, 90, 97, 101
Cox Broadcasting Corp. v. Cohn, 215
Croly v. Matson Nav. Co., 118
Cronkite, Walter, 4
Crowley, John Powers, 116
Cummings, Walter J., 202
Curtis Publishing Co. v. Butts, 28, 50, 72, 73, 75, 218; elements of malice in, 86–87

Daily News, 30
Daily Worker, 3, 151, 155, 169
Daley, Richard J., 6
Damages (*see also* Punitive damages; Reputation), 21–22, 67, 181–82, 235, 237, 244–45; amount awarded, 68, 183, 184, 203; amount claimed, 40, 41, 113, 177; appellate decision regarding, 206–7; defendant's arguments regarding, 76, 189, 197; Gertz' testimony regarding, 149–50, 151, 154–55; Supreme Court ruling in *Gertz* on, 106–7, 111, 203, 246
Darrow, Clarence, 155
Decalogue Society of Lawyers, 59, 149

Decker, Bernard B., 42, 43–45, 96, 97, 113, 121; and failure to produce Stang as witness, 53; and fair comment plea, 187, 198; grants motion for judgment notwithstanding the verdict, 70–74; and jury instructions, 62–68; rulings on pretrial motions, 46–47, 49
Declaratory judgments, 227
Defamation (*see also* First Amendment; Libel; *and specific cases*): common law elements of, 25–26; legal commentary on, 226–32; *Restatement* on, 235–36; as state law issue, 109–10
"Defamation Law in the Wake of Gertz v. Robert Welch, Inc.: The Impact on State Law and the First Amendment," 229
Dellinger, David, 3
Democratic National Convention (1968), 3–5, 9, 25
DePaul Law Review, 229–30
Depositions, 46, 54–55, 60, 115, 121, 130–31; of Stang, 76, 162
Dieringer, Henry, 31, 32
Dilling v. Illinois Publishing and Printing Company, 47
Directed verdict, motion for, 184–85
Discovery (*see also* Depositions), 45–46, 60, 76, 121
Dissent and Disorder, 4, 9, 164, 171, 178; Gertz' testimony regarding, 58, 152, 153
Diversity of citizenship, 36
Donaldson, Ronald. *See* Nelson, Ronald
Douglas, William O., 90, 93, 94, 232, 233; dissent by, 103, 108–9
Dow Jones & Company, 242
Due process, 86–87, 89–90, 96, 97
Dulles, John Foster, 7, 143, 162, 170, 200

Dun & Bradstreet, Inc. v. Greenmoss Builder, Inc., 229, 239, 247; history of, 240–42; Supreme Court opinions in, 242–46

Echeles, Julius Lucius, 12, 44–45, 54, 56, 190; representation of Nuccio by, 13, 14, 16; Stang's testimony regarding, 168, 171, 172; testimony of, 123, 130–31
Egan, John, 58
Eisenhower, Dwight D., 7, 45, 98, 103, 162
Eldridge, Carleton G., Sr., 234
Epstein, Benjamin T., 34
Epton, Saul, 12
Ernst, Morris, 155
Evans, Joseph, 58

Fahey, John, 164
Fairchild, Judge Thomas, 202
Fair comment (*see also* Privilege), 26, 49, 70, 76, 126, 235; and requirement to prove malice, 123, 173, 174, 185, 187, 198
Farnsworth, Myrtle, 31, 32
Farnsworth v. Tribune Company, 31–32, 33, 71, 214, 225
Field Enterprises, Inc., 223
Fink, Eli E., 54, 132, 147
Firestone, Mary Alice, 216
First Amendment Lawyers' Association, 233
First Amendment (*see also* Malice; Public figures; Public issues; Public officials; *and specific cases*), 25, 49, 72, 87, 235–37; "absolutionist" position regarding, 90, 108–9, 233; applicability to commercial information, 241–43; applicability to defamation, 110; and compulsory access laws, 213; and freedom of speech vs. right to privacy, 89, 90–91, 95; and Illinois standard for liability, 224–25; and matters of private concern, 243; and nonmedia defendants, 215, 229, 241, 245; opinion vs. fact under, 105, 111, 200, 210; and truth as defense to libel, 31–32, 214–15
First National Bank of Boston v. Bellotti, 243
Fisher, Harry M., 29
Fitzgerald, Richard, 2, 4, 12–13, 14, 130
Fitzpatrick, Tom, 14–15
Flaum, Joel M., 42, 113, 123, 126, 161, 202; appeal bond set by, 208; denial of defendant's posttrial motions by, 190; denial of motion for directed vedict, 172; evidentiary rulings by, 130, 132, 158, 163–64, 168; and fair comment plea, 123, 126, 185, 187; Heldrich on, 184–85; jury instructions by, 173, 174, 180–82, 206; qualifications of, 116–17; questioning of Stang by, 165, 166–67; ruling on motion to dismiss malice count, 173; rulings on summary judgment motions, 117–20, 121
Follett, Dwight, 43
Ford, Gerald, 116, 232
Ford, Henry, 184, 211
Forster, Arnold, 34
Fourteenth Amendment (*see also* First Amendment), 49, 72, 73–74, 108–9, 214–15; and civil-rights action, 18, 20
Fourth Amendment, 93
Fraenkel, Osmond, 155
"Frame-Up, Richard Nuccio and the War on Police" (*see also* *American Opinion*): checking of facts in, 52, 72, 132, 133, 139, 157, 158, 160, 206; commissioning of, 52, 139, 157, 159–60, 171–72;

content of, 1, 2–6, 15, 155; distribution of, 37–38, 40; Gertz' reaction to, 1, 149–50, 151–52; as matter of public interest, 73, 79; provided to jurors, 129–30; research for, 114–15, 119, 164–69, 171, 172, 177, 178, 179
Frankfurter, Felix, 92
Franksville Restaurant, 2, 11–12
Freedom of speech. *See* First Amendment
Freedom of the press. *See* First Amendment; Media
Freedom of the Press (McCoy), 234

Gertz, Elmer: acquaintance with Supreme Court justices, 232–33; age of, 121; *American Opinion* allegations regarding, 1, 3, 4, 5, 6, 155; *American Opinion*'s ignorance of, 52–53, 66, 139, 147; cross-examination of, in retrial, 152–55, 156; direct examination of, in retrial, 147–52; and Heldrich, 113–14, 115–16, 123–24; and Illinois Constitutional Convention, 33, 95, 153–54, 155, 196; and Illinois Police Association, 134, 147, 149, 176; impact of case on personal life of, 234; informal encounters with Stanley, 233; at inquest, 17, 69, 78, 88–89, 94, 99–100, 153; and law school classes, 122, 124–25; libel cases handled by, 28–33; libel complaints by, 37–41, 112–13; representation of, 42–43, 44, 74, 83; Stang's failure to contact, 60, 119, 172; Stanley's failure to contact, 144; testimony of, in first trial, 57–62; trip to Soviet Union by, 126; and verdict in retrial, 182–83
Gertz, Mamie, 193
Gertz v. Robert Welch, Inc. (S. Ct. 1974) (*see also* United States Supreme Court), 191, 203; companion cases to, 213–14; concurring opinion in, 108; dissenting opinions in, 108–11; legal commentary on, 228–32, 234–35, 236–40; majority opinion in, 102–8; Supreme Court application of, 216–17, 218–19, 242–46; unanswered questions in, 214–16
Giampietro, Mary, 1, 92, 162, 182; testimony of, 51, 129, 158, 159
Giampietro, Wayne B., 1, 44, 124, 131–32, 157, 163; appellate arguments by, 77, 200, 201; brief on second appeal, 197–99; closing arguments by, 68, 174–77, 179–80; as co-counsel with Gertz, 74, 83; and delays, 121; deposition of Echeles by, 130–31; and distribution of article to jurors, 129–30; examination of Gertz by, 57–60, 147–52, 155; examination of Jenner by, 134–37; examination of Stanley in retrial, 132–34, 139–45; examination of Stanley in second trial, 146–47, 159–61; filing of complaint by, 36; *Illinois Bar Journal* article by, 227–29; and jury instructions, 62–63, 65–66, 173, 174; maturation of, 42–43, 123; and motion to dismiss malice count, 173; opening statement in retrial, 128; oral argument in Supreme Court, 92, 93–97, 101; response to defendant's appeal to Supreme Court, 210; on ruling on conditional privilege, 185; and verdict in second trial, 182–83
Gideon's Trumpet (Lewis), 190
Goldberg, Arthur J., 90, 152, 233
Goldwater v. Ginsburg, 50
Gordon, David, 122
Grady, John, 184

Grant v. Reader's Digest Ass'n, 47
Greenberg, Frank, 54, 64, 131–32
Greenmoss case. *See Dun & Bradstreet, Inc. v. Greenmoss Builder, Inc.*
Gross negligence, 223, 225
Guide to Subversive Organizations and Publications, 133, 165–66

Hagerty, Mildred F., 197
Hallcraft, Betty, 127
Hallett, Albert, 23
Handy, Gary R., 124, 126
Hanley, Robert F., 230
Harlan, John Marshall, 226, 244
Harvard Law Review, 237
Hearst newspapers, 29
Heldrich, Gerard C., Jr., 113–16, 123–24, 126, 132, 147, 167; appeal by, 194; closing argument by, 177–79; cross-examination of character witnesses by, 128–29, 131, 135, 136, 138; cross-examination of Gertz by, 152–55, 156; examination of Stang by, 162–66, 172; and jury instructions, 173, 174; motions by, 120–21, 173, 184–85, 186–90; opening statement by, 128; on payment of judgment, 211; and Stanley's testimony, 138–39, 141, 142, 144, 145–46, 156–59, 160–61
Herbert, Anthony, 221–22
Herbert v. Lando, 221–22
"He's Earned a Moral Fortune" (Pick), 231–32
Houchins v. KQED, 222
House Committee on Un-American Activities (HUAC), 4, 149, 151, 155, 169
Humphrey, Hubert, 6, 142, 143, 200
Hunt, N. B., 34
Hutchinson v. Proxmire, 219–20

Illinois: constitution of, 31–32, 95, 214–15, 225; procedural rules in, 45–46; typical damage awards in defamation actions, 184
Illinois Bar Journal, 227
Illinois Constitutional Convention, 33, 95, 153–54, 155, 196
Illinois Law Forum, 231
Illinois Police Association, 134, 147, 149, 176
"Impact of *Gertz* in the Law of Libel in Illinois, The" (Stonecipher and Trager), 231
Information Industry Association, 242
"Injury to Reputation and the Constitution: Confusion Amid Conflicting Approaches" (Christie), 236–37
Innocent-construction rule, 29, 30, 80, 97, 185, 231
Intercollegiate Socialist Society, 3, 38, 46, 104, 120
Interrogatories (*see also* Discovery), 46, 60, 121; special, 174
Irons, Peter, 247
Isaacs, Alexander J., 44
It's Very Simple (Stang), 143

Jalovec, Richard, 16
Jenner, Albert E., Jr., 123, 134–37, 150, 207
John Birch Society, Inc., The (*see also American Opinion*; Robert Welch, Inc.), 1, 2, 16, 25, 38, 98; and assets of Robert Welch, Inc., 208; beliefs of, 7–10; house counsel for, 124; power of, 33–35; second jury's attitude toward, 184; Stang's association with, 53–54, 144, 156, 166; subsequent history of, 211–12
John Marshall Journal of Law Practice and Procedure, The, 230

Index ■ 289

John Marshall Law School, 122, 124
Johnson, Lyndon B., 45, 103, 143, 170
Journal of the American Bar Association, 247
Judgment, collection of, 208–9, 210–11
Judgment notwithstanding the verdict, 69–74, 174
Jurisdiction, 27, 36
Jury: instructions in first trial, 62–68, 70, 71–72, 76; instructions in retrial, 160, 173, 174, 180–82, 206; request for, 36–37; selection in retrial, 127–28; verdict in first trial, 68; verdict in retrial, 182–84

Kachigian, Michael M., 13, 54, 131, 168, 172; testimony of, 56–57, 138
Kaufman, Irving, 221–22
Kennedy, John F., 7, 8, 45, 103, 143, 170
Kennedy, Robert F., 9
Kiley, Roger, 30, 77, 80–81
King, Martin Luther, Jr., 7, 9, 128, 143, 170
Kissinger, C. Clark, 3
Kitchen, Noel, 169
Klepak, Ralla, 18, 19, 41, 59, 161; as character witness, 55; Stang's failure to contact, 168, 172; testimony of, 54, 55, 147, 156, 166
Knoch, Win, 77
Koenig, Kathryn, 130, 147
Krueger, Kathryn, 182
Khrushchev, Nikita, 8
Kupcinet, Irving, 128–29
Kurland, Philip, 232

Laski, Harold, 81
Law-of-the-case doctrine, 118, 197, 198, 204–5
LDRC. *See* Libel Defense Resource Center

Leighton, George N., 44, 115, 126
Leopold, Nathan F., Jr., 33, 234
Levin, Steven Michael, 229
Lewis, Anthony, 190
Lezak, Carl, 5, 164
Liability, state standards for (*see also* Malice; Negligence), 106, 111, 191, 204, 223
Libel (*see also* Damages; Defamation; First Amendment; Libel per se; Malice; Reputation; *and specific cases*), 25; accusation of crime as, 93, 94, 98; cases handled by Gertz, 28–33; elements of, 181; Illinois liability standard for, 118, 123, 173, 185, 186–87, 223–26, 230–31; and innocent-construction rule, 29, 30, 80, 97, 185, 231; media views on, 192–93; per quod, 230; state setting of liability standards for, 106, 111, 191, 204, 223; truth as defense to, 31–32, 97, 214–15; typical damage awards for, 184, 192
Libel Defense Resource Center (LDRC), 191
Libel per se, 27, 70, 72, 78, 102; accusation of Communist affiliation as, 29, 47, 67, 76, 174; and presumed damages, 203, 207, 230
Libel, Slander and Related Problems (Sack), 234–35
Ligtenberg, John, 54, 55, 132, 147
"Long-arm" statutes, 27, 36
Lorillard v. Field Enterprises, 47
Loyola University of Chicago Law Journal, 229

McCarthy, Joseph, 212
McCormick, Colonel, 115
McCoy, Ralph E., 234
McDonald, Lawrence P., 211
Machanic, David, 194, 199, 200–201, 209
McMullen, John C., 230–31

Magazine Publishers Association, 191
Malice, 26, 27–28, 32, 186, 210; allegations in pleadings regarding, 39, 48, 49, 112; appeals court holdings on, 78, 80, 203–5, 206; appellate arguments regarding, 75–76, 197–99, 200–201; closing arguments on proof of, 175–76; denial of opportunity to prove, 82, 86, 89, 96; and fair comment claim, 123, 173, 174, 185, 187, 198; and judgment notwithstanding the verdict, 69, 72, 73–74; and jury instructions, 62–63, 65, 181; plaintiff's arguments to Supreme Court on, 85, 86–87, 91–92; and punitive damages, 119, 203, 246; states following standard of, 223; and summary judgment motions, 49–50, 119; Supreme Court opinions in *Gertz* on, 105–6, 109
Marovitz, Abraham Lincoln, 184
Marshall, George C., 45
Marshall, Prentice H., 116, 117
Marshall, Thurgood, 102, 103, 233, 238, 239, 245; in *Firestone*, 217–18
Martin, Henry, 127
Marxist League for Industrial Democracy, 3, 38, 46, 57, 104, 120
Mass Media and the Law in Illinois (Stonecipher and Trager), 231
Media, 28–29, 105, 110–11, 192–93, 212, 245; and applicability of *Gertz*, 215, 229, 241
Media Law Reporter, 194–95
Mental anguish (*see also* Damages), 22–23, 107, 113, 177, 182, 207
Meserve, Robert W., 234
Metromedia case. See *Rosenbloom v. Metromedia, Inc.*
Miami Herald Publishing Co. v. Tornillo, 213–14, 227

Michigan Law Review, 236–37
Minnis, Michael, 194
Mirabelli, Enrico, 125
Motions, 46–47, 49, 76, 125, 184–85; posttrial, 69–74, 174, 186–90; for summary judgment, 20, 21, 49–50, 117–20, 187, 203
Municipal liability, 23

Napoli, Alexander J., 20, 21, 22
Nation, 192–93
National Association of Broadcasters, 191
National Enquirer, 121–22, 192
National Law Journal, 200–201
National Lawyers Guild, 38–39, 46, 47, 78, 120, 135; *American Opinion* assertions regarding, 4, 5; Gertz' testimony regarding, 59, 148–49, 152, 155; Stang's source of information regarding, 172, 176, 205, 206; Stanley's testimony regarding, 139; Supreme Court findings on, 103–4
National Lawyers Guild, Foremost Legal Bulwark of the Community Party, 133
National Mobilization Committee to End the War in Vietnam, 3
National Newspaper Association, 191
Negligence, 109, 112, 174, 181, 191; comparative, 188; contributory, 121, 187–88, 230; as standard in Illinois, 118, 123, 173, 185, 186–87, 223–26, 230–31; states adopting as standard, 223
Nelson, Douglas, 19
Nelson, Priscilla V., 22–23
Nelson, Ronald (*see also* Coroner's inquest), 2, 9, 16, 19, 20; killing of, 11, 12; Nuccio's harassment of, 13, 22; proof of damages for death of, 21–22
Nelson family. See Civil suits

Index ■ 291

Nelson v. Nuccio (*see also* Civil suits), 23
New York Times, 151, 222
New York Times v. Hill, 73
New York Times v. Sullivan, 32, 46, 50, 75, 90, 214; appeals court application of, 79, 80; applied in *Farnsworth*, 32; applied in retrial, 185; and Brennan's dissent in *Gertz*, 109; and *Gertz* distinguished by Supreme Court, 99, 100, 105–6, 107; holding of, 26–27; and judgment notwithstanding the verdict, 70, 71, 72, 73; and jury instructions in first trial, 62–63, 64, 65; legal commentary on, 226–27, 228, 236, 238, 239; reaffirmation of, 111; White's reservations regarding, 244–46
Nixon, Richard M., 7, 45, 103, 200
Northwestern University Law Review, 229
Nuccio, Richard, 18–21, 39, 75, 78, 94, 120; *American Opinion* statements regarding, 1, 2, 3, 4, 5, 6; harassment of Nelson by, 13, 22; at inquest, 6, 17, 88–89; judgment against, 23; plaintiff's witnesses on prosecution of, 44, 56–57, 59–60, 130–31, 138, 166; prosecution and conviction of, 11–16, 103, 112, 113; Stang's testimony regarding, 164, 168–69, 171, 172, 178, 198; Stanley's testimony regarding, 53, 134, 139, 145–46, 157

Obstruction of justice, 93, 94
O'Connor, Sandra Day, 239, 242
Ogren v. Rockford Star Printing Company, 47
Old Dominion Branch No. 496, National Association of Letter Carriers v. Austin, 92, 214, 237

Opening statements, 128
Opinion, vs. fact, 105, 111, 200, 210, 235, 236–37
Oral argument: in appellate court, 77–78, 199–201; for petitioner in Supreme Court, 92, 93–97, 101; for respondent in Supreme Court, 93, 97–101
Otwell, Ralph, 215–16

Parks, Gordon, 127
Parmelee, Maurice, 29
Parmelee v. Hearst Publishing Co., 29–30, 80
Paul, Les, 169
Pegler, Westbrook, 29
Pelelle, Michael J., 230
Pell, Eve, 193
People v. Nuccio (1969), 13–14
People v. Nuccio (1973), 16
Pick, Grant, 231–32
Pierson, Ball and Dowd, 194, 199
Pleadings, 45, 46; in civil-rights case, 19–20; in first libel action, 36–41, 47–49, 76; in second libel action, 113–14, 133, 156
Police (*see also* Chicago police), 49, 157, 159–60, 171–72; alleged war on, as public issue, 72, 73, 79, 84–85, 96; *American Opinion* allegations of war against, 5, 40–41, 75; John Birch campaign for, 34
Posner, Richard A., 200
Posttrial motions, 69–74, 174, 186–90
Powell, Lewis F., 95–96, 101–2, 215, 239, 242–43; *Gertz* opinion by, 102–8
Practicing Law Institute (PLI), 234–35
Pretrial memorandums, 121
Prior restraint, 26, 87
Privacy, right to, 89, 90, 95
Private persons (*see also* Public issues), 75, 107, 215–16, 235, 236;

Supreme Court holding on, 106–8, 111
Privilege (*see also* Fair comment), 33, 125, 174, 203, 204; appeals court ruling on, 205–6; *Restatement* on, 235; under Speech or Debate Clause, 219
Probable cause, 93
Protess, David, 122
Proxmire, William, 219
Public figures (*see also* Public officials), 28, 47, 48–49, 61–62, 235, 237; appeals court holding on, 204–5; attorneys as, 33, 75, 85–86, 88, 94, 99, 102, 108; criminals as, 218–19; *Firestone* decision on, 216–18; under *Hutchinson v. Proxmire*, 219–20; and judgment notwithstanding the verdict, 69, 71–72; and jury instructions in first trial, 63–66; summary judgment on, 118, 119; Supreme Court opinions in *Gertz* on, 102, 105–6, 107, 108, 109; under *Wolston v. Reader's Digest*, 218–19
Public issues, 89, 95–96, 99, 102; appeals court rulings on, 78–79, 80–81, 203, 204; Blackmun's position on, 108; Brennan's dissenting opinion on, 109; certiorari petition arguments regarding, 85, 86, 87; *Firestone* decision on, 216–17; and judgment notwithstanding the verdict, 72, 73–74
Public officials (*see also* Public figures), 27–28, 60, 94, 99–100, 235; defendant's allegations regarding Gertz as, 48–49, 69; and proposed limitations on damage awards, 244–45; Supreme Court opinions in *Gertz* on, 105–6, 109
Punitive damages (*see also* Damages), 119, 122, 156, 182, 187,
227; amount awarded to Gertz, 183, 184, 203; Gertz' request for, 40, 113, 177; proposed limitations on, 244–45; Supreme Court ruling in *Gertz* on, 106, 111, 203, 246

"Radical Changes in the Law of Libel" (Hanley), 230
Radical Right, The—Report on the John Birch Society and Its Allies (Epstein and Forster), 34–35
Rankin, Judy, 169
Reagan, Ronald, 211
Reckless disregard (*see also* Malice), 50, 72, 79–80, 112, 157, 235; *New York Times v. Sullivan* on, 105–6
Red Guild, 58
Rehnquist, William H., 94, 95, 98, 102, 103, 218; in *Firestone*, 216–17; in *Greenmoss*, 239, 242
Reputation (*see also* Damages), 44, 67, 174–75, 225, 228, 246–47; accusation of communism as injury to, 112, 131, 132, 136, 137–38; allegations of complaint regarding, 38, 40; and attorneys as representatives, 89; as heart of defamation claim, 31, 54; proposed limitations on damages for injury to, 244–45; and requirement to prove actual injury, 102, 106–7, 182, 189
Requests to produce (*see also* Discovery), 46
Res judicata, 204
Restatement (Second) of Torts, 235–37
Return to Runnymede (Boyle), 43
Reuben, Don, 31, 32, 229, 232
Review of the News, 156, 168
Robert Welch, Inc. (*see also American Opinion*; John Birch Society, Inc.), 6, 34, 36, 145, 161; assets

of, 156, 208; payment of judgment by, 211
Rodriguez, Joe, 169
Roger Baldwin Foundation, 4, 136, 137, 148, 164
Rosenbloom v. Metromedia, Inc., 108, 109, 223, 239, 245, 247; and *Gertz* compared, 80, 96, 101–2, 237; rationale of, 104; Supreme Court repudiation of, 101–2, 216–17, 238
Rossen, John, 3, 152, 155
Rosson, Barbara, 127
Rosten, Leo, 190
Ruby, Jack, 1, 3, 43, 115, 127, 137, 149
Ryan, Edward, 169

Sack, Robert D., 234–35
St. Amant v. Thompson, 27–28, 50
St. Louis Post-Dispatch, 192
Salomon, Kurt J., 29
Schaefer, Walter V., 135, 223, 225–27
Scheel, Linda, 169
Schlesinger, Arthur, Jr., 238
Schomp, Gerald, 8, 9
Schwartz, Bernard, 101, 102
Scott, William, 116
Seventh Circuit Court of Appeals. *See* United States Court of Appeals
Simon, Seymour, 196
"60 Minutes," 221
Southern Illinois University Law Journal, 231
Sparling, Edward J., 58, 148, 190
Sparling Commission, 58–59, 115, 148, 171, 172
Special verdicts, 174
Speech or Debate Clause, 219
Spiegel, Jack, 3, 152, 172
Split-Second Decisions: Shootings of and by Chicago Police, 23–24
Sprecher, Robert A., 201, 202–6

Spreyer, Abigail, 81
Stang, Alan, 40, 76, 198; association with *American Opinion*, 53–54, 112, 144, 156, 158, 162; commissioning of article by, 52, 139, 157, 159–60, 171–72; content of article by, 1, 2–6, 15, 155; cross-examination of, 113, 123, 166–72; direct examination of, 162–66; and Echeles, 130, 131, 168; failure to testify in first trial, 53–54, 68; Gertz' testimony regarding, 60; Kachigian's testimony regarding, 57; later accusations by, 150, 151, 168; pattern of calling people Communists, 45, 139–40, 142, 143–44, 180, 200; and proof of malice, 176, 206; reliance on government documents by, 165–66, 206; research by, 114–15, 119, 164–69, 171, 172, 177, 178, 179; Stanley's belief in reliability of, 49–50, 133, 146, 158, 159; Stanley's reliance on, 49–50, 51, 52, 78, 134, 201
Stanley, Winfield Scott, Jr., 34, 42, 49, 72, 171–72, 179; adverse examination of, 51–53, 132–34, 138–45, 146–47; appeals court rulings on malice of, 78, 79–80, 206; after cessation of *American Opinion*, 211; cross-examination of, 145–46, 159–61; Heldrich's direct examination of, 156–59; informal encounters with Gertz, 233; plaintiff's arguments on malice of, 173, 175–76; reliance on Stang by, 49–50, 51, 52, 78, 134, 201
Statutes of limitations, 25, 31
Stevens, John Paul, 202, 232–33, 239, 245; on appeals court, 77, 78–80, 97
Stewart, Potter, 96, 102, 103
Stonecipher, Harry W., 231

294 ■ Index

Strict liability, 26, 106, 107, 111, 224
Student Lawyer, 231
Summary judgment, 20, 21, 49–50, 117–20, 187, 203
Support Your Local Police campaign, 34

Thompson, James R., 116
Thornhill v. Alabama, 243
Time, Inc. v. Firestone, 216–18
Tischner, Margaret, 14–15
Tobriner, Matthew, 238
Tone, Joffrey R., 231
Tornillo. See Miami Herald Publishing Co. v. Tornillo
Trager, Robert, 231
Tribe, Lawrence H., 238–40
Troman v. Wood, 118, 123, 173, 185, 187, 230; opinion in, 223–26
Trudeau, Pierre, 142, 200
Tully, Thomas, 169, 172
Turkington, Richard C., 229–30
Tybor, Joseph F., 200–201

"Unconstitutionality of the Qualified Truth Defense to Libel Actions, The" (Pelelle), 230
Underwood, Robert, 13–14
United Medical Laboratories v. Columbia Broadcasting System, 73
United States Constitution. *See* First Amendment; Fourth Amendment; *and specific cases*
United States Court of Appeals, 194, 207–8; briefs and argument in first appeal to, 74–78; briefs and argument in second appeal to, 196–201; opinion in first appeal to, 78–82, 97–98; opinion in second appeal to, 202–7
United States District Court (*see also* Motions; Pleadings; *and specific witnesses*), 19, 36, 184

United States Supreme Court (*see also Gertz v. Robert Welch, Inc.*), 26–28; and companion cases to *Gertz*, 213–14; concurring opinion in, 108; conference in, 101–2; dissenting opinions in, 108–11; majority opinion in, 102–8; petitioner's briefs in, 89–92; petitioner's oral argument in, 92, 93–97, 101; petitions for certiorari to, 83, 84–89, 209–10; post-*Gertz* defamation decisions of, 215, 216–20, 221–23, 239, 242–46; procedure in, 83, 84, 92–93, 101; reluctance to review libel cases, 194–95; representation in, 83–84; respondent's oral argument in, 93, 97–101
University of Colorado Law Review, 226
University of Illinois Law Forum, The, 230

Verdict: in first trial, 68; in retrial, 182–84
Viereck, George Sylvester, 233–34
Viereck, Peter, 233

Walker, Dan, 232
Walker, Edwin, 76, 97
Walker Report, 4, 58, 72
Wall Street Journal, 242
Walsh, Matthew, 15, 16, 169, 172
Waltz, Jon R., 137–38, 232
Ward, Harry F., 3
Warden, Rob, 184, 185–86
Warren, Earl, 7, 233
Washington Post, 151
Watts, Clyde J., 76, 77, 84, 88–89, 114, 194; oral argument in Supreme Court, 93, 97–101
Weiler, Daniel A., 230
Weiss, Ron, 15–16
Welch, Robert, 7, 34, 38, 113, 150, 211

Western Islands Publishing Company, 34
Whitby v. Associates Discount Group, 47
White, Byron R., 98, 100, 102, 103, 213–14, 222; dissenting opinion in *Gertz*, 109–11; in *Greenmoss*, 239, 244–45
Whiting, Carol, 169
Wigmore, John Henry, 226
Will, Hubert, 184
Witnesses. *See specific individuals*

Wolfson, Jo-Anne F., 13
Wolston v. Reader's Digest Association Inc., 218–19
Woodward, Carol, 172
Wrongful death action, 18

Zeinfeld, Seymour, 32
Zeinfeld v. Hayes Freight Lines, 33, 230
Ziskin, Edgar, 58
Zurcher v. Stanford Daily, 222

Best known as a lawyer, Elmer Gertz has made waves in literary circles with books, pamphlets, book reviews, magazine articles, radio plays, and as publisher of a weekly newspaper. His range of interests is best indicated by some of the organizations he has founded or joined and headed: the Civil War Round Table, the Shaw Society (Bernard, that is) of Chicago, the Decalogue Society of Lawyers, the American Jewish Congress, the Public Housing Association, The First Amendment Lawyers Association, and the Blind Services Association. An avid theatergoer all his life, he has an almost equal interest in gourmet dining (though his wife says he talks more food than he actually eats).

His chief joys are his wife, his three children, and his six grandchildren. As for accomplishments, he is proudest of the State of Israel Prime Minister's Medal, awarded to him in 1972.

92009824

```
KE       Gertz, Elmer, 1906-
228      Gertz v. Robert
.G47     Welch, Inc.
G47
1992
```

DATE DUE